All About How to Become A Successful Exporter | Any Origin

Dr. Vijesh Jain

Global Management Consultant, Corporate trainer,
Ex Director, United World School of Business
Ex Dean, IILM Business School

DEDICATION

I wish to dedicate this book to my distinguished professors at IIFT, New Delhi, who so passionately taught me theoretical aspects of business management way back in 1980s. I also dedicate this book to my numerous B School students, corporate students who have so passionately attended my various Topics and workshops on especially the topics related to How to successfully carry out export business in last 20 years. I also wish to dedicate this book to my wife and children who supported me wholeheartedly and with contribution to write this book.

CONTENTS

ACKNOWLEDGMENTS

This text is a result of inputs provided by several experts in the field of exports and imports, from industry as well as from academic world. I specially thank *Shri Rakesh Roshan*, Professor and *Shri Amit Kumar Rajvanshi*, Chief Manager-Global Supply Chain, at *Dabur India* for showing the correct path for contents formation for this book through valuable discussions. I am also thankful to my student of International Business *Arshvardhar* for arranging the text in correct order and seeing that layout is correct. Finally I wish to acknowledge the frequent support of *Shri Anil Kumar, Dr. Mukesh Porwal, Prof Navneet Saxena* and *Prof. Deepak Tandon* for their support and constantly guiding me to fine tune the information provided in this book.

INTRODUCTION

In an era of global interconnectedness and dynamic economic landscapes, the role of an exporter has never been more crucial. The ability to navigate the complex terrain of international trade, understand diverse economic environments, and efficiently manage the intricacies of export procedures is an invaluable skill set. "All About How To Become A Successful Exporter | Any Origin" is a comprehensive reference book meticulously crafted to empower working executives and students of international business management with the essential knowledge and skills required to thrive as successful exporters.

This reference book serves as a practical guide, offering a systematic exploration of key topics that are fundamental to excelling in the field of international trade. From laying the groundwork with important background and economic concepts behind international trade to delving into the nuances of export documentation, each chapter is designed to equip readers with the insights and proficiency needed to navigate the complexities of the export business.

The journey commences with an exploration of crucial foundational concepts, including important background and economic principles that underpin international trade. Readers will familiarize themselves with common terms and abbreviations used in the export business, ensuring a solid understanding of the language integral to the global marketplace.

Before taking the plunge into the export business, it is imperative to be armed with the right knowledge. The book guides readers through essential considerations, providing insights into what one needs to know before embarking on the export journey. Understanding the intricacies of foreign trade policy is paramount, and the book uses examples, such as India's Foreign Trade Policy, to illuminate the practical implications.

A deep dive into the international business environment follows, exploring the various facets that exporters must navigate. Where to acquire market intelligence is a critical question, and this book addresses it comprehensively, complete with case studies illustrating effective methods of gathering export market information.

Tracking progress is key to success, and the book includes a dedicated section to evaluate and reflect on one's journey so far. Understanding the updated INCOTERMS® 2020, securing international payments, comprehending export procedures, and mastering export documentation are pivotal aspects that the book covers in detail.

As the journey concludes, a comprehensive case study ties together the theoretical knowledge presented throughout the book, providing a real-world application of the principles discussed. "All About How To Become A Successful Exporter | Any Origin" is more than a reference book; it is a roadmap to success in the dynamic realm of international trade, offering valuable insights and practical skills that will empower aspiring exporters to thrive in the global market.

Thank you very much.

Chapter 1: All About What is Covered in This Book

Topics 1 to 3:

Embarking on the journey to become a successful exporter is akin to navigating a vast and intricate landscape. In this chapter, we delve into the heart of our comprehensive guide, "All About How To Become A Successful Exporter | Any Origin," unveiling the roadmap that will equip you with the knowledge and skills essential for triumph in the dynamic world of international trade.

Our aim is to provide a detailed overview of the diverse topics covered in this book, each meticulously chosen to address the multifaceted challenges and opportunities inherent in the export business. As you turn the pages, you will find a strategic progression that starts with building a solid foundation, traverses through the complexities of international trade, and culminates in practical insights and case studies that illuminate the real-world application of the principles discussed.

Key Topics Covered:

Important Background and Economic Concepts Behind International Trade: Lay the groundwork with an exploration of the foundational principles that govern global trade.

Common Terms and Abbreviations Used in Exports Business: Equip yourself with the language integral to the international marketplace.

Things to Know Before You Plunge into Export Business: Gain insights into essential considerations before venturing into the export arena.

Understanding Foreign Trade Policy: Example India's FT Policy: Navigate the intricacies of foreign trade policy through a focused examination, using India as a practical example.

Understanding All About International Business Environment: Explore the dynamic and multifaceted international business landscape.

Where to Get the Market Intelligence: Learn effective methods of gathering export market information through practical insights and case studies.

Case Study Related to Gathering Export Market Information: Apply theoretical knowledge to real-world scenarios, enhancing your practical understanding.

Your Progress So Far: Reflect on your journey, evaluate your progress, and chart your course for future success.

Understanding INCOTERMS® 2020: Navigate the updated International Commercial Terms to ensure smooth transactions.

Getting International Payments: Master the intricacies of securing international payments in a global business environment.

Understanding Export Procedures: Gain in-depth insights into the procedures involved in exporting goods internationally.

Understanding Exports Documentation: Navigate the complexities of export documentation to ensure compliance and efficiency.

Moving Goods Internationally: Explore the logistics and considerations involved in transporting goods across borders.

How to generate export business, find buyers, find markets and new trade leads?

Concluding Case Study: Tie together the knowledge gained throughout the book with a comprehensive case study, providing a practical application of the principles discussed.

As you immerse yourself in the following chapters, envision the transformation from an aspiring exporter to a confident and successful participant in the global marketplace. "All About How To Become A Successful Exporter | Any Origin" is not just a book; it is your guide, mentor, and companion on this exciting and rewarding journey. Welcome to a world of possibilities and success in international trade.

Chapter 2: Opening Case Study: Bringing Indian Service Industry to the World

Topics 4: The birth of an idea

There are many success stories of entrepreneurs who remarkably expanded globally in a very short time based on great ideas. One such success story is that of Mukesh Ambani, the chairman and largest shareholder of Reliance Industries, based in Mumbai, India.

Mukesh Ambani joined Reliance Industries, founded by his late father Dhirubhai Ambani, in 1981 and has since transformed it into one of India's largest conglomerate companies with interests in petrochemicals, refining, oil and gas exploration, and retail.

Under his leadership, Reliance Industries has become a significant player in the global market, with its oil and gas subsidiary, Reliance Petroleum, being one of the largest refineries in the world. The company has also made significant investments in developing new technologies, such as the launch of Jio, a 4G LTE mobile network that disrupted India's telecommunications market and brought affordable internet access to millions of people in India.

Mukesh Ambani's entrepreneurial vision, business acumen, and leadership skills have made Reliance Industries a globally recognized brand and a shining example of Indian entrepreneurship on the world stage.

In the next topics, Dr. Jain shares with you another interesting story of a highly successful person from India who, while based in Paris on a work assignment, founded a million-dollar global business company in Europe that became an instant success.

Topics 5: Case Study Overview

Case Study: Bringing Indian Service Industry to the World

Hello friends, in this section, I'm thrilled to share with you a captivating case study that I've developed specifically for this course. This real-life account, although with discreet details to protect the identities of the individuals and the company involved, is crafted with a purpose – education.

The essence of this case study lies in shedding light on the transformative journey of simple ideas evolving into thriving global businesses. As we delve into the narrative of Mr. Krishna Reddy, an ambitious individual from India navigating the corporate landscape in France, we aim to unravel the intricacies of entrepreneurship, global trade, and the challenges faced by business professionals on an international scale.

This story serves as a window into the genesis of a new business idea and the remarkable journey of Mr. Krishna Reddy as he transforms his vision into a formidable global enterprise. Each twist and turn in his narrative unveils the realities of the business world, offering valuable insights into the complexities involved in the pursuit of success.

Throughout this case study, we will explore the hurdles faced by global business professionals, the strategic decisions made to overcome challenges, and the pivotal role played by an individual's determination and ingenuity in shaping the destiny of a business.

So, fasten your seatbelts as we embark on the fascinating journey of Mr. Krishna Reddy – a journey that encapsulates the essence of turning aspirations into achievements and dreams into a global reality. Get ready to witness the power of a single idea and the myriad of factors that contribute to the triumph of a business on the global stage.

Topics 6: The birth of a potentially successful business idea

So here begins the captivating tale of Mr. Krishna Rao, an IIT and IIM graduate hailing from Bangalore, India. Despite being on a promising trajectory within the technology department of a multinational corporation headquartered in Paris, France, his heart harbored a different aspiration — that of becoming a global entrepreneur.

Krishna Rao, having never ventured beyond the borders of India, saw this overseas opportunity not just as a career move but as a gateway to understanding the intricacies of global businesses. Impressed by the dynamism of global entrepreneurs, he envisioned himself joining their ranks and transforming his dreams into a global reality.

As an individual deeply rooted in his Indian heritage, Krishna Rao sought ways to remain connected with his cultural origins while living in France. Through WhatsApp groups connecting Indian families across France and neighboring countries, he established vibrant connections. His role in the technology department took him on work-related travels across European countries, offering him the chance to remain in touch with the Indian diaspora.

Krishna Rao's social nature, inherited from his father and grandfather in India, compelled him to actively participate in events and family functions organized by the Indian community. His genuine interest in attending these gatherings revealed a unique opportunity.

During one such event, hosted by an Indian family in France, Krishna Rao observed the challenges faced by Indian expatriates in organizing events that mirrored their cultural traditions. The cost of arranging such events, with authentic merchandise and services reminiscent of India, proved to be exorbitant. This realization struck a chord with Krishna Rao, igniting the spark of an entrepreneurial idea.

Recognizing the demand for affordable event services within the Indian expatriate community, Krishna Rao envisioned a venture that could bridge this gap. His plan involved leveraging the latest technology and products not only from India but also from countries like China. His entrepreneurial spirit, kindled by inspiring stories of global success shared during his MBA at IIM Ahmadabad, drove him to explore this innovative business concept.

Krishna Rao understood that by organizing and sourcing services in an efficient manner, these events could be made available at a fraction of the cost. He envisioned providing these services using the latest digital tools and technologies, making them accessible to Indian families across Europe and potentially on a global scale. This realization marked the beginning of his journey from a corporate professional in Paris to a visionary entrepreneur with a mission to bring the richness of Indian culture to the world stage.

Topics 7: A little more about this opening case study and the business journey of Krishna

Now, let's delve into the event that followed and sparked Mr. Krishna Rao's entrepreneurial journey, leading him to successfully establish a services cum merchandise venture in Europe and beyond. The focal point of his venture was to cater to the diverse needs of the Indian diaspora, providing them with authentic services and products related to religious and general events.

The journey commenced with Krishna Rao recognizing the untapped potential for such services, not just in Europe but in various other countries with a significant Indian expatriate population. This realization became the catalyst for his ambitious venture that sought to bring the essence of Indian culture to the global stage.

In the upcoming segments of this case study, we will unravel the intricacies of Krishna Rao's seven-year journey, from the inception of his idea to the current turnover of over €250 million. The narrative will touch upon the highs and lows, the triumphs, and the near-collapse scenarios that Krishna Rao encountered during this transformative period.

His perseverance and resilience in the face of adversity will be highlighted, showcasing how he navigated challenges that could have potentially derailed his entrepreneurial dreams. The story will be a testament to the strategic decisions, innovations, and sheer determination that propelled Krishna Rao's venture to remarkable success.

So, stay tuned as we embark on this captivating journey, dissecting the highs and lows, the challenges and triumphs, that shaped Mr. Krishna Rao's path from a corporate professional in Paris to the visionary entrepreneur behind a thriving global enterprise. Keep watching as we unfold the story of turning a simple idea into a €250 million business within a span of just seven years.

Topics 8-10: Converting the idea into successful business

Continuing the saga of Krishna Rao's entrepreneurial journey, let's delve into the birth of his business—an idea sparked by the realization of the challenges faced by Indian families in Europe when organizing cultural events. Krishna, a food enthusiast and a social individual, enjoyed connecting with Indian families in Europe during his work tours and social visits.

The turning point came during one of these events when Krishna observed the financial strain on Indian families trying to organize culturally rich gatherings. This observation led to a profound realization—that professional and organized event services, catering specifically to the diverse cultural backgrounds of the Indian diaspora, could be offered at a fraction of the cost.

Recognizing the need for customized services tailored to different regional and cultural backgrounds, Krishna saw an opportunity in event management services and merchandise related to Indian traditions. From "Puja" items to services of "Panditji" for Hindu families, Krishna identified various aspects that families were willing to pay for, given the challenges of accessibility and affordability in certain European locations.

With the vision of solving a real problem and providing value to the Indian diaspora, Krishna embarked on a journey to bring his idea to life. Confident in his observations and passionate about addressing the challenges faced by Indian families in Europe, Krishna took a sabbatical from his job and immersed himself in research.

Stationing himself in India for several months, Krishna studied different ways of conducting events, identified required products, and explored sources for these items. His research covered a spectrum of events, from religious functions and ceremonies to marriages, birthdays, and festival celebrations. Krishna's comprehensive study also included the idea of offering traditional dresses for such events.

During this research phase, Krishna serendipitously crossed paths with Rama Rao, who shared similar ideas and aspirations. Rama Rao, working in France with a successful family event management business in India, saw the potential for a collaborative venture. Their meeting in a pub in Bangalore evolved into a solid business partnership.

Krishna and Rama Rao decided to join forces, leveraging Krishna's marketing expertise for the front end of the business and Rama Rao's experience in managing the men and material aspect, including sourcing products from India and overseeing operations. The vision was clear—to start a company catering initially to Indian families in France and select

European countries.

This dynamic partnership marked the transformation of a conceptualized idea into a tangible and ambitious business venture. The stage was set for Krishna and Rama Rao to embark on their entrepreneurial journey, armed with passion, research, and a shared vision for providing indispensable services to the Indian diaspora in Europe. The journey, however, was just beginning, with challenges and triumphs awaiting them on the road to success. Stay tuned as we unfold the chapters of Krishna Rao's venture from inception to its remarkable growth over seven years.

In the initial phases of operations, Krishna Rao, now fully dedicated to the marketing side of the business, relied heavily on digital marketing and WhatsApp marketing. Leveraging the social groups he had diligently cultivated over the last two years in France, Krishna found an initial flip from these networks. The first years of operations saw brisk business, and both partners, having left their jobs, were fully committed to making their venture a success.

Krishna's marketing efforts were comprehensive and personal. He spent his time visiting various contacts, families, and social events organized on a community basis. Through these interactions, he shared his ideas with Indian families and the diaspora, creating a network that spanned not only France but also neighboring countries. His keen insight enabled him to uncover unexplored opportunities, and the response from Indian families was overwhelmingly positive.

In the first year alone, the company's turnover had already reached an impressive 2 million Euros. Their service offerings covered a broad spectrum, including services related to religious functions, general events, and even small marriage functions in the traditional Indian way. The company also ventured into supplying wedding dresses, both online and offline, catering to the preferences of their clients. Services like Panditji were made available through both online and offline channels.

The success of the business in its initial year was attributed to the strategic marketing initiatives led by Krishna and the efficient operational support provided by Rama Rao. Their combined efforts not only made the company a well-known brand among Indian families in France but also gained recognition in some neighboring countries.

The company had successfully carved its niche in providing indispensable services and merchandise to the Indian diaspora, addressing the unique needs of cultural events and traditions. As word of mouth spread and their reputation grew, Krishna and Rama Rao's venture became synonymous with quality, reliability, and innovation in serving the vibrant Indian community abroad.

The foundation for success had been laid, and the next chapters of their journey would witness further expansion, challenges, and triumphs as they continued to navigate the complex landscape of event management and merchandise provision for the Indian diaspora in Europe and beyond. Stay tuned for the unfolding of the next stages of this remarkable entrepreneurial odyssey.

Topics 11-13: The first shock

European Newspaper Article: Allegations of Child Labor Shake Krishna Reddy's Business

In a shocking turn of events, one of the prominent service and merchandise providers for the Indian diaspora in Europe, Krishna Reddy's company, is facing severe backlash following allegations of employing child labor in India. The accusations, reported in a recent article in a European newspaper targeting migrant populations, claim that the reason behind the seemingly affordable products and services offered by Krishna Reddy's company is the unethical use of child labor in its supply chain.

The news of the alleged exploitation of child labor has resulted in a widespread boycott of Krishna Reddy's company by the Indian migrants residing in France and neighboring countries. This sudden and impactful response has sent shockwaves through the business, causing a significant downturn in sales and leading to the near-collapse of the enterprise in its second year of operation.

Krishna Reddy vehemently denies the allegations, asserting that the news article was not well-researched and was based purely on hearsay. He suspects the involvement of European competitors and rivals within India in spreading false information to tarnish the reputation of his business. Despite facing financial troubles and the threat to his company's existence, Krishna Reddy maintains that the allegations are unfounded.

Adding to the turmoil, Krishna's business partner, Rama Rao, decides to return to India and rejoin his family's successful event management business. Rama Rao also expresses his desire to sell his stake in the company, further complicating the already challenging situation for Krishna Reddy. Despite the financial strain, Krishna manages to buy out Rama Rao's stake in the company to the satisfaction of both parties. Remarkably, the two friends maintain a strong and enduring friendship even in the face of the turbulent times their business is enduring.

The future of Krishna Reddy's company hangs in the balance as it grapples with the aftermath of the child labor allegations and the departure of a key partner. As investigations into the veracity of the claims continue, the resilience of Krishna Reddy and the fate of his once-thriving business remain uncertain.

Krishna Reddy's Resilience: Triumph After Turmoil

After weathering the storm of the allegations and the subsequent boycott, Krishna Reddy, the determined entrepreneur behind the Indian service and merchandise venture, managed to swim through the turbulent second year. Remarkably, by the third year, the company experienced an exponential surge in sales growth, marking a remarkable turnaround for Krishna Reddy's business.

Undeterred by the challenges faced in the past, Krishna Reddy took bold steps to expand and strengthen his operations. In a strategic move, he established a new operations training and sales management office—a sizable facility dedicated to providing comprehensive training for new recruits. The scope of recruitment extended beyond India, reaching out to the erstwhile East European countries.

The training program aimed not only to serve the Indian clients but also to cater to individuals from other nationalities. The influx of new recruits received top-notch training, equipping them to provide services not only to the Indian migrants but also to a diverse range of clients hailing from various parts of Europe and beyond.

By the third year, Krishna Reddy's venture had transcended its initial focus solely on Indian migrants. The company received inquiries from across Europe, as well as from the United States, Canada, Japan, and even Australia. The remarkable expansion saw the business extending its services not only to Indian migrants but also to migrants from a myriad of other nationalities.

Recognizing the diverse needs of the growing clientele, Krishna Reddy strategically tailored services to meet the unique cultural requirements of various nationalities. The company created a niche for itself by providing services that resonated with the cultural roots of clients from different countries. Krishna Reddy's thorough understanding of these requirements allowed him to train his team effectively, ensuring that they could serve clients from a multitude of backgrounds.

The product line also expanded, with merchandise being sourced not only from India but also from China. The company successfully carved out a distinct position in serving the diverse needs of migrants, becoming a go-to resource for individuals seeking services that reflected their cultural heritage.

The healthy and robust growth of the company marked a turning point for Krishna Reddy. The vision he had pursued, despite facing setbacks and challenges, was finally coming to fruition. The venture that had once faced near-collapse was now thriving, serving a clientele that extended far beyond its initial scope.

Krishna Reddy's resilience, strategic vision, and commitment to quality services propelled the company to new heights. The once-turbulent entrepreneurial journey was now characterized by triumph and success. As the business continued to flourish, Krishna Reddy looked back at the challenges overcome and forward to the continued growth and expansion of his thriving venture.

Topics 14-15: The Second Shock

Krishna Reddy's Trial by Fire: Financial Setback and the Lifeline

As Krishna Reddy's company soared to new heights, a sudden and unforeseen challenge emerged. The main financier from Europe, a crucial supporter of the operations, unexpectedly backed out. Faced with a financial crunch, the situation forced the company to consider selling the majority stake held by Krishna Reddy—an emotionally painful decision for the visionary entrepreneur.

During this challenging period, Krishna Reddy found solace and support from an unexpected source—his wife. Having married a year after starting the company, Krishna's wife had become an integral part of the business, bringing her financial background to the forefront. As the company entered its third year, marked by ambitious expansion plans, Krishna's wife actively participated in the operations.

The dire situation unfolded as the company faced the dual pressures of rapid expansion and the sudden withdrawal of a key financier. New orders had been placed, and operational units in different countries were under development. Krishna Reddy found himself constantly on overseas trips to monitor the progress of the expanding offices and operations in the United States, Japan, and various European countries.

The withdrawal of the main European financier posed a significant setback. The company urgently required financing to sustain its expansion plans, and the valuation was not favorable for selling the majority stake. Selling a significant portion of the company at that juncture would have resulted in substantial losses, undermining the hard work and time invested by Krishna Reddy over the past two years.

In this critical moment, Krishna's wife, leveraging her financial acumen, stepped up to secure the future of the company. She managed to secure a favorable and much-needed loan from an Indian state bank, aligning with the new export promotion schemes initiated by the government of India. This soft finance on accommodating terms served as a godsend opportunity, offering a lifeline to the struggling company.

The availability of this loan on favorable terms became the turning point that allowed the company to weather the financial storm without resorting to selling the majority stake. Krishna Reddy's resilience, combined with the strategic financial support from his wife, enabled the company to not only survive but also continue its trajectory of growth and expansion.

The unforeseen financial setback became a testament to Krishna Reddy's ability to navigate challenges and adapt to unexpected circumstances. With the financial lifeline in place, the company emerged stronger, reaffirming Krishna Reddy's commitment to his vision and the sustained success of the thriving venture.

Krishna Reddy's Company: A Beacon of Integrity and Unmatched Success

As Krishna Reddy's company navigated the complexities of expansion, the sales growth remained consistently robust. The enterprise had evolved into a major brand name and a household phenomenon, not just among Indian migrants but also among individuals from diverse nationalities. The success story was not just about numbers; it was about healthy expansion and efficiently managed internal affairs.

Krishna Reddy, demonstrating his astute leadership, implemented Standard Operating Procedures (SOPs) based on three years of invaluable experience. These SOPs, coupled with the integration of smart technologies and high-quality international logistics, played a pivotal role in ensuring seamless internal operations. The company's journey was a testament to Krishna's commitment to excellence and the pursuit of innovation in the face of growth.

A key pillar of success, according to Krishna, lay in the principles of integrity and honesty that guided every facet of the business. In an industry where challenges could easily sidetrack even the most promising ventures, Krishna's unwavering commitment to ethical business practices set his company apart. The success of the enterprise was not solely attributed to financial gains; it was built on a foundation of trust and transparency.

The standard set by Krishna extended beyond the company's internal operations. The integrity and honesty displayed in dealings with vendors, partners, and franchisees garnered widespread praise. In an era where shortcuts and compromises were tempting, Krishna adhered to a principle that prioritized doing the right thing over immediate gains. His steadfast commitment to ethical business practices became a beacon of trust and reliability in the industry.

While others may have succumbed to dishonest practices for short-term gains, Krishna's unwavering stance proved to be the linchpin of his company's enduring success. The integrity, honesty, and principled approach adopted by Krishna were not just values; they were the cornerstones of the company's achievements.

As the company continued its upward trajectory, Krishna Reddy's unwavering commitment to principles served as an inspiration for aspiring entrepreneurs and a model for sustainable business success. The story of Krishna Reddy's venture became a testament to the enduring power of integrity and honesty in steering a business towards unparalleled heights of achievement.

Topics 17: The third shock faced by the company

Resilience Amidst Adversity: Krishna Reddy's Company Emerges Stronger

The relentless surge of the COVID-19 pandemic sent shockwaves through global businesses, and Krishna Reddy's company was no exception. As Europe grappled with the impacts, the company faced a dire situation with declining sales and a severe financial strain. The global sales, which had once thrived, came to a standstill, leaving the company struggling to pay salaries and trapped in financial uncertainties.

During the peak of the pandemic, numerous advance payments were stuck in countries like India, China, and Southeast Asia. Challenges in delivering goods, compounded by genuine reasons related to the pandemic, further aggravated the situation. Despite the gradual recovery of sales at the end of the pandemic's most severe conditions, the company's financial health remained precarious.

By mid-2021, the company found itself on the verge of closure, not due to a lack of orders but because of financial constraints resulting from the business collapse. However, in a turn of fate, the virtues of integrity, honesty, and principles for which Krishna Reddy and his company were known became the beacon of hope. By divine intervention, one of the largest event management companies in the world extended an offer to acquire 50.5% of the company's stake, allowing Krishna and his dedicated team to retain control.

Under this acquisition, Mr. Krishna continued as the Chairman of the company, maintaining a 49.5% stake and overseeing the helm of affairs. Retaining 50% of the existing staff, the new company offered a golden handshake to the rest. This strategic move not only secured the future of the company but also ensured the welfare of the loyal staff who stood by Krishna during the company's highs and lows.

Krishna's wife, who had been an integral part of the company as the

Chief Financial Officer, continued in her role. The acquisition marked a turning point for the company, catapulting it into the ranks of the world's largest event management companies, primarily serving migrant working families.

Topics 18: Concluding Remarks

In 2022, the total worldwide turnover of the company exceeded €220 million, a remarkable achievement that surpassed even Krishna Reddy's dreams. The journey, though fraught with challenges and adversities, showcased the remarkable resilience of the company. From facing three distinct difficult situations that brought the company to the brink of collapse, Krishna Reddy's unwavering commitment to integrity and principles emerged as the driving force that steered the company towards unparalleled success.

The story of Krishna Reddy's venture is a testament to the indomitable spirit of entrepreneurship, unwavering dedication, and the transformative power of resilience in the face of adversity. The company, having weathered the storms, now stands as a shining example of triumph and success in the ever-evolving landscape of global business.

Assignment: Unraveling the Challenges and Triumphs

After delving into the intricate details of the case study, I invite you, dear readers, to embark on an enlightening assignment. The purpose of this assignment is to encourage thoughtful reflection, critical analysis, and a deeper understanding of the complexities faced by Krishna Reddy in his entrepreneurial journey. Here are the questions for your consideration:

Identify the key challenges faced by Krishna Reddy's company during its three critical periods of difficulty. How did these challenges impact the company's operations and financial health?

Examine the role of integrity, honesty, and principles in Krishna Reddy's business approach. How did these virtues contribute to the success of his company, especially during challenging times?

Analyze the impact of the COVID-19 pandemic on Krishna Reddy's business. How did the company navigate through the financial strain and operational challenges caused by the pandemic?

Evaluate the decision of the largest event management company to acquire a majority stake in Krishna Reddy's company. What implications did this acquisition have on the future of the business, its stakeholders, and the overall industry landscape?

Reflect on the lessons learned from this case study that could be applicable to aspiring entrepreneurs in the field of international business and event management. What strategies and principles can be derived from Krishna Reddy's journey?

I encourage you to ponder over these questions, draw insights from the case study, and formulate your responses. Once you've crafted your answers, please share them as instructed. Subsequently, you will have the opportunity to explore my solutions and comments, providing valuable insights to enhance your understanding.

Your engagement with this assignment will not only deepen your comprehension of the case study but also foster a richer learning experience. I look forward to your thoughtful responses, and together, we can unravel the intricate tapestry of challenges and triumphs in Krishna Reddy's remarkable entrepreneurial journey. Keep watching for further insights and discussions.

Chapter 3 : Important Background and Economic Concepts Behind International Trade

Topics 20: Chapter Overview

As you embark on this insightful journey through the book, it is my pleasure to delve into a crucial chapter that lays the foundation for a deeper understanding of international trade. In this chapter, we will unravel the historical and economic threads that have woven the intricate tapestry of global commerce.

In the preceding sections, we have outlined the course's objectives and structure, providing you with a roadmap to navigate the complexities of how to become a successful exporter. Now, let us take a step back in time to explore the evolution of international trade. Understanding the past is pivotal, for it shapes our comprehension of the present and guides us toward a more informed future.

In the not-so-distant past, the landscape of international trade was vastly different. Technological advancements, particularly in the last 50 years, have transformed the global marketplace. The accessibility of everyday items from overseas, at remarkably affordable prices, is now taken for granted. However, it was not always so.

To enrich your learning experience, I will share insights into the economic concepts and historical perspectives that characterized international trade in bygone eras. This exploration will provide you with a valuable background, facilitating a more profound grasp of the chronology of events and the evolution of economic theories.

This chapter will not delve excessively into historical minutiae but will instead illuminate the major highlights, offering a panoramic view of the economic theories and events that shaped international trade. By gaining insight into the prevailing thoughts and expectations surrounding international trade, you will develop a comprehensive understanding of its foundations.

Moreover, we will bridge the gap between history and the contemporary economic landscape by exploring the latest theories and thinking on the benefits of international trade. This section is not a mere retrospective; it is an exploration of the current understanding that underpins the global economic order.

As we navigate through this chapter, my aim is clear—to cultivate a thought process that will serve as a solid foundation for the subsequent lessons. I am confident that these chapters and topics will ignite an engaging intellectual journey, simplifying complex concepts and providing clarity to enhance your learning experience.

So, buckle up for an exciting exploration of the historical and economic landscapes that have shaped the world of international trade. Let's embark on this enriching voyage together!

Topics 21-22: A Brief History of International Trade

Greetings, fellow learners! As we embark on our quest to uncover the secrets of becoming successful exporters, it's essential to ground ourselves in the rich tapestry of international trade history. Join me on a journey through time as we explore the evolution of commerce and the fascinating origins of global exchange.

From time immemorial, trade has been a cornerstone of human interaction, connecting people across different continents. The earliest evidence we have points to a form of trade known as barter, where goods were exchanged directly. Picture a world where rare metals, agricultural commodities, and precious stones served as the currency of the day.

In various eras, creative solutions emerged to facilitate the exchange of goods. Intermediate commodities, akin to the currencies we use today, entered the scene. The historical records are replete with instances of experimentation, with diverse items playing the role of facilitators in this intricate dance of global commerce.

Venturing into the Middle Ages marked a turning point in the history of international trade. The European era brought with it a more organized approach, with the introduction of official currencies and precious metals like gold. This era witnessed the rise of intermediaries, including the advent of banks, which played a crucial role in facilitating the movement of goods between continents and countries.

During this period, political analysts, philosophers, and economists keenly observed the evolving dynamics of international trade. Their ideas, often articulated in the form of classical and modern theories, laid the groundwork for the shaping of the trade landscape. Traders, in turn, gleaned insights from these theories to maximize profits and expand their businesses.

In the upcoming chapters, I will delve into some of the classical and modern theories that emerged from these intellectual pursuits. These theories have not only captivated traders but also influenced the strategies and policies of countries engaged in foreign trade. Join me as we explore these popular ideas in bite-sized sub topics that promise to unravel the complexities of international trade theories.

So, stay tuned and keep reading as we navigate the intriguing landscapes of international trade history together. The insights we gain will undoubtedly enrich our understanding and pave the way for success in the world of export.

Topics 23: Classical theories explaining the most common reasons of international trade

In our exploration of the fascinating realm of international trade, let's delve into some of the most influential classical and historical theories that have shaped the course of nations and their engagement in global commerce. To kick off this exploration, let me share with you one of the earliest and most impactful theories that emerged during the Middle Ages and the era of European colonization.

During this transformative period, marked by European countries embarking on expeditions to explore new routes across the seas, economic and philosophical thinking surrounding international trade underwent significant developments. Sponsored sea expeditions enabled countries to conquer the high seas, facilitating long-distance trade and exploration.

Topic 24: Theory of Mercantilism

At the heart of this era was the Theory of Mercantilism, which advocated for a nation's industrialization as a means to accumulate wealth and power. According to this theory, countries should focus on producing value-added goods that could be exported at high prices. In return, these nations would import raw materials and commodities necessary for the manufacturing process. The ultimate goal was to amass gold reserves, viewed as a symbol of wealth and strength, thereby enabling these nations to dominate the global stage.

The connection between industrialization, international trade, and the pursuit of gold reserves became a driving force behind the expansion of trade routes and the establishment of colonial dominance. European countries, following the tenets of Mercantilism, engaged in extensive industrial activities to strengthen their export capabilities and bolster their economic standing on the international stage.

The question of whether the surge in industrialization and international trade was a direct result of the Theory of Mercantilism or if the theory was crafted to justify and capitalize on these emerging economic trends remains a subject of debate. Nevertheless, the undeniable fact is that, during this time, nations subscribing to Mercantilist principles did achieve a level of global dominance, with vast regions falling under their colonial rule.

This theory, often considered the first classical theory of international trade, laid the groundwork for subsequent economic thought and policy. In the chapters to come, we will explore additional classic and historical theories that have shaped the landscape of international trade, each offering unique perspectives on why countries engage in trade and how this interaction influences the global stage.

Stay tuned for an enlightening journey through the theories that have defined the dynamics of international trade over the centuries.

Topic 25: Classical theories of International Trade

In our journey through the evolution of international trade theories, we've now arrived at a pivotal moment—a transition from the unsustainable theory of Mercantilism to the groundbreaking theories of absolute and comparative advantages. Let's unravel this historical narrative that marked a significant shift in economic thinking and laid the foundation for the wealth of nations.

In the previous Topic, we explored how Mercantilism, with its focus on accumulating gold reserves through industrialization and exports, started facing challenges. Imperialist activities began to recede due to political and commercial backlashes from the colonies, leading to a decline in the viability of Mercantilist principles. This period of flux set the stage for a fresh perspective on international trade—one that aimed at sustainable benefits for all nations.

Enter Adam Smith, hailed as the father of economics, who presented a groundbreaking idea in his seminal work, "Wealth of Nations." Smith proposed that for international trade to benefit all nations, the focus should shift to economic terms. He introduced the theory of absolute advantage, suggesting that countries, whether industrialized or not, should concentrate on producing goods where they possess an absolute advantage—producing more with limited resources than other nations.

The theory of absolute advantage gained widespread popularity and importance, marking the decline of imperialistic pursuits. It paved the way for a more inclusive wave of industrialization, shaping the world in ways that resonate with us today.

However, the evolution did not stop there. Another influential social scientist, David Ricardo, proposed the theory of comparative advantages. According to Ricardo, when countries have absolute advantages for multiple products, they should focus on producing only a few products where they have a comparative advantage over others. The rest of the products can be produced by countries with a comparative advantage in those specific areas. This approach, Ricardo argued, would lead to increased wealth for all nations involved in trade.

The theory of comparative advantage further extended the principles of absolute advantage, emphasizing the importance of specialization in international trade. Countries focusing on their comparative advantages could maximize production efficiency and resource utilization, contributing to the overall wealth of nations.

These classical theories—absolute advantage and comparative advantage—are not relics of the past; they remain highly relevant in today's global landscape. The principles laid out by Smith and Ricardo have withstood the test of time, providing valuable insights into the dynamics of international trade.

As we conclude our exploration of classical theories, stay tuned for the next Topic, where we will delve into modern theories that continue to shape our understanding of international trade in more sophisticated ways.

Exciting times lie ahead on our learning journey!

Topics 26-28: Modern theories explaining the international trade

As we venture further into the dynamic landscape of international trade theories, let's explore two influential modern theories that have captivated countries and firms engaged in global commerce. These theories offer fresh perspectives on why countries share similarities in trade patterns and how the life cycle of a product can be extended through international trade.

The first theory on our exploration is Linder's Country Similarity Theory, introduced by the Swedish social scientist Stefan Linder in 1961. Linder proposed that firms, successful in their domestic market, naturally seek new markets abroad. The key to their success lies in entering countries that bear similarities to their home country, whether in terms of economic development, per capita income, or cultural affinities.

According to Linder's theory, firms excel in understanding the demands and preferences of their domestic customers. By focusing on countries with similarities, firms can leverage their experience and modify their goods to cater to the preferences of the new market. This theory emphasizes the importance of economic and cultural similarities, making it a valuable tool for firms venturing into international trade. It has proven especially useful for new entrants looking to navigate the complexities of global markets.

Moving on, let's delve into the Product Life Cycle Theory, a modern concept proposed by Raymond Vernon. This theory, initially developed to understand the marketing stages of a product within a single market, has profound implications when extended to the realm of international trade.

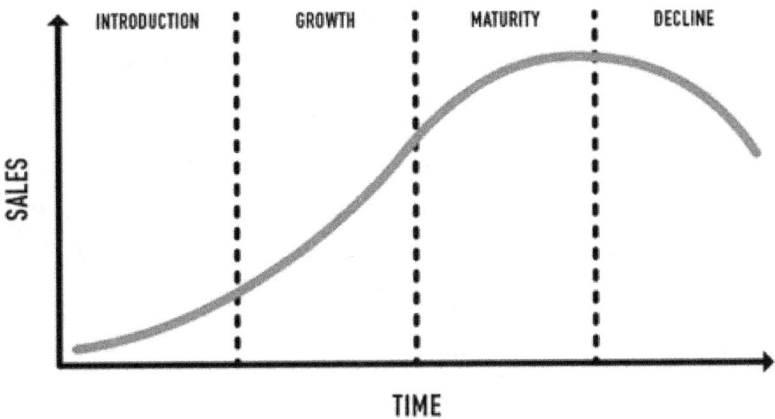

Figure: Product Life Cycle Theory

The Product Life Cycle Theory posits that a product, innovated and introduced in the home country, undergoes four phases: introduction, growth, maturity, and decline. When applied to international trade, the theory suggests that the same product, when introduced in a new market, will experience a similar four-phase cycle but at a different time. The result is an elongated product life cycle, offering significant advantages for innovators and manufacturers.

The extension of the product life cycle means that a product, which might have declined or faced obsolescence in one market (Time T1), gets a new lease on life when introduced in another market (Time T2). This prolonged product life cycle becomes an attractive proposition for international traders, allowing them to continue reaping the benefits of their innovations for an extended period.

To illustrate the Product Life Cycle Theory in action, consider the introduction of desktop and laptop computers by U.S. companies in developing countries. These products, having undergone their life cycle phases in the U.S., were later introduced in developing countries, witnessing a renewed cycle and extended longevity. This example showcases the practical implications and benefits of the theory in the context of international trade.

As we wrap up our exploration of these modern theories, stay tuned for the next Topic, where we will unravel additional concepts that shed light on the intricate dynamics of international trade.

Our journey through modern theories of international trade continues as we explore two influential concepts that shed light on the strategic advantages driving global commerce and the intricate interplay of push-pull forces on firms navigating the international market.

1. Porter's Diamond Theory: Unlocking Strategic Advantage

In the realm of strategic advantages, a cornerstone theory emerges— Porter's Diamond Theory. Michael Porter proposed that a combination of factors could propel a specific industry in a particular country to international competitiveness. The four pivotal factors constituting this diamond model include:

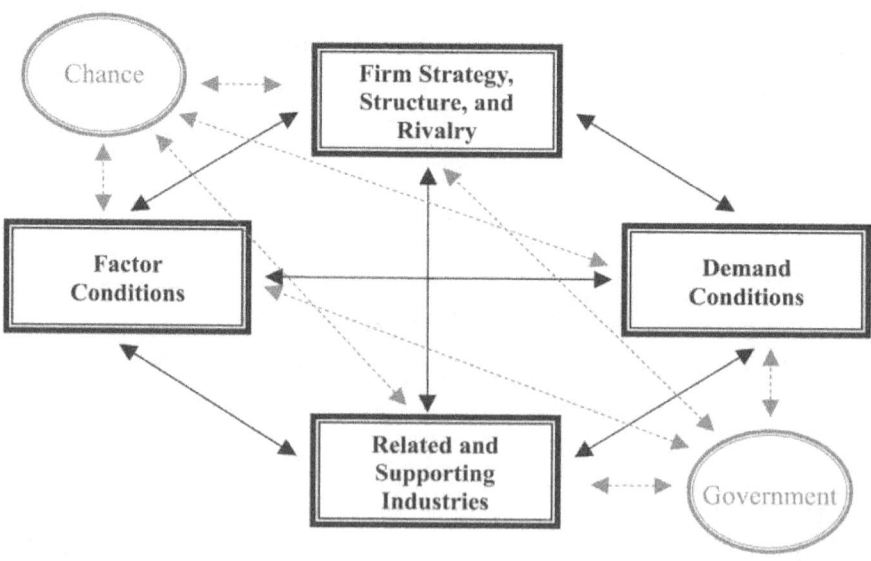

Source: Porter (1990)

Figure: Porter's Diamond Theory

Factor Conditions: These encompass the skills, resources, infrastructure, and finances necessary for manufacturing. When favorable, these conditions significantly contribute to strategic advantage.

Firm Strategy, Structure, and Rivalry: Healthy competition, sound strategies, and an open industry structure foster competitiveness. Professional strategies and an economically tenable environment contribute to reduced manufacturing costs and enhanced product features.

Demand Conditions: The existence of continuous, healthy demand for a specific set of products within a particular industry. For instance, the sustained demand for small cars in India has propelled its auto manufacturers to global competitiveness.

Related and Supporting Industries: The availability of vendors and supporting industries providing essential inputs, coupled with a seamless global supply chain, contributes to the overall competitive advantage of the industry.

Supported by factors such as a favorable environment, government policies, and a bit of good fortune, this combination of elements provides the strategic, national competitive advantage that positions a specific industry as a leading global supplier.

2. Push-Pull Forces Theory: Navigating Firm Perceptions

In the dynamic landscape of international trade, firms often experience push and pull forces influencing their decisions. Push factors, arising from adverse conditions in the domestic market (e.g., market saturation, limited size), prompt firms to explore international markets. Pull factors, on the other hand, attract companies to international markets due to attractive opportunities, favorable pricing, and the potential for economies of scale.

These factors can be sector-specific or firm-based. Sector-specific factors may include market attractiveness and size, while firm-based factors can range from internal capabilities to the visionary outlook of founders. The push-pull forces theory provides a nuanced understanding of the dynamics that drive firms toward or away from international expansion.

As we unravel these sophisticated theories, stay tuned for our next Topic, where we will delve into additional concepts that continue to shape our understanding of the multifaceted world of international trade.

Exciting discoveries await!

Topic 29: Chapter Conclusion

As we conclude this chapter on the theories and ideas behind international trade, I want to express my gratitude for your engagement and dedication to understanding the intricate dynamics of global commerce. Our exploration has taken us through a rich tapestry of historical accounts and sophisticated modern theories, equipping you with a solid foundation of knowledge and economic rationale.

The primary aim of this section was to provide you with the intellectual tools to navigate the complex world of international trade successfully. Armed with this understanding, you now possess the ability to engage in meaningful conversations with your business partners overseas. You can confidently articulate the rationale behind your trade decisions, showcasing a thoughtful approach rooted in the gems of economic theories that have evolved over time.

In the historical context, we delved into the evolution of international trade, uncovering the motivations and economic philosophies that propelled goods from one corner of the globe to another. Now, with a firm grasp of these concepts, you have the power to impress upon your international counterparts that your approach to trade is not just transactional but founded on a deep understanding of the historical, economic, and strategic aspects of global commerce.

The diverse range of theories explored, from Linder's Country Similarity to Porter's Diamond and beyond, serves as a toolkit for you, the successful exporter. These theories are not mere abstractions but practical tools that can be wielded in your conversations, negotiations, and strategic decision-making processes. Your newfound confidence and knowledge will undoubtedly contribute to building and maintaining strong relationships with your business partners, fostering trust and cooperation.

As you move forward in your journey as an exporter, remember that these theories are not static. They are dynamic, evolving in response to changes in the global landscape. Stay curious, stay informed, and continue to explore emerging ideas that will shape the future of international trade.

Thank you for your dedication to learning, and I wish you continued success in your endeavors as a global trader.

Chapter 5: Things to Know Before You Plunge into Export Business

Welcome back to the book, where we embark on the next crucial chapter in our journey toward mastering the intricacies of export business. In the previous sections, we delved into the foundational elements of this complex field, exploring common terms and gaining insights from international trade theories and history. Now, as we progress further, it becomes imperative to equip ourselves with essential knowledge that will serve as a solid foundation for success in the export arena.

Topic 29: Chapter Overview

In this section, we will unravel critical aspects that demand your attention before you take the plunge into the dynamic world of export. Much like our earlier discussions, the information shared here is designed to enhance your confidence and understanding of the entire export process.

First and foremost, we will explore the mindset and attitude necessary for triumph in the realm of export operations. Success in this field often hinges on possessing the right mindset, and I will guide you through the characteristics that distinguish a successful exporter.

Additionally, we'll delve into the crucial prelude to soliciting orders— home research. I'll walk you through the preparations essential for success, offering insights into the meticulous product research that lays the groundwork for prosperous export ventures.

To further illuminate the landscape, this section will unveil a typical export transaction framework. Understanding the game plan of both this course and the broader export business will provide you with a strategic advantage. By comprehending the rules that govern the export game, you will navigate the complexities with clarity and purpose.

So, fasten your seatbelts as we explore the nuanced facets that will fortify your foundation and set the stage for a successful journey in the export business.

Topics 34-35: Personal Skills And Attitude Required For Export Success

Welcome back to our exploration of the fundamental aspects of becoming a successful exporter. As we venture deeper into the intricacies of export business, it's crucial to spotlight a key factor that can significantly influence your journey—the personal skills and attitude required for export success.

In the realm of export operations, possessing the right mindset is often the differentiating factor between those who thrive and those who face challenges. So, what kind of attitude should you cultivate to ensure triumph in this dynamic field?

Adaptability: Export business operates in a rapidly changing global landscape. Being adaptable to shifting market trends, evolving regulations, and unforeseen challenges is paramount. We'll explore how cultivating adaptability can position you for success in an environment that demands constant adjustment.

Resilience: The export journey is rarely a smooth ride. Resilience in the face of setbacks and obstacles is essential. I'll guide you through strategies to develop resilience, ensuring that challenges become stepping stones rather than stumbling blocks.

Cultural Sensitivity: Successful exporters recognize the significance of cultural nuances in global business. Understanding and respecting diverse cultures can open doors to new opportunities. I'll provide insights into how cultural sensitivity can be a powerful tool in your arsenal.

Effective Communication: Clear and effective communication is a cornerstone of successful export transactions. We'll delve into the importance of communication skills, whether it's negotiating deals, resolving conflicts, or establishing lasting partnerships.

Risk Management: Export business inherently involves risks. Developing a keen sense of risk management is crucial. I'll share strategies to identify, assess, and mitigate risks, empowering you to make informed decisions and safeguard your business interests.

As we navigate this discussion, remember that these personal skills and attitudes are not static; they can be cultivated and refined over time. By incorporating these principles into your approach, you'll be better equipped to tackle the challenges and seize the opportunities that the export business presents.

So, let's embark on this exploration of the mindset and skills that can elevate you to new heights in the world of international trade.

Topics 36-37: Preparation required before soliciting orders from overseas

In the pursuit of a successful export transaction, meticulous preparation is the cornerstone of achievement. Before embarking on the journey of soliciting orders from overseas, it is imperative to conduct thorough home research, a critical process that lays the groundwork for a prosperous venture.

Identifying the Right Product:

The first step in this preparatory phase is the meticulous selection of the export product. While it may not necessarily be the best in the market, it should possess world-class quality. Whether manufacturing the product or procuring it from manufacturers, a well-thought-out product strategy is essential. This involves deciding on the range of products— few items of large consumption or a diverse range for merchant exporters.

Conducting Product Research:

Comprehensive product research is the key to success. Understanding the product specifications, acquiring high-quality photographs and video clips, and gathering all possible details are crucial components of this stage. The product strategy should address the easy availability of the product at competitive international prices. Desk research, discussions with industry bodies, government entities, and trade promotion bodies become vital to compare prices with competitors and gather market intelligence.

Market Focus Strategy:

Creating a product that aligns with the needs of the target market is essential. Even if the product isn't the best or doesn't have the lowest price, coupling it with an attractive offer for international customers can make it stand out. Later, we will delve into the market focus strategy, where a deeper understanding of markets and customer needs is crucial.

Documentation and Compliance:

In today's digital age, preparing a comprehensive database with high-quality images, video clips, and detailed text about the product is essential. Additionally, understanding all types of compliance, both in the home country and potential host countries, is crucial. This includes researching regulations, standards, and certifications required for the target markets.

Creating an Entry Barrier:

While the depth of research may seem daunting, remember that these efforts act as a safeguard. The information gathered becomes your private asset, creating an entry barrier for competitors. This exclusive knowledge, encompassing product details, market insights, and compliance requirements, positions you for success and minimizes challenges in the later stages of export business.

So, as we delve into the intricacies of this preparation phase, keep in mind that the effort invested now will serve as a catalyst for a smoother and more successful export journey in the long run.

Topics 38-40: Understanding the Basic Rules of the Game: The Export Transaction Framework

In this crucial phase of our discussion, let's delve into the fundamental rules that govern the export business. Understanding the flow of goods, documents, and payments is paramount for a seamless and successful international trade venture. So, let's unravel the framework of the export transaction.

1. Product Research and Strategy:

The journey commences with meticulous product research, as discussed in the previous Topic. Armed with knowledge and a well-crafted product strategy, the exporter positions themselves as either a manufacturing exporter or a merchant exporter, with the ultimate goal of securing business.

2. Export Contract:

Once business opportunities are identified, the next step is to formalize the arrangement through an export contract. This document encapsulates the terms and conditions, delivery terms, payment terms, and any commercial agreements between the exporter and the overseas buyer.

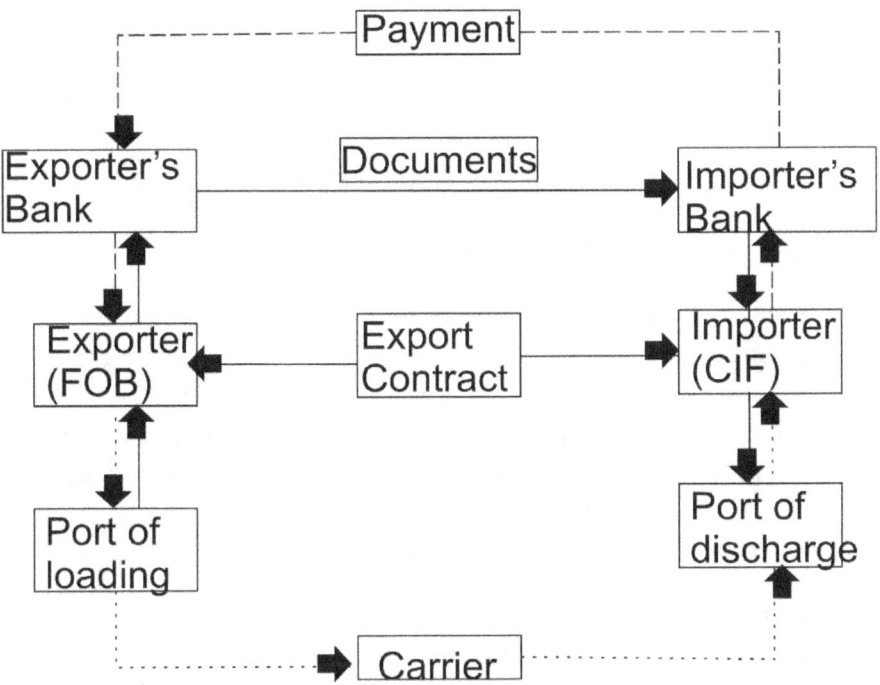

Figure: A Typical Export Transaction Framework

3. Letter of Credit (LC) Opening Instruction:

In many international transactions, payment is facilitated through a Letter of Credit (LC). The exporter prepares a draft LC opening instruction based on the export contract and shares it with the overseas buyer. This instruction guides the buyer's local bank in issuing the LC, ensuring payment upon meeting specified documentary conditions.

4. Advising and Issuing Banks:

The overseas buyer approaches their local bank, the issuing bank, with the final LC opening instruction. The issuing bank then sends the LC, in the form of a Swift code, to the correspondent bank of the exporter.

This correspondent bank, acting as the advising bank, translates the LC into understandable terms for the exporter.

5. Acceptance of Letter of Credit:

Upon receiving and reviewing the LC, the exporter may seek professional assistance if needed. Once satisfied that the terms align with the export contract, the exporter accepts the letter of credit. This marks the beginning of the actual export transaction.

6. Shipment and Document Preparation:

With the accepted LC in hand, the exporter proceeds to prepare the goods, complying with local and international regulations. The goods are then shipped, whether by sea or air, as agreed upon in the contract. Simultaneously, the exporter gathers all necessary documents, such as invoices, packing lists, certificates, and bills of lading or air waybills.

7. Negotiating Bank and Document Presentation:

The exporter forwards these documents to their local bank, acting as the negotiating bank. This bank, after due diligence, forwards the documents to the issuing bank. The issuing bank accepts the presentation and verifies compliance with the terms of the LC.

8. Payment:

If all conditions are met, the issuing bank makes the payment to the exporter, either immediately (in the case of a sight LC) or after a specified period (in the case of a Usance LC). This marks the successful completion of the export transaction.

Understanding this framework provides clarity on the sequential steps involved, ensuring that each party involved plays their role efficiently. In the upcoming sections, we will delve into the intricacies of export contracts, LC structures, and the nuances of document preparation in greater detail. Stay tuned for a comprehensive exploration of these essential aspects of the export business.

As discussed previously, the completion of the export transaction involves a meticulous process, and understanding the roles of different intermediaries is crucial.

9. Importer's Settlement with Issuing Bank:

Upon receiving the compliant set of documents, the issuing bank fulfills its duty and makes the payment to the exporter. Simultaneously, the goods have reached the port of discharge, and now the responsibility and interest lie with the importer. The importer, in possession of the documents held by the issuing bank, proceeds to settle any dues, including bank charges and interest, with the issuing bank.

10. Handover of Documents and NOC:

If all dues are settled, the issuing bank hands over the documents, along with a No Objection Certificate (NOC) if the transport documents were consigned to the bank. This NOC signifies the importer's authorization to collect and possess the goods.

11. Importer's Customs Clearance:

Armed with the documents and NOC, the importer approaches the shipping company to take possession of the goods. The next crucial step involves clearing the goods through the customs of the host country. The importer ensures all necessary procedures are followed for a smooth customs clearance process.

Understanding Intermediaries' Roles:

In this intricate export transaction framework, various intermediaries play pivotal roles:

Issuing Bank: Acts as the guarantor of payment and oversees the settlement between the importer and the exporter.

Advising Bank: Translates the LC into terms understandable by the exporter and assists in understanding the conditions.

Negotiating Bank: Receives documents from the exporter, performs due diligence, and forwards them to the issuing bank, playing a crucial role in the document negotiation process.

Customs and Border Control: Both in the home country and host country, these entities ensure regulatory compliance and facilitate the movement of goods across borders.

Carrier (Shipping Company or Airline): Responsible for physically transporting the goods from the port of loading to the port of discharge.

Freight Forwarder or C and F Agent: Handles logistics, ensuring the smooth movement of goods, and may assist in customs clearance.

Significance of the Export Transaction Framework:

This framework is indispensable in navigating the complexities of international trade. With transactions occurring between countries governed by different legal systems, this structure provides a standardized and logical approach to manage complications. Understanding the rules of the game becomes paramount to ensuring the smooth flow of goods, documents, and payments.

Conclusion:

As we delve deeper into the intricacies of export operations in subsequent Topics, remember that this export transaction framework forms the foundation. Your success in finding markets, buyers, and securing orders will be amplified when built upon this solid understanding of the transaction's fundamental structure.

Stay tuned as we further explore market strategies, buyer identification, and the nuances of becoming a successful exporter in the forthcoming Topics.

Topic 41: Chapter Conclusion

As we conclude this chapter, "Things to Know Before You Plunge into

Export Business," it's essential to reflect on the critical aspects we've explored. The journey began with a comprehensive understanding of product research and strategy, emphasizing the need for intense and deep research. We delved into the strengths and weaknesses of products, stressing the importance of a complete and appealing package for the international market.

The pinnacle of this chapter was the unveiling of the typical export transaction framework. We navigated through the intricate steps involved in securing business, signing export contracts, and the seamless flow of goods, documents, and payments. Recognizing the roles of key intermediaries such as issuing banks, advising banks, negotiating banks, customs, border control, carriers, and freight forwarders highlighted the collaborative nature of international trade.

Key Takeaways:

Meticulous Preparation: The early introduction of the export transaction framework emphasizes the need for meticulous preparation. Any oversight in documents or processes can have severe consequences in the international market.

Confidence in the Process: Understanding the complete framework instills confidence. The clarity gained from this early Topic sets a strong foundation for subsequent sections in the course.

Global Landscape: Acknowledging the differences in economic standards, cultures, and histories among countries, we recognize the varying landscape of the international business environment. Geopolitical factors play a significant role in shaping this landscape.

Looking Ahead:

Market Strategies: In the upcoming Topics, we will delve into market strategies, buyer identification, and marketing approaches tailored for the international arena.

International Business Environment: The next section will focus on understanding the global landscape, delving into the economic, cultural, and geopolitical factors that influence international trade.

Final Thoughts:

As you progress through this book, remember that each concept introduced serves as a building block for a comprehensive understanding of the export business. If any aspect seems challenging, know that it will be revisited and clarified in subsequent Topics.

Feel free to reach out with any queries or concerns. This book aims to equip you with the knowledge and skills needed to navigate the complex world of international trade successfully. Embrace the journey, and let's continue unraveling the intricacies of becoming a successful exporter.

Chapter 6: Where to Get the Market Intelligence

Topic 42: Chapter Overview

Welcome back to the book! In this chapter, we embark on a crucial exploration into the realm of business intelligence, a compass that guides you through the intricacies of international trade. The objective is clear: to equip you with the knowledge of diverse avenues where you can source valuable business intelligence.

Importance of Business Intelligence:

Understanding the market landscape is akin to having a treasure map in the world of export business. The more precise and informed your decisions are, the higher the likelihood of success. Therefore, investing time in acquiring robust business intelligence becomes the cornerstone of your export journey.

Navigating Avenues of Intelligence:

Throughout this section, we will delve into various avenues, both online and offline, where you can extract business intelligence. These insights will not only help you identify potential markets but also provide strategies on how to connect with potential buyers effectively.

Diverse Ideas for Your Toolkit:

Recognizing that different products may benefit from distinct strategies, we'll discuss a plethora of ideas. Some may align perfectly with your product, while others might spark creative adaptations. The goal is to present you with a diverse toolkit of ideas and avenues to explore.

Case Study Exploration:

In the subsequent section, we will dive into a practical case study involving exporters from India. By dissecting how they seek information, you will gain insights applicable not just to your situation but also to exporters worldwide. The goal is to empower you with the skills to identify similar sources in your own country.

Building Confidence and Generating Ideas:

By the end of this section and the subsequent one, you should feel more confident and armed with an abundance of ideas. Your ability to find and harness business intelligence sources and avenues will be enhanced, providing a robust foundation for your export endeavors.

Join me on this journey as we explore the myriad ways to gather business intelligence. The information you acquire will not only shape your understanding of potential markets but will also guide you in establishing meaningful connections with buyers. Let's dive into the world of market intelligence and pave the way for your success in

Topics 43-44: Typical Steps of Doing Export Market Research

Embarking on the journey of export market research involves a strategic approach with several key steps. Understanding these steps is pivotal for making informed decisions and obtaining valuable business intelligence. Let's delve into the typical steps involved in conducting export market research:

1. Secondary Research:

The first step is to engage in secondary research. Unlike primary research, this phase is more general but significantly cheaper and quicker. Secondary research provides an overall understanding of the market landscape, acting as a foundation for more specific investigations. It serves as a preliminary exploration before delving into more focused primary research.

2. Primary Research:

Following secondary research, the next step involves primary research. This phase is product-specific, honing in on the particular goods earmarked for export. While primary research is more focused, it tends to be costlier and time-consuming. However, it provides targeted data and information, offering insights into the export market potential specific to your product line.

3. Choosing the Export Entry Route:

The third step involves selecting the right export entry route or method. This decision is crucial and requires the creation of an initial export plan. Your export plan outlines the strategic approach, addressing questions such as whether you'll focus on product strength or tailor your offerings based on market requirements. This strategic decision influences the subsequent steps in your export journey.

4. Developing an International Marketing Plan:

For those focusing on the market and understanding its intricacies, the fourth step involves creating a professional international marketing plan. This plan goes beyond surface-level insights; it is a comprehensive document that includes a country note. This country note delves deeper into the chosen market, exploring trends and providing a roadmap for success. These documents are to be closely guarded and continually updated as your export efforts progress.

5. Creating Trade Leads:

The final step entails creating trade leads based on the insights gathered in the previous steps. Leveraging the strength of your export plan, you delve into finding ways to generate trade leads. This step involves exploring various sources, methods, avenues, and platforms to create leads. The success of this phase hinges on the foundation laid in the earlier steps.

In the subsequent Topic, we will dive deeper into the intricacies of creating trade leads. Understanding the options available for generating leads is crucial, and these options will be tailored to the insights gained from the comprehensive export market research conducted in the initial steps. Stay tuned to explore the nuances of creating trade leads and enhancing your export endeavors.

Topics 45-46: Common Export Methods and Routes

In the realm of international trade, understanding the common export methods and routes is crucial for any aspiring exporter. As we delve into the various avenues available, we find two overarching categories: the digital route, or eCommerce, and the offline routes, which encompass physical transactions.

Digital Route - eCommerce:

1. Online Marketplaces:

Platforms like Amazon Global Selling, Etsy.com, and Rakuten offer expansive international reach.

Each platform has distinct rules and guidelines, necessitating a comprehensive understanding.

Dedicated courses, such as the VJ Global MBA Course Series on Udemy, provide insights into successfully establishing a digital export business.

2. Own Shopping Portals:

Create customized international shopping portals tailored to your organization's needs.

Free services, like the one provided by the Federation of Indian Export Organization in association with Global Linkers, offer a cost-effective option for Indian exporters.

Offline Routes:

1. Direct Exports:

Direct Shipments to Importers:

- Engage with well-established importers in the target market.

- Requires meticulous discovery of potential importers through a detailed export plan and country-specific strategies.

Overseas Commission Agents:

- Agents act as intermediaries, selling goods to overseas wholesalers and generating orders on behalf of the exporter.

Setting up Own Company Abroad:

- Establish a local company or branch office abroad to directly manage marketing and distribution.

Strategic Partnerships or Joint Ventures:

- Partner with overseas entities for complementary strengths, potentially accelerating market entry and reducing costs.

2. Indirect Exports:

Exporting through Merchant Exporters, Buying Houses, or Government Trading Companies:

- Utilize existing exporters or government-run agencies for overseas sales.

- Government-controlled canalized exports may have specific regulations.

Deemed Exports:

- Common in countries with special economic zones.

- Refers to sales from Domestic Tariff Areas to 100% export-oriented units, with associated benefits.

Pros and Cons:

Digital Route (eCommerce):

Pros:

- Potential for high profits and significant growth.

- Direct interaction with customers fosters better market understanding.

Cons:

- Higher risks and initial costs.

- Time-consuming process to establish and break even.

Offline Routes (Direct and Indirect Exports):

Pros:

- Better risk management in indirect exports.

- Lower learning curve in deemed exports.

Cons:

- Lower profits and growth in indirect exports.

- Limited market understanding due to indirect involvement.

Understanding these common export methods and routes is essential for exporters to make informed decisions and navigate the complexities of the international market successfully. In the subsequent sections, we will delve deeper into the intricacies of direct and indirect exports to provide a comprehensive guide for aspiring exporters.

Topic 47: Common Overseas Market Research Methods

In the quest to become a successful exporter, market research plays a pivotal role, providing the foundation for informed decision-making. Let's explore the common overseas market research methods, crucial for acquiring business intelligence and shaping successful export strategies.

Primary Research vs. Secondary Research:

1. Primary Research:

Definition:

Involves the physical collection of data through market surveys, visits to overseas markets, and targeted research.

Methods:

- Participation in trade fairs, exhibitions.

- Customized market surveys, either self-conducted or through third-party research firms.

- Face-to-face interviews with individuals possessing specific data about products or markets.

Characteristics:

- Time-consuming and costly.

- Focuses on specific product lines and selected markets.

- Data collected through offline sources.

2. Secondary Research:

Definition:

Involves desk research using online resources, published data, and information from trade bodies or organizations.

Methods:

- Utilizes online resources and databases.

- Social media research for insights from digital communities.

- Face-to-face meetings with trade development bodies for additional insights.

Characteristics:

- More cost-effective and less time-consuming compared to primary research.

- Relies on both offline and online sources.

- Covers a wide range of markets, providing a broad overview.

- Trends and potential markets identified through analysis of published data.

Choosing the Right Sequence:

While both primary and secondary research have their merits, the ideal strategy involves a sequential approach. Extensive secondary research should precede specific primary research efforts. This ensures a comprehensive understanding of potential markets and products before investing in more resource-intensive primary research activities.

Advantages and Disadvantages:

Primary Research:

Advantages:

- Highly specific insights into chosen product lines and markets.

- Direct interaction provides firsthand information.

Disadvantages:

- Time-consuming and costly.

- Limited coverage of markets due to resource constraints.

Secondary Research:

Advantages:

- Cost-effective and less time-consuming.

- Wide coverage of markets and potential trends.

Disadvantages:

- Information may be more general and less specific.

- Limited ability to capture nuanced market nuances.

Conclusion:

In the pursuit of successful export endeavors, a judicious combination of primary and secondary research methods is crucial. Secondary research lays the groundwork, offering a broad understanding of potential markets, while targeted primary research provides specific insights needed for strategic decision-making. By following a well-defined sequence and leveraging the strengths of each approach, exporters can gather the intelligence necessary to navigate the complexities of international markets and pave the way for success.

Topic 48: Typical Steps For Secondary Market Research

Embarking on the journey to become a successful exporter requires a systematic approach to secondary market research. These steps are essential for extracting valuable insights and identifying potential markets and products. Let's delve into the typical steps involved:

1. Mining Trade Statistics and Figures:

- Utilize International Trade Classification Harmonized System (ITC HS Code) to categorize products.

- Explore trade statistics and figures available on various websites, both paid and free.

- Analyze data based on product lines, regions, and market categories.

2. Filtering Top Potential Markets or Products:

- Extract relevant data from the initial analysis.

- Filter out the top ten potential markets or products based on the situation at hand.

- This step lays the groundwork for a more focused evaluation in subsequent stages.

3. Evaluating Potential Markets:

- Assess the top ten potential markets or products identified in the previous step.

- Evaluate markets based on factors such as market size, growth potential, and trade dynamics.

- Refine the list further to pinpoint markets with the most promising opportunities.

4. Analyzing Customers and Trends:

- Dive into customer behavior, preferences, and emerging trends.

- Analyze product trends, fashion preferences, and customer needs in the potential markets.

- Base the analysis on the statistical data gathered earlier to ensure data-driven insights.

5. Mining Data about Comparable Products and Competition:

- Investigate the landscape of comparable products in the chosen markets.

- Examine pricing trends, sales volumes, and market shares of comparable products.

- Identify direct and indirect competition to understand the competitive environment.

Conclusion:

In the realm of secondary market research, these five steps provide a structured approach to gathering and analyzing critical information. From the initial mining of trade statistics to the in-depth analysis of customer behavior and competition, each step contributes to the exporter's understanding of potential markets and product lines.

By following these typical steps, exporters can make informed decisions, prioritize their efforts, and strategically position themselves in the global marketplace. This comprehensive secondary research process sets the stage for success, enabling exporters to navigate the complexities of international trade with confidence and intelligence.

Topic 49: Typical Steps for Primary Market Research

In the pursuit of becoming a successful exporter, primary market research holds a pivotal role in gathering firsthand information about potential markets and products. Let's explore the typical steps involved in primary research, following the structured sequence advocated for effective export market research.

1. Product Research and Sample Collection:

Objective:

- Understand every aspect of the chosen product.

- Collect information on composition, manufacturing processes, and required inputs.

Activities:

- Gather detailed product information, including specifications and reports.

- Collect samples, photographs, and even videos showcasing production processes.

Importance:

- Essential groundwork for engaging with foreign buyers.

- Provides a comprehensive understanding of the product.

2. Desk Research and Correspondence:

Objective:

- Prepare for physical visits and engagements in foreign markets.

- Establish contacts with overseas agencies, buyers, wholesalers, and importers.

Activities:

- Conduct desk research to identify potential contacts and events.

- Correspond with overseas entities, inquire about events, and schedule participation.

Importance:

- Lays the foundation for the next steps in primary research.

- Facilitates the planning and organization of physical activities.

3. Market Surveys, Trade Fairs, and Buyer-Seller Meets:

Objective:

- Gather firsthand information by engaging directly with potential buyers.

Activities:

- Conduct market surveys to understand buyer preferences and trends.

- Participate in trade fairs or buyer-seller meets to interact with industry players.

Importance:

- Enables direct interaction with the market.

- Provides an opportunity to showcase products and build relationships.

4. Visits to Potential Buyers Overseas:

Objective:

- Establish a personal connection with potential buyers.

Activities:

- Plan and undertake visits to potential buyers' locations.

- Conduct face-to-face meetings to understand buyer needs and expectations.

Importance:

- Builds trust and rapport with potential buyers.

- Allows for a deeper understanding of the market dynamics.

5. Budget Planning and Financial Involvement:

Objective:

- Ensure effective allocation of resources for primary research activities.

Activities:

- Develop a detailed budget considering travel costs, event participation fees, and other expenses.

- Assess the financial feasibility of planned activities.

Importance:

- Ensures financial preparedness for the resource-intensive nature of primary research.

- Enables a strategic allocation of funds for maximum impact.

Conclusion:

In the realm of primary market research, these steps form a comprehensive guide for exporters aiming to establish a strong presence in international markets. By systematically progressing from product research to direct engagement with potential buyers, exporters can gather invaluable insights, build relationships, and lay the groundwork for successful export operations.

Financial prudence and strategic planning are crucial throughout these steps to ensure that primary research efforts yield maximum benefits and contribute to the exporter's journey toward success in the global marketplace.

Topics 50-51: Most Common Sources of Information World Wide

In the quest to become a successful exporter, tapping into reliable and diverse sources of information is imperative. Whether you are exporting from any corner of the world, several common sources provide valuable insights into the dynamics of international markets. These sources are essential for comprehensive market intelligence, aiding exporters in making informed decisions. Here are some of the most common and globally accessible sources:

1. Industry Associations:

Description:

- Local and foreign industry associations play a crucial role in providing sector-specific information.

- Often sponsored by local governments, quasi-government bodies, or private organizations.

Importance:

- Offer insights into industry trends, regulations, and best practices.

- Facilitate networking opportunities within the industry.

2. Foreign Trade Development Bodies:

Description:

- Organizations sponsored by local governments dedicated to fostering international trade.

- Maintain archives of valuable information related to trade and market dynamics.

Importance:

- Provide a wealth of data on export opportunities, market trends, and regulatory frameworks.

- Act as conduits for connecting exporters with potential partners.

3. Online Sources:

Description:

- A plethora of online platforms, both paid and free, offer valuable information for research.

- Include databases, market reports, and insights relevant to primary and secondary research.

Importance:

- Enable quick access to a vast repository of global market data.

- Facilitate cost-effective information gathering.

4. Trade Consulates and Embassies:

Description:

- Trade consulates of potential markets in the exporter's home country.

- Embassies of the exporter's home country in different countries.

Importance:

- Offer on-the-ground insights into local markets, regulations, and cultural nuances.

- Facilitate direct communication with local authorities and industry players.

5. American Trade Centers:

Description:

- Network of centers in many capital cities worldwide.

- Comprehensive resources and databases often available free of cost.

Importance:

- Provide access to hard-to-find data and specialized information.

- Serve as valuable hubs for exporters seeking detailed market intelligence.

Conclusion:

These common sources of information form the backbone of successful export market research, irrespective of the exporter's origin. Leveraging these resources empowers exporters to navigate the complexities of international trade, make strategic decisions, and establish a strong presence in global markets. As technology advances, online sources continue to play a pivotal role, offering convenience and accessibility to a wealth of information at the fingertips of aspiring exporters.

Topic 52: Top 5 Global Sources of Market Intelligence Data

In the dynamic landscape of international trade, accessing accurate and comprehensive market intelligence is crucial for success. Here are the top five global sources of market intelligence data that can provide valuable insights into business, market trends, and international trade information:

1. United Nations Statistical Yearbook:

Description:

- A repository of data encompassing almost 220 countries.

- Provides statistical data on international trade for both products and nations.

Importance:

- Authentic and extensive source of international trade information.

- Covers a wide range of countries, offering a holistic view of global trade dynamics.

2. ITC Trade Map (International Trade Center):

Description:

- Online platform offering international trade statistics and figures.

- Provides free information on trade volumes, growth rates, and market shares.

Importance:

- Detailed product-wise and country-wise trade data available.

- Offers monthly, quarterly, and yearly trade information for both imports and exports.

3. OECD Surveys Series:

Description:

- Annual surveys based on original research and interviews.

- Focuses on 24 member countries but provides insights applicable globally.

Importance:

- Offers detailed information in qualitative and quantitative terms.

- Valuable source for understanding global trade dynamics through original research.

4. WITS (World Bank's World Integrated Trade Solution):

Description:

- Provides access to external trade information from various international sources.

- Integrates data from UN COMTRADE, UNCTAD TRAINS, WTO, IDB, and CTS databases.

Importance:

- Simplifies complex international databases for user-friendly access.

- Comprehensive information on external trade from key global organizations.

5. ORU Library (Global Business Information Pages):

Description:

- Digital library with a focus on country profiles, cultural information, and global data.

- Includes links to authentic web sources for updated and reliable information.

Importance:

- Provides a curated list of sources for global business

information.

- Offers access to the most updated and authentic data on various international aspects.

Conclusion:

Navigating the complexities of the global market requires a wealth of information, and these top five global sources of market intelligence data serve as invaluable tools for exporters. Whether delving into trade statistics, understanding market trends, or conducting in-depth research, these sources offer a wealth of data to inform strategic decisions and enhance the chances of success in the international trade arena. As the business landscape evolves, leveraging these sources becomes essential for staying ahead in the competitive world of global commerce.

Topic 53: Some more examples of global sources of market information

In addition to the top five sources previously discussed, there are several other valuable global sources of market information that exporters can leverage for comprehensive insights. While these may not be among the top five, they play a crucial role in providing diverse and specific data for successful international trade:

1. World Bank Atlas:

Description:

- Similar to the United Nations Statistical Yearbook, providing a vast repository of data.

- Offers more general information compared to the detailed insights of the United Nations Statistical Yearbook.

Importance:

- Serves as an additional resource for a broader understanding of global economic trends.

- Complements other sources by providing a general overview of various countries.

2. Exporter's Encyclopedia:

Description:

- An extensive handbook updated annually, covering over 220 countries.

- Encompasses areas such as international communication, trade regulations, documentation, transport, and travel.

Importance:

- Comprehensive guide offering practical information for exporters.

- Provides valuable insights into the regulatory environment and logistics of international trade.

3. Local State Departments and Trade Organizations:

Description:

- State departments, ministries, and trade promotion bodies sponsored by local governments.

- Examples include export promotion councils (EPCs), Indian Trade Promotion Organization (ITPO), and product-specific boards like the Coffee Board or Tea Board.

Importance:

- Maintain updated records of trade statistics and offer support to exporters.

- Provide product-specific information and support for various export promotion activities.

4. Chambers of Commerce and Industry Bodies:

Description:

- Local industry bodies often acting as joint ventures between local and overseas governments.

- Examples include FIEO (Federation of Indian Export Organization), FICCI (Federation of Indian Chambers of Commerce and Industries), and CII (Confederation of Indian Industries).

Importance:

- Serve as bridges between exporters and policymaking bodies.

- Provide valuable information, support, and act as advocates for exporters.

5. Foreign Trade Institutes:

Description:

- Specialized institutions funded by local governments, such as the Indian Institute of Foreign Trade.

- Provide market surveys, reports, and library resources to support exporters.

Importance:

- Offer specialized knowledge and training in foreign trade.

- Maintain archives of valuable information and contribute to the education and development of exporters.

Conclusion:

Exploring a variety of global sources ensures a well-rounded understanding of the international trade landscape. Each of these additional sources plays a unique role in providing exporters with the information and support needed to navigate the complexities of global markets successfully. By tapping into this diverse array of resources, exporters can make informed decisions, enhance their market intelligence, and increase the likelihood of becoming successful players in the global trade arena.

Topics 54-55: Local governments sponsored trade portals

In the digital age, local governments across the globe are actively contributing to the facilitation of international trade by establishing online trade portals. These portals serve as invaluable resources for exporters, offering a wealth of information and tools to enhance their global market intelligence. Let's delve into the significance and functionality of such portals, using the Indian Trade Portal as an illustrative example.

Indian Trade Portal: A Case Study

The Indian Trade Portal, sponsored by the Indian government in collaboration with the Federation of Indian Export Organizations (FIEO), stands as a comprehensive platform supporting exporters. Here's a glimpse of what these portals typically provide:

**Top Trading Partners and Products:

Detailed insights into India's top 25 trading partners, along with information on exported and imported goods.

Foreign Buyers Platform:

A platform where foreign buyers can list their requirements, fostering collaboration between Indian exporters and global businesses.

**Trade Policy and Procedures:

In-depth information on Indian trade policies, documentation procedures, and regulations.

Tariffs and Incentives:

Access to details on tariffs, preferential tariffs, Goods and Services Tax (GST), and local export incentive schemes.

Product-Specific Information:

Utilizing the International Trade Classification Harmonized System (ITC HS) code or product descriptions, exporters can obtain specific data for both exports and imports.

**Logistics Support:

Information on easing logistics challenges, ensuring smooth transportation of goods from the manufacturing facility to international destinations.

Export Registration Guidance:

Guidelines on how to register with export promotion bodies and interact with key officials for valuable insights.

**Regulatory Instruments:

Understanding the regulatory instruments shaping and implementing effective trade policies.

News and Events:

Latest news and upcoming events relevant to Indian exporters, including participation in international events and sponsored delegations.

Banking Regulations:

Insights into banking regulations governing exports from India.

Global Application:

While the Indian Trade Portal serves as a specific example, similar trade portals are prevalent in most trading nations worldwide. These portals, sponsored by local governments, have become standard tools for exporters seeking comprehensive market intelligence. The wealth of data, insights, and support services they offer significantly contribute to empowering exporters in their global endeavors.

In the next section, we will explore a case study demonstrating how a specific exporter utilized the Indian Trade Portal to gather crucial international trade information, shedding light on the practical benefits of such platforms.

Topics 56-57: Generating Trade Leads - Digital Methods

In the contemporary landscape of international trade, leveraging digital methods is instrumental in generating trade leads effectively. Let's explore the various strategies employed in the digital realm to identify potential business opportunities and enhance global market presence.

1. Marketplaces Data Mining:

Overview: International marketplaces like Amazon Global Selling, Etsy, Rakuten, and eBay are vast digital communities generating substantial data.

Method: Utilizing data mining tools and platforms such as JungleScout.com to extract valuable insights.

Application: JungleScout.com provides data generated by Amazon Global Selling, allowing users to explore product trends, top suppliers, and prominent buyers.

2. Export Sales Funnel:

Overview: A strategic combination of social media advertising and lead collection on your own website.

Method: Creating a systematic export sales funnel to guide potential customers from social media platforms to your website.

Benefits: Enables the collection of trade leads and contact information through an orchestrated process.

3. LinkedIn Sales Funnel:

Overview: Business-to-business sales funnel program on LinkedIn.

Method: Leveraging LinkedIn Sales Funnel software to identify and engage potential business partners.

Significance: Provides a platform for B2B networking and lead generation, especially valuable for professional connections.

4. Email Marketing:

Overview: A powerful tool to collect targeted email addresses and disseminate marketing messages globally.

Method: Employing email marketing software to send promotional offers, company updates, and product information.

Effectiveness: An efficient and direct communication channel to reach a global audience.

5. Live Advertising on Social Media:

Overview: Utilizing live videos on social media platforms, with a focus on product features, production processes, and company values.

Platform: Instagram's live advertising is particularly effective for engaging audiences.

Engagement: Live videos foster real-time interaction, enabling companies to showcase their offerings and values.

6. Social Advertising:

Overview: Crafting social messages and spreading them across various social media platforms.

Method: Providing freebies or valuable content on the company website to encourage user registrations and contact collection.

Benefits: By using social advertising effectively, businesses can attract a substantial online audience and collect valuable contacts.

In conclusion, these digital methods offer exporters a diverse toolkit for generating trade leads. Whether through data mining, sales funnels, email marketing, live advertising, or social media campaigns, businesses can strategically position themselves in the global market. Each method serves as a digital gateway to connect with potential buyers, establish valuable partnerships, and navigate the intricate landscape of international trade.

Topic 58: Generating Trade Leads - Top Offline Methods

While digital methods play a crucial role in trade lead generation, exploring offline avenues is equally essential. Let's delve into some of the top offline methods to obtain valuable trade leads in the physical world.

1. Trade Publications Subscriptions:

Description: Subscribing to publications offering weekly or fortnightly trade leads received by local trade development bodies.

Relevance: Local trade bodies, Chambers of Commerce, and Export Promotion Councils (EPCs) often compile and share product inquiries based on HS codes.

Access: These subscriptions provide updated and live trade leads, delivered through emails, online downloads, or physical booklets.

2. Market Survey Reports:

Description: Exploring market survey reports from overseas business development delegations sponsored by local trade bodies.

Significance: Delegation reports contain valuable information on product inquiries, importers, and market trends from major trading partners.

Availability: Market survey reports are often available online or can be obtained from local bodies, offering insights into potential export opportunities.

3. Embassies and Consulates:

Description: Engaging with embassies and consulates to gather information on potential importers in the countries they represent.

Benefits: Consulates maintain data on importers seeking suppliers; regular visits and communication help establish fruitful connections.

Recommendation: Regular appointments or telephonic inquiries can lead to obtaining lists of importers seeking specific products.

4. Overseas Chambers of Commerce:

Description: Utilizing the services of overseas Chambers of Commerce that act as bridges between countries.

Example: The Indo-German Chamber of Commerce (IGCC) serves as a model, providing information and trade leads for businesses interested in the India-Germany trade relationship.

Membership Benefits: Joining such chambers as a member allows access to trade leads, participation in buyer-seller meets, and other valuable services.

5. State-Funded Trading Corporations and EPCs:

Description: Collaborating with state-funded trading corporations, such as the State Trading Corporation (STC) and Minerals and Metals Trading Corporation (MMTC).

Role: These organizations, with specific product mandates, receive inquiries beyond their scope and are obligated to share these inquiries with local exporters.

Access: As a member of relevant EPCs or recognized organizations, one can approach these corporations for authentic trade leads.

6. Local Trade Development Bodies:

Description: Leveraging local Chambers of Commerce, EPCs, and trade promotion bodies to access trade leads.

Participation: Active involvement in local trade bodies provides recognition and facilitates the receipt of valuable trade leads.

Networking: Engaging with industry-specific bodies ensures exposure to potential export opportunities and collaborations.

In conclusion, these offline methods complement digital strategies, providing exporters with a holistic approach to trade lead generation. Whether through publications, overseas chambers, consulates, or collaborations with state-funded corporations, the physical world remains a rich source of real and actionable trade leads. Regular interactions, membership participation, and strategic engagements enhance the effectiveness of these offline methods in uncovering new business prospects.

Topic 59: Generating Trade Leads - Other Offline Methods

While email marketing remains a stalwart in international trade, there are additional offline methods that can significantly contribute to lead generation. These methods, although traditional, continue to be effective and offer unique opportunities for exporters seeking new markets.

1. Correspondence and Email Marketing:

Approach: Sending detailed inquiries and correspondence through emails to potential buyers worldwide.

Execution: Building a comprehensive database of email addresses through digital methods or by visiting trade development bodies and institutes.

Enhancement: Coupling email marketing efforts with visits to overseas markets for face-to-face engagements based on the responses received.

2. Participation in Buyer-Seller Meets:

Definition: Buyer-seller meets organized by various trade development bodies, industry associations, and network groups.

Opportunities: Events where buyers and sellers converge with mutual interests, often arranged by entities like CII, FIEO, FICCI, and product-specific EPCs.

Accessibility: Identifying and participating in such meets, which can be either free or paid, offers a direct platform for engaging with potential buyers.

3. International Trade Fairs and Exhibitions:

Strategic Involvement: Participation in international trade fairs and exhibitions, a glamorous and exciting method requiring significant preparation and research.

Benefit: Attracts serious inquiries and potential clients, with Germany being a hub for such events organized by entities like Frankfurt Messe.

Importance: Essential for both new and established exporters to showcase products and capture the interest of buyers seeking a variety of goods.

4. Sample Marketing:

Tactic: Generating interest through samples, suitable for product categories with manageable sample costs.

Execution: Crafting a strategy for sample marketing, either on a paid or free basis, to showcase products and garner interest in the international buying community.

Effectiveness: Particularly suitable for items where samples play a pivotal role in attracting potential buyers.

5. Sponsoring Events:

Strategic Branding: Identifying and sponsoring relevant overseas events, conferences, industry meets, or buyer-seller gatherings.

Visibility: Ensuring the company's brand is visible in events attended by the target audience, thereby increasing the chances of generating serious trade leads.

Smart Decision-Making: Assessing the financial involvement in sponsoring events and evaluating the potential return on investment in terms of quality trade leads.

6. Local Trade Development Bodies:

Engagement: Active participation in local Chambers of Commerce, EPCs, and trade promotion bodies.

Recognition: Establishing recognition within local trade bodies facilitates the receipt of valuable trade leads and enhances networking opportunities.

Networking: Regular involvement in industry-specific bodies ensures exposure to potential export opportunities and collaborations.

In conclusion, these offline methods, ranging from buyer-seller meets and trade fairs to sample marketing and event sponsorships, provide exporters with diverse channels to explore and expand their global reach. While traditional, these approaches remain integral to the multifaceted nature of international trade, offering tangible opportunities for engagement and the generation of high-quality trade leads.

Topic 60: Generating Trade Leads: Some More Offline Methods

In the pursuit of expanding your export business, exploring diverse offline methods for generating trade leads is crucial. These methods, while traditional, offer unique opportunities to connect with potential buyers and establish a robust presence in international markets.

1. Private Demo Events:

Strategy: Organizing exclusive overseas private demo events for invited buyers.

Execution: Advertise the event, display products in selected venues like hotels or business centers, and invite buyers for a personalized experience.

Applicability: Particularly effective for luxury items such as jewelry, high-value fashion, wedding dresses, cosmetics, where showcasing the product range in person enhances buyer engagement.

Product Information Kits: Utilize product information kits to increase awareness, reinforce branding, and generate serious inquiries.

2. Business Network Groups:

Networking Opportunity: Join international business network groups with local chapters.

Example: Groups like Business Network International (BNI) facilitate interactions with prospective international buyers.

Benefits: Networking opportunities and annual membership charges provide avenues for building relationships and exploring potential trade leads.

3. Local Advertising:

Placement: Advertise in local publications and newspapers to announce events, meetings, or visits by marketing representatives.

Outreach: This method attracts new clients and generates interest from buyers, especially in regions with limited communication infrastructure or smaller countries.

Effectiveness: Public advertisements can be powerful tools to connect with a diverse audience and establish a local presence.

4. Commission Agents:

Local Expertise: Engage commission agents in overseas markets who possess local expertise and understand the dynamics of the market.

Facilitation: Commission agents can share contact details of prospective buyers, with the understanding that a commission will be paid upon successful business transactions.

Benefits: Leverage the knowledge of these agents to navigate local markets and establish fruitful connections with buyers.

5. Overseas Trade Bodies:

Collaboration: Connect with overseas trade associations and Chambers of Commerce in target markets.

Engagement: Understand the interests of local industries and exporters and showcase your value proposition.

Support: Overseas trade bodies, when approached appropriately, can provide valuable assistance in obtaining trade leads.

These practical offline methods complement digital strategies discussed earlier, offering exporters a comprehensive approach to lead generation. The combination of private demo events, network group participation, local advertising, commission agent engagement, and collaboration with overseas trade bodies empowers exporters to diversify their outreach and explore untapped markets. By strategically implementing these methods, exporters can position themselves for success in the competitive landscape of international trade.

Topic 60: Chapter Take Away

In this comprehensive exploration of export market research and business intelligence gathering, our journey has unveiled a myriad of methods, avenues, and opportunities to equip you with the knowledge needed to thrive as a successful exporter. The significance of each idea and strategy discussed in this section is intended to guide you through the intricacies of international trade.

If there are aspects that remain unclear or if certain ideas require further clarification, I encourage you to revisit the Topics, immersing yourself in the content. Many insights shared here are drawn from extensive research, training experiences, and, significantly, practical encounters in the corporate world and international trade. Some information might be unique and not readily available in published form, making this section a valuable resource for your export journey.

In the upcoming section, I will leverage the tools and methodologies discussed earlier to present a real-world case study. Through this detailed examination, you'll witness how a company utilized these strategies to gather crucial business intelligence, laying the foundation for a successful foray into the export business. This case study aims to provide you with practical, hands-on insights, reinforcing the concepts discussed in this section.

To enhance your understanding and familiarity with these ideas, an assignment based on the case study will be provided. This assignment is designed to deepen your grasp of the concepts and empower you with practical skills that can be applied to your own ventures.

As we move forward, remember that successful exporting is not just about products and markets; it's about understanding the nuances, leveraging information, and making informed decisions. This section serves as your compass, guiding you through the vast landscape of international trade. Embrace the knowledge, apply the strategies, and embark on your journey towards becoming a thriving and accomplished exporter.

Chapter 7: Case Study Related to Gathering Export Market Information

Topics 62-63: Overview

Here is an interesting case study of a small-town Indian exporter, wishing to enter the international markets with a modest background. The most challenging part of such export projects is getting an initial understanding of the export markets and finding the sources of information. Even bigger challenge is to ascertain where to start.

Introduction to the case study

Hello, dear readers,

Welcome to the exciting realm of practical knowledge in the world of exporting. This section builds upon the foundations laid in the previous segment, where we delved into the intricacies of desk research and initial exploration in the realm of international trade.

In this chapter, we aim to immerse you in a hands-on learning experience through a detailed case study. Our protagonist is Sahi Samay Carpets Industries, a thriving enterprise nestled in the quaint town of Hathras, near the historical city of Agra in India.

Specializing in the creation of exquisite cotton dhurries, particularly the unique chenille cotton rugs crafted through traditional handloom techniques, Sahi Samay Carpets Industries has been a local success story for the past 15 to 20 years. Although their products possess global appeal, they have primarily been channeled through Indian exporters based in cities like Mumbai, Delhi, and Bangalore.

Enter Mr. Neerav, the dynamic second-generation entrepreneur and son of the company's owner. Armed with training and knowledge in exporting, Mr. Neerav is eager to steer the family business towards the international market. His mission: to unravel the intricacies of exporting cotton dhurries, specifically the chenille cotton rugs that are meticulously crafted by skilled artisans.

In the upcoming chapters, we will accompany Mr. Neerav on his journey of exploration and discovery. His initial focus lies on understanding the market dynamics, creating trade leads, and unraveling the mysteries of international marketing. Mr. Neerav is prepared to invest two to three months in extensive desk research to gather crucial insights into the global export scenario.

The next Topic will provide a detailed account of Mr. Neerav's pursuit, including his methodology for uncovering information such as ITC HS codes, potential international markets, and India's standing in the global export landscape. Join us in decoding the strategies employed by Mr. Neerav as he navigates through the labyrinth of information to pave the way for Sahi Samay Carpets Industries' successful foray into the international market.

Stay tuned for an enlightening journey into the world of export market exploration. Keep watching, and let the insights unfold.

Topic 64: Where to start the desk research?

Our protagonist, Mr. Neerav, stands at the crossroads of exploration, eager to unravel the intricacies of exporting chenille rugs, also known as Chenille dhurries or Chenille carpets.

The initial step in Mr. Neerav's quest is to understand the position of Chenille dhurries in the international market. His inquiries revolve around fundamental aspects that shape an exporter's path to success. First and foremost, he grapples with the question of where to begin this journey of comprehension.

Addressing his primary concerns, Mr. Neerav is keen on identifying the right websites to kickstart his research. As an Indian exporter, he understands the pivotal role of accurate and up-to-date data in shaping export strategies. Thus, his second question centers on pinpointing the most reliable sources for gathering pertinent information.

Delving deeper into the complexities of international trade, Mr. Neerav recognizes the importance of product classification from the customs perspective. Acknowledging the significance of the ITC HS code, the international trade classification harmonized system, he aims to grasp the intricacies of this eight-digit code to navigate the export landscape effectively.

In his pursuit, Mr. Neerav acknowledges that a crucial starting point is the Indian Trade Portal. Drawing from his export training, he recognizes the portal as a valuable resource for Indian exporters. This platform serves as the gateway for Mr. Neerav to access essential information, understand government policies, explore export benefits, and decode the foreign trade policy pertaining to Chenille Rugs.

As Mr. Neerav immerses himself in the Indian Trade Portal, he seeks answers to key questions: Is export allowed? What benefits can he avail himself of? What is the government's stance on exporting chenille rugs? And crucially, what are the top countries that actively import Chenille dhurries?

Join us in the upcoming chapters as we unravel Mr. Neerav's exploration, navigating the labyrinth of information on the Indian Trade Portal and beyond. Discover with him the foundations of successful export market research and the strategic decisions that will shape Sahi Samay Carpets Industries' international venture.

Stay tuned for a captivating exploration into the world of export market dynamics. Happy reading!

Topic 65-66: Finding the 8 digit HSN code

In the global landscape of customs and border control, a harmonized classification system reigns supreme – the ITC HS classification. This system aligns and harmonizes products and goods, ensuring a standardized approach to categorization. Each product category is meticulously organized into chapters, identified by 2-digit numbers. Subentries within these chapters are further delineated into 4 digits, 6 digits, 8 digits, 10 digits, and 12 digits numerical codes.

Our protagonist, Mr. Neerav, faces his first crucial objective: obtaining the ITC HS Code. This code serves as the gateway to understanding the export profile of the item in question. In his pursuit of knowledge, Mr. Neerav starts by inputting "Chenille Carpets" into the classification system.

His initial discovery unfolds in the form of a 6-digit code – 570500. This code signifies that the product falls under Chapter 57 in the ITC HS classification. The first two digits always denote the chapter, representing different categories of products.

However, Mr. Neerav's quest doesn't end here. His focus sharpens on obtaining the specific 8-digit code that will provide comprehensive insights into the product classification. Understanding the critical role of the eight-digit code, he navigates to the export section on the Indian Trade Portal.

This strategic move proves fruitful, as Mr. Neerav discovers an 8-digit code – 57050024 – where Chenille dhurries are explicitly mentioned. The eight-digit code not only refines the classification but also serves as the precise starting point for Mr. Neerav's exploration into the export world.

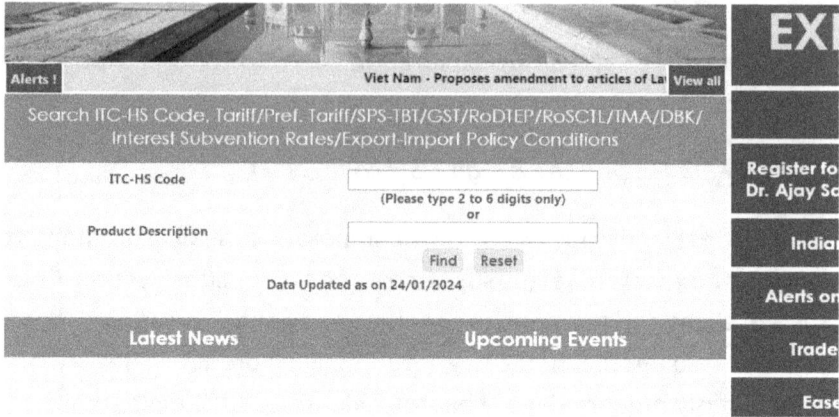

Figure: Search HSN Code for export items on Indian Trade Portal

Armed with the knowledge of the ITC HS code 8 digits, specifically 57050024, Mr. Neerav lays the foundation for further investigations into the international market scenario. The Indian Trade Portal emerges as a valuable ally, providing him with the key to unlocking the intricate details of Chenille dhurries' export dynamics.

Join us in the upcoming topics as Mr. Neerav navigates through the intricacies of export market research, armed with the power of the precise ITC HS code. Witness the unfolding of strategies that will shape Sahi Samay Carpets Industries' successful foray into the international market.

Stay tuned for an insightful exploration into the world of export market dynamics. Happy reading!

Topic 67: Finding top destinations

Continuing our exploration into Mr. Neerav's quest for export market information, let's follow his journey as he strives to identify the top destinations for Chenille dhurries, specifically under the ITC HS code 57050024.

Mr. Neerav begins by visiting the homepage of the Indian Trade Portal to access trade statistics for India. His aim is to understand which countries are the primary importers of Indian goods. What he discovers is a comprehensive list of import statistics for 116 countries, showcasing India's contributions to their imports.

Delving further into this data, Mr. Neerav identifies the top 25 export markets for India. These markets range from the USA and UAE to China, Bangladesh, and the Netherlands. Recognizing the significance of these countries, he narrows down his focus, realizing that among them lie potential destination countries for Sahi Samay Carpets Industries.

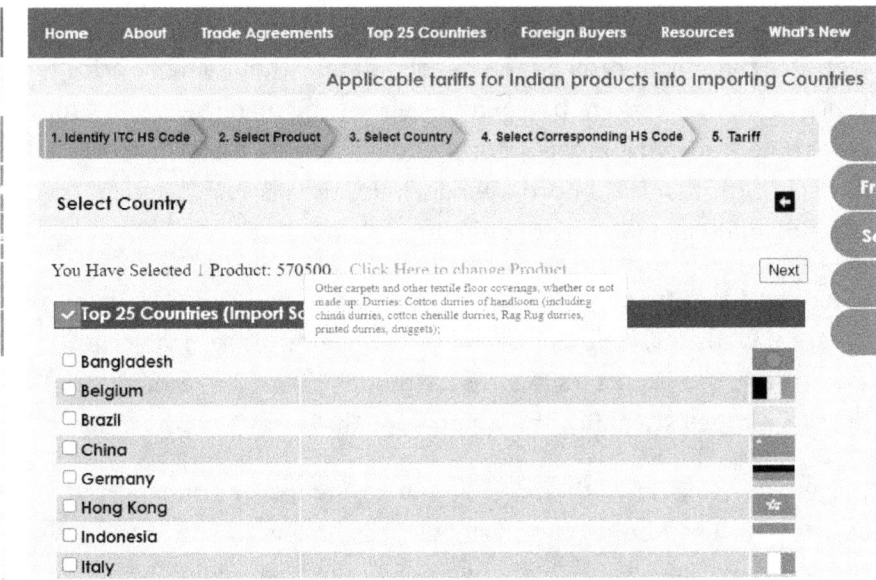

Figure: Top 25 importers of interested export goods

Starting with the USA, Mr. Neerav attempts to explore the specific HS code chapters that dominate its imports. However, to his disappointment, he finds that Chapter 57, which encompasses Chenille carpets, is absent from the list of top import items. This lack of representation suggests that Chapter 57 may not be a major commodity for the USA.

Undeterred, Mr. Neerav extends his search to the United Kingdom and other potential markets, only to encounter a similar absence of Chapter 57 in their top 25 imported commodities. The realization dawns that Chenille carpets may not be prominently featured among the major imports of these countries.

Facing a roadblock in the trade statistics, Mr. Neerav shifts his approach. Turning to Google, he directly searches for the ITC HS code 57050024, hoping to find export data specific to this code. However, the available information is behind a paywall, posing a challenge due to budget constraints.

Undeterred by this obstacle, Mr. Neerav perseveres, seeking alternative websites that might provide the needed data without a hefty price tag. While most sites require payment for access, he manages to find some older data from November 2016, shedding light on the export of Chenille dhurries. This information includes details such as prices, sizes, ports of loading, and ports of discharge.

In a remarkable turn of events, Mr. Neerav discovers more data on different websites, including the names of countries receiving the exports and the exporters involved. Notably, the USA, Germany, and Russia emerge as significant markets for Sahi Samay Carpets Industries.

Diligently noting down the sizes, varieties, and designs of exported cotton rugs, Mr. Neerav gains valuable insights into the preferences of the target markets. He also discovers rare information about the number of shipments, exporters, and buyers involved in the trade, emphasizing the importance of the US, France, and Germany as primary destinations.

Armed with this newfound knowledge, Mr. Neerav is well-equipped to make informed decisions as he continues his exploration into the world of export market dynamics. Join us in the upcoming chapters to witness the strategic choices and actions that will shape Sahi Samay Carpets Industries' successful venture into international markets.

Stay tuned for an insightful journey into the intricate details of export market research. Happy reading!

Topic 68: Finding top destination's import policy data and tariffs

Continuing our journey with Mr. Neerav, let's delve into his strategic approach to understanding the import policies and tariffs of the top destination countries – the USA, Germany, and France – for Sahi Samay Carpets Industries' Chenille dhurries.

Armed with the knowledge that these three countries are the major markets, Mr. Neerav returns to the Indian Trade Portal. Focusing on the specific HS code 57050024, he navigates to the details of the top 25 countries importing this item. Aiming to unravel the import policies and tariffs, he selects the target countries – USA, Germany, and France.

For the USA, Germany, and France, Mr. Neerav explores any special trade agreements or preferences in the Indian Trade Portal. However, he discovers that there are no distinct agreements for Chenille dhurries, indicating that the import duties will be standard without any preferential treatment.

Undeterred, Mr. Neerav continues his investigation by examining the ten-digit codes recognized by the customs of these three countries. This step is crucial for determining the specific categorization of Chenille dhurries and accessing accurate import policies. As he hovers over each code, he carefully reads the descriptions to identify the most fitting classification.

In the case of Germany, he finds a ten-digit code (5705008091) that precisely defines Chenille dhurries made of cotton. This code becomes a valuable tool for future interactions with buyers, customs, and border control.

Similarly, Mr. Neerav explores the ten-digit codes for the USA and France, selecting those that align with the characteristics of Chenille dhurries made of cotton. These codes (5705002020 for the USA and 5705008091 for France) offer specificity, providing a clear understanding of the product for customs clearance.

Pressing the next button, Mr. Neerav reaches the detailed results page for Germany, the USA, and France. Here, he finds that the import duty under Most Favored Nation (MFN) tariff is 8% for Germany and France, and 3.3% for the USA. This information indicates that there are no special preferences or bilateral agreements between these countries and India for Chenille dhurries.

Although Mr. Neerav doesn't enjoy any specific advantages in terms of import duties, he gains a crucial understanding of the standard tariffs applicable to his product. This knowledge empowers him to calculate costs accurately and positions Sahi Samay Carpets Industries competitively in these markets.

Join us in the upcoming chapters to witness how Mr. Neerav strategically navigates the complexities of export market research, import policies, and tariff calculations. Stay tuned for further insights into the world of international trade dynamics. Happy reading!

Topic 69: Finding about home country government export policy

In the wake of Mr. Neerav's comprehensive exploration of international markets, it's time to unravel the intricacies of the Indian government's export policies, incentives, and benefits related to the identified HS code 57050024 for Chenille dhurries.

Building on his wealth of knowledge gathered from previous research, Mr. Neerav shifts his focus to the export policies of the Indian government. He navigates to the relevant section on the Indian Trade Portal to scrutinize the specifics of exporting products falling under the ITC HS code 57050024.

Upon selecting the product description that aligns with Sahi Samay Carpets Industries' offerings, Mr. Neerav discovers that the export policy for handmade woolen or cotton carpets is "free." This implies that there are no restrictions on exporting this product from India to other countries.

However, a notable restriction surfaces – the prohibition of exporting Chenille carpets on Documents Against Acceptance (DA) basis. As explained in earlier Topics, DA is one of the international payment methods. In this case, Mr. Neerav learns that he must opt for Letter of Credit (LC) terms, specifically payable at sight, unless he secures a special guarantee from the Export Credit Guarantee Corporation (ECGC) of India.

Mr. Neerav delves deeper to explore the incentives provided by the Indian government for the identified HS code. Noting the duty drawback code, he records that the benefit is provided in square meters, with a drawback rate of 5.3%. Additionally, there is a cap of ☐44per unit, emphasizing the maximum benefit per square meter.

Moving on to other incentives, Mr. Neerav unearths the Interest Equalisation Scheme for pre and post-shipment rupee exports. As Sahi Samay Carpets Industries qualifies as a small and medium-sized enterprise (MSME), they are eligible for a 3% interest rate benefit on loans obtained from commercial banks.

Another notable incentive is the Remission of Duties and Taxes on Exported Products (RoDTEP). For cotton rugs under HS code 57050024, Mr. Neerav discovers a rate of 3.5% on the Free on Board (FOB) value, with a capped benefit of ☐17.20per square meter.

Having meticulously documented these incentives, Mr. Neerav concludes his research by acknowledging the GST rates for domestic sales in India. Although GST is not applicable to exports, this information provides a holistic view of the overall taxation scenario.

With this comprehensive understanding of the Indian government's export policies and the array of incentives available, Mr. Neerav is well-equipped to navigate the international trade landscape with strategic foresight.

Stay tuned for the unfolding chapters as Mr. Neerav continues his journey, making informed decisions to propel Sahi Samay Carpets Industries towards success in the global market. Happy reading!

Topic 70: What is next?

Buoyed by the wealth of information acquired through his extensive research, Mr. Neerav is now poised for the next phase of his venture into international exports. His meticulous investigation has established India as the top exporter of the specific item he intends to trade—Chenille dhurries. Armed with this knowledge, he outlines a strategic plan for further exploration and preparation.

First on his agenda is to visit key organizations that can offer valuable insights and connections. Mr. Neerav plans to make a trip to the Indo German Chamber of Commerce, recognizing Germany as one of his target markets. This visit is strategic, aiming to gather information, build relationships, and understand the nuances of the German market.

In pursuit of his U.S. market aspirations, Mr. Neerav plans to visit the American Central Library. His objective is to compile a list of potential importers in the USA, enriching his understanding of the market dynamics and identifying key players.

Similarly, Mr. Neerav sets his sights on the French consulate trade office in New Delhi, seeking to establish connections and gather market intelligence for the French market. The proximity of the consulate to Hathras, his base, makes this visit a practical and valuable step in his research process.

To further strengthen his market presence, Mr. Neerav resolves to explore international trade fairs in Germany. Armed with the information obtained from data archives and paid services, he plans to showcase his samples at these fairs, capitalizing on the exposure to potential buyers and market trends.

Recognizing the importance of detailed preparation, Mr. Neerav anticipates dedicating another two to three months to refine his product samples and designs. The information gleaned from various sources, including shipment details and paid services, will be cross-verified to ensure the accuracy of his findings.

In essence, Mr. Neerav's journey has transformed from a quest for initial knowledge to a well-informed strategy for entering the international market. His comprehensive understanding of the HS codes, market trends, and potential challenges has positioned him as a savvy exporter ready to navigate the intricacies of global trade.

As we follow Mr. Neerav's progress, the next chapters will unveil the outcomes of his visits to key organizations, the refinement of his product offerings, and the strategic steps he takes to establish Sahi Samay Carpets Industries as a formidable player in the international market. Stay tuned for the unfolding chapters of this exciting journey!

Assignment: Starting with a new products for exports

This assignment's objective is to allow you to explore all possible business intelligence about a new product you may wish to enquire about for export potential from your home country. Some questions are posed in this assignment. But you can go beyond these questions and collect information.

Assignment instructions: Based on the case study shared in this section, you would be required to answer certain questions related to a product of your choice for exporting from your country. You may use all you have learned from this case study to find solutions to the questions raised in this assignment. It will be better if you prepare a market research report based on the questions asked in this assignment. And submit the same for review and comments by the VJ Global MBA Courses Series team.

Question 1:

Write down a short note on your export idea stating the product description, country of origin, and background of the promoter of the new startup in this chosen product. Describe as much as you like to highlight all you know at the starting stage about your new export project.

Question 2:

Find out the HSN code at least 8 digit code/s of the product/s you have chosen to enquire about.

Question 3:

Collect all relevant statistics and figures to know at least 4 potential export markets for the product/s in question. Support your choices with suitable references and sources of information.

Question 4:

Find out the highlights of the local government export policy provisions for the product/s in question. Also, list out what government support and incentives are available for the export of the proposed goods. Specifically, point out if there are any local government restrictions or compliances required for the products proposed for exports.

Question 5:

Prepare an initial export plan and marketing strategy for the chosen product/s exports and the project in hand. Also prepare a initial export market research report based on this assignment.

Chapter 9: International Commercial Terms INCOTERMS 2020

Topics 72-73: Overview

As we continue our journey in the world of international trade, you've undoubtedly gained valuable insights into generating leads, bargaining, negotiating, and soliciting orders. You've mastered the art of creating interest in overseas buyers and are now at a crucial stage – finalizing the deal.

In the intricate landscape of international commerce, the process of sealing the deal involves providing quotations, generating proforma invoices, and, in some cases, drafting elaborate contracts. The complexity of these transactions necessitates a nuanced understanding of various elements, one of which is the pivotal aspect of delivery terms.

When we discuss delivery terms, we're delving into the realm of commercial terms. International business transactions involve countries that are not only geographically distant but also differ legally, culturally, and administratively. This disparity creates a significant gap between the point of origin and the destination, with numerous intermediaries and processes involved in the journey of goods.

Understanding this journey is crucial – it spans from the seller's location to the agreed-upon destination, usually the buyer's country. The transfer of obligations and risks is not a straightforward process; it varies at different points along the way.

To address the complexities of international trade, the International Chamber of Commerce, based in Paris, France, has published a charter known as Incoterms – an abbreviation for International Commercial Terms. These terms, recognized globally, provide a standardized set of rules defining the obligations and risks associated with the transfer of goods from seller to buyer.

In this section, we'll explore the 11 Incoterms of 2020 in detail. These terms play a vital role in determining when the obligation and risk transfer occurs in the journey from the origin to the destination. As we delve into these terms, we'll uncover the nuances that distinguish one point from another, shedding light on the complexity inherent in international trade.

Join me in unraveling the intricacies of the latest version of Incoterms, INCOTERM 2020, as we navigate through the journey of goods from the seller's warehouse to the buyer's, understanding the crucial points where obligations and risks shift hands.

Topic 74: About INCOTERMS 2020

INCOTERMS have weathered the test of time, adapting to the ever-changing landscape of international trade, transportation, and document delivery systems. The latest iteration, INCOTERMS 2020, serves as a beacon, providing a framework that transcends borders and languages, offering a concise and binding set of contractual conditions.

Within these terms, exporters and importers find a common ground, a shared language that ensures the satisfaction of each party involved in a transaction. These terms serve a triple purpose:

Completion of a Sale to Satisfaction: INCOTERMS 2020 facilitates the seamless completion of a sale, ensuring that all parties involved are satisfied with the terms of the contract.

Establishing Basic Terms: In a format that is both short and simple, INCOTERMS outline the fundamental terms governing the transportation and delivery of goods, fostering clarity in international transactions.

Clarifying Costs, Risks, and Obligations: The terms explicitly define the roles of each contracting party concerning the delivery of goods. From the completion of delivery to the transfer of risk, INCOTERMS answer crucial questions:

a) At what stage does the seller fulfill their delivery obligation?

b) How can one party ensure the other meets the desired standards outlined in the contract?

c) When does the transfer of the risk of loss or damage occur?

d) What documents and notices are required during the transportation and transfer of title?

e) How are transport costs distributed among the parties?

f) Who is responsible for obtaining licenses, permissions, and handling government-imposed formalities?

g) What constitutes the 'delivery terms,' and what proofs signify the completion of delivery?

h) What are the modes and terms of carriage?

Join me as we delve into the specifics of INCOTERMS 2020, unraveling the language that binds international trade, and equipping you with the knowledge to navigate the intricacies of successful exporting.

Continuing with our exploration of INCOTERMS 2020, it's imperative to understand that these terms are traditionally categorized into four distinct groups, each delineating the roles and responsibilities of the contracting parties. These categories, identified by the first letter of their respective terms, provide a framework for negotiating and tailoring the terms to meet the unique needs of each trade transaction.

Group E - Ex Works (EXW): In this category, denoted by the letter 'E,' the seller fulfills their obligation by making the goods available to the buyer at their own premises. The buyer assumes all responsibilities and costs associated with transportation, insurance, and import duties from the seller's location. EXW, falling under Group E, marks the initiation of the INCOTERMS journey, where the buyer takes charge of the entire logistical process.

Group F - Free Carrier (FCA), Free Alongside Ship (FAS), Free On Board (FOB): Moving on to Group F, these terms involve the seller in delivering the goods to a first carrier, usually selected by the buyer. The 'F' terms, which include FCA, FAS, and FOB, dictate the point at which the seller fulfills their obligation. Whether it's at the seller's premises, the port of shipment, or when the goods are loaded onto the carrier, Group F offers flexibility in negotiating the terms based on the preferences of the contracting parties.

Group C - Cost and Freight (CFR), Cost, Insurance and Freight (CIF), Carriage Paid To (CPT), Carriage and Insurance Paid To (CIP): Transitioning to Group C, the seller in these terms undertakes the responsibility of entering into a contract for the main carriage at their own cost. This group, denoted by the letter 'C,' includes CFR, CIF, CPT, and CIP. Here, the seller handles the main transportation costs, but the risk transfers at different points depending on the specific term chosen.

Group D - Delivered at Terminal (DAT), Delivered at Place (DAP), Delivered Duty Paid (DDP): Concluding our categorization with Group D, these terms require the seller to bear both the costs and risks necessary to bring the goods to the agreed-upon destination. The 'D' terms, comprising DAT, DAP, and DDP, place a higher degree of responsibility on the seller, making them accountable for the entire transportation process, including unloading at the buyer's premises.

As we progress in this chapter, we'll delve into the intricacies of each INCOTERM within these categories, exploring how they address the fundamental questions related to delivery terms, risk transfer, and obligations. Join me in unraveling the nuances of INCOTERMS 2020 and mastering the language that underpins successful international trade transactions.

Topic 75: INCOTERMS 2020 Explained

Continuing our journey through the intricacies of INCOTERMS 2020, let's dive deeper into the specifics of each term and their implications in the international trade landscape.

Ex Works (EXW): The starting point of our journey, where the seller's obligation concludes as the goods are made available at their premises. This point, known as "WORKS," signifies the completion of the seller's responsibility.

Free Carrier (FCA): As we progress, FCA marks the point where the goods are loaded onto the first carrier, typically a truck. This term offers flexibility, allowing the parties to negotiate the precise location where the seller fulfills their obligation.

Free Alongside Ship (FAS): Our journey then takes us to the point where goods are lying beside the ship, ready for loading. Known as "Free Alongside Ship," FAS highlights the location alongside the ship at the port of loading.

Free On Board (FOB): FOB denotes the moment when the goods are loaded onto the ship at the port of loading. It is at this point that the seller's responsibility is fulfilled, and the risk and obligation begin to shift to the buyer.

Cost and Freight (CFR): Transitioning into Group C, CFR emphasizes that not only have the goods been loaded onto the ship, but the cost of main carriage to the port of discharge is borne by the seller.

INCOTERMS® 2020-Point of Delivery & Transfer of Risk

Figure: Summary of all 11 INCOTERMS 2020

Cost, Insurance, and Freight (CIF): Extending the obligations further, CIF includes not only the cost of carriage but also the insurance cost until the goods reach the port of discharge. Here, the seller assumes a higher degree of responsibility.

Cost Paid To (CPT): Taking a leap to Group D, CPT signals that the seller covers all costs involved in the entire journey, from the first carrier to the buyer's warehouse. The risk transfer points may vary, emphasizing the importance of the buyer's understanding of these terms.

Cost, Insurance, and Paid To (CIP): In CIP, the seller goes beyond CPT by also covering the insurance cost. This term reflects the comprehensive nature of the seller's responsibility in ensuring the safe arrival of goods at the buyer's premises.

Delivered at Place Unloaded (DPU): Introducing the D terms, DPU signifies that the goods have been delivered at the agreed place in the buyer's country, unloaded and ready for the buyer to take possession. The risk and obligation shift to the buyer's country.

Delivered at Place (DAP): In DAP, the goods reach the premises of the buyer, specifically the buyer's warehouse. The seller's obligation extends to the buyer's designated location, offering a clearer delineation of responsibility.

Delivered Duty Paid (DDP): Concluding our exploration with DDP, this term signifies that the seller not only delivers the goods at the buyer's place but also takes care of all import duties and taxes. The buyer's obligations begin only after the goods are safely delivered and all duties are settled.

Understanding these terms empowers exporters and importers to negotiate and agree upon a framework that aligns with their needs. The clarity provided by INCOTERMS 2020 ensures that international trade transactions can proceed smoothly and with minimal risk of disputes. As you delve into the specifics of each term, you'll gain a comprehensive understanding of the obligations, risks, and costs associated with the journey of goods from the seller's premises to the buyer's warehouse.

Chapter Conclusion: Navigating the Landscape of INCOTERM 2020

In concluding our exploration of the International Commercial Terms, INCOTERM 2020, we've embarked on a journey through the intricacies of international trade, from the seller's premises to the buyer's warehouse. These terms, steeped in tradition and continuously adapting to the evolving global trade landscape, provide a standardized framework for negotiating, defining obligations, and mitigating risks in cross-border transactions.

Starting with the foundational concept of "WORKS" in Ex Works (EXW), we traversed through the various categories, each denoted by a letter symbolizing the primary point of obligation transfer. From the flexibility of Free Carrier (FCA) to the loading of goods alongside the ship in Free Alongside Ship (FAS) and onto the ship in Free On Board (FOB), each term represents a pivotal moment in the seller's journey to fulfill their obligations.

Transitioning to Group C, we explored Cost and Freight (CFR) and Cost, Insurance, and Freight (CIF), where the seller's responsibilities extend to the main carriage and insurance, adding layers of complexity and care.

Group D introduced a comprehensive approach with Cost Paid To (CPT) and Cost, Insurance, and Paid To (CIP). These terms signify not just the completion of the seller's obligation but also the covering of transportation and insurance costs.

The D terms, Delivered at Place Unloaded (DPU), Delivered at Place (DAP), and Delivered Duty Paid (DDP), mark the culmination of the seller's journey as the goods reach the buyer's designated location. DDP, in particular, signifies a comprehensive obligation, including the settlement of import duties and taxes by the seller.

The accompanying chart serves as a visual aid, mapping out the points of obligation transfer and risk transfer across the 11 INCOTERMS. The clarity provided by these terms enhances international trade transactions, fostering smooth negotiations and reducing the risk of disputes.

As you delve into the specifics of each term, remember that the beauty of INCOTERMS lies in their ability to create a universal language for traders worldwide. By understanding these terms and incorporating them into your contracts, you empower yourself to navigate the complex web of global trade with confidence, ensuring that every party involved comprehends their roles, risks, and responsibilities.

In the world of international trade, where distances are vast, cultures diverse, and legal frameworks distinct, INCOTERMS 2020 stands as a beacon, guiding exporters and importers towards successful, dispute-free transactions. May this knowledge serve you well on your path to becoming a skilled and successful exporter, regardless of your origin.

Chapter 10: Receiving International Payments

Topic 76: Different methods

Welcome to a crucial chapter in "All About How to Become A Successful Exporter, Any Origin." As you embark on your journey into the world of international trade, one of the paramount considerations is navigating the landscape of international payments. This chapter is dedicated to unraveling the intricacies of receiving payments from overseas partners, ensuring a secure and seamless financial transaction process.

Understanding the fundamentals of international payments is indispensable for exporters, laying the groundwork for successful and risk-mitigated transactions. In this exploration, we will delve into the various options available for receiving payments and discuss the nuances of each method. Moreover, the chapter will shed light on the inherent risks associated with different payment options, presenting a comprehensive view that caters to both exporters and importers.

The world of international finance is complex, and what may be a secure payment option for one party could pose risks for the other. Hence, it becomes imperative to strike a balance between security and convenience, considering the perspectives of both the exporter and the importer. This chapter aims to equip you with the knowledge and insights needed to make informed decisions about international payments, fostering a secure and prosperous journey in the realm of global trade.

Join me in unraveling the intricacies of getting international payments, as we explore the methods, risks, and best practices that define this critical aspect of successful exporting.

Options for Receiving International Payments in Export Transactions

In the intricate landscape of international trade, understanding the nuances of receiving payments is pivotal for exporters. The journey from negotiating the deal to ensuring the secure transfer of funds involves careful consideration of various options, each laden with its own set of risks and advantages.

The Role of Letters of Credit (LC)

As we previously delved into the Letter of Credit, a widely used method involving the collaboration of banks, let's briefly revisit the key points. In this scenario, the importer's local bank issues the LC, which is advised by the exporter's bank. The exporter, upon accepting the terms, ships the goods, and the negotiating bank releases the documents to the importer upon payment. While this method introduces a layer of complexity, it provides a secure framework for both parties.

Exploring Alternative Payment Options

However, there exist other avenues for international payments, each carrying its unique risk profile. One extreme involves the importer making a 100% advance payment. While this is the safest option for the exporter, it poses the highest risk for the importer. On the contrary, consignment sales, where payment occurs after the importer receives and takes possession of the goods, are safest for the importer but significantly riskier for the exporter.

Risk Ladder of Payment Options

Let's visualize the spectrum of risk involved in different payment options:

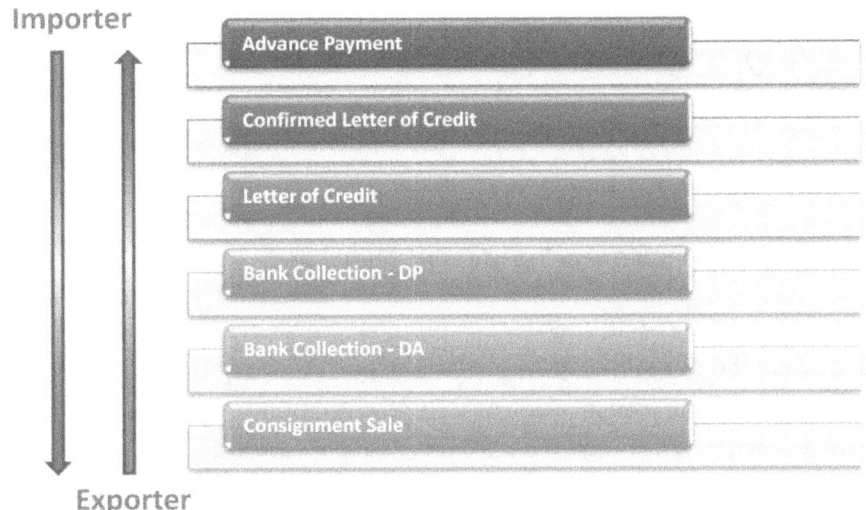

Figure: Payment Risk Ladder For Exports

Advance Payment:

- Riskiest for the importer.

- Safest for the exporter.

Confirmed Letter of Credit:

- Second safest for the exporter.

- Involves a second layer of local confirmation by the confirming bank.

Letter of Credit (LC):

- A secure method but less so compared to a confirmed LC.

Bank Collection (Documentary Payment or Acceptance):

- More risk for the exporter.

- Involves selling documents to the importer against payment or acceptance.

Consignment Sale:

- Riskiest for the exporter.

- Safest for the importer.

Topic 77: Factors Influencing Method Selection

The choice of payment method is influenced by a myriad of factors, including the bargaining power of the exporter, the nature of the product, and the transaction cost. The transaction cost varies significantly, with confirmed LCs and LCs being costlier due to the risk premium charged by banks. Bargaining power, product type, and cost considerations collectively guide both parties in selecting the most suitable method for international payments.

As we proceed in this chapter, we will dissect each of these payment options, shedding light on their intricacies, advantages, and potential pitfalls. The goal is to empower exporters with a comprehensive understanding of the options at their disposal, enabling informed decisions in the dynamic realm of international trade.

Conclusion: Navigating International Payments in Export Transactions

In the intricate dance of international trade, the chapter on "Different Methods of Receiving International Payments in Export Transactions" serves as a compass, guiding exporters through the labyrinth of payment options. As we conclude this exploration, it becomes evident that the world of commerce is not one-size-fits-all; rather, it is a tapestry of choices, risks, and strategic considerations.

The journey commenced with a revisit to the tried-and-tested method of Letters of Credit (LC), a robust mechanism involving banks to secure transactions for both exporters and importers. The complexities were dissected, and the nuances appreciated. However, the landscape expanded beyond LCs, unraveling a spectrum of options, each with its distinctive risk profile.

The risk ladder, extending from advance payments—safest for the exporter yet riskiest for the importer—to consignment sales—safest for the importer but laden with risk for the exporter—provided a visual roadmap for understanding the trade-offs involved. Confirmed LCs emerged as a noteworthy intermediary, introducing an additional layer of security for the exporter through local bank confirmation.

This chapter underscores the importance of recognizing the multifaceted factors influencing the selection of payment methods. Bargaining power, product nature, and transaction costs collectively shape the strategic decisions of both exporters and importers. The delicate balance between risk and security becomes the fulcrum upon which successful international transactions pivot.

As exporters delve further into the world of international trade, armed with insights from this chapter, they are equipped to make judicious decisions. The nuanced understanding of risk and the intricate dance of payment methods empowers exporters to navigate the dynamic terrain of global commerce. With this knowledge, they stand better prepared to negotiate, strategize, and forge secure and mutually beneficial transactions in the ever-evolving global marketplace.

Chapter 11: Understanding Export Procedures

Topic 78: Overview

So far in our journey through the intricacies of becoming a successful exporter, we've delved into various aspects of the international trade landscape. Now, as we navigate further in this course, our focus turns to a critical juncture in the export journey – understanding the export procedures.

Have you ever wondered what exactly constitutes the export procedure from its initiation to its culmination? The realm of international trade is governed by a series of intricate steps that demand attention to detail and adherence to regulations. In this chapter, we will unravel the complexity and shed light on approximately 13 key steps that form the backbone of the complete export procedure.

Embarking on a global trade venture requires a comprehensive understanding of the legal formalities that each country mandates. From the moment a decision is made to engage in export activities, a series of crucial steps must be meticulously followed. It is important to note that these procedures might exhibit subtle variations from one country to another, making it imperative for exporters to grasp the intricacies of the specific regulations in their target markets.

Join us as we dissect each step of the export procedure, providing you with valuable insights and practical guidance to navigate through the maze of international trade regulations. Whether you are a novice exporter or a seasoned professional seeking a refresher, this chapter aims to equip you with the knowledge necessary to successfully traverse the export landscape with confidence and efficiency.

Topics 79-80: Legal compliance

So, fasten your seatbelts as we embark on a journey through the 13 fundamental steps that define the export procedure – an indispensable guide for any origin.

Step 1: Legal Compliance

As we embark on the journey through the labyrinth of export procedures, our first crucial checkpoint is legal compliance. Navigating the legal landscape is paramount for the success of any export venture. In this section, we will explore the fundamental legalities that lay the groundwork for a smooth and lawful export process.

Figure: Legal Compliance For Export

1. Creating a Legal Entity: Setting the Stage for Export Success

The initial and pivotal legal compliance in the export journey involves the creation of a legal entity, a business structure that will serve as the backbone of your export operations. Whether you opt for a simple proprietorship or venture into more complex forms like partnerships, LLPs, private limited, or public limited entities, the choice rests on factors such as budget constraints, long-term vision, and mission.

For those entering the export domain on a tight budget or seeking to test the waters, a straightforward business entity like a proprietorship, widely used in countries such as India, provides a quick and cost-effective starting point. The flexibility of such entities allows for easy establishment and closure based on business needs.

2. Import-Export License: Navigating the Regulatory Seas

Following the establishment of your legal entity, the next critical step is obtaining an import-export license. In some jurisdictions, this may be as straightforward as utilizing your tax ID number, while in others, a more intricate process, such as acquiring an importer-exporter code (IEC) number, may be required.

In countries like the United States, the tax ID number itself can act as the import-export license. Conversely, in India, obtaining the IEC code, acting as the import-export license, is a relatively streamlined process. Applicants can apply online, and the government fee is a nominal amount, making it accessible for businesses of varying sizes.

3. Registering with Local Tax Authorities: Navigating the Fiscal Terrain

A critical legal compliance in most countries involves registering with local tax authorities to navigate the fiscal landscape. This includes obtaining registrations such as the Goods and Services Tax (GST) number in India. Depending on the product and jurisdiction, businesses might also need to register with other tax authorities such as sales tax, VAT, or excise.

The primary objective of these registrations is to facilitate tax-exempt exports, aligning with the common goal of governments to encourage and promote international trade. By becoming a registered entity with local tax authorities, exporters can steer clear of direct and indirect taxes that could otherwise impede the competitiveness of their products in the global market.

Join us as we delve deeper into the legal intricacies, unraveling the layers of compliance that form the bedrock of a successful and legally sound export operation. In the next sections, we will explore the subsequent steps in the export procedure, providing insights and practical tips for each stage.

Topic 81: Step 2: Registrations for Getting Support and Export Assistance

Having laid the groundwork with legal compliance, the next pivotal step in the export procedure involves strategic registrations aimed at securing essential assistance, fostering trade generation, and obtaining valuable business intelligence. In this section, we explore the diverse organizations that can provide support and the registrations that open the door to a myriad of opportunities.

1. Trade Development Bodies: Navigating Export Opportunities

One avenue for comprehensive support in international trade is through registrations with trade development bodies. In India, for instance, Export Promotion Councils (EPCs) serve as vital platforms for trade development. Product-wise classification within these organizations, often requiring a Registration Cum Membership Certificate (RCMC), facilitates access to archives and data. This wealth of information becomes an invaluable resource, aiding exporters in understanding market dynamics and trends.

Similar entities exist in various countries, sponsored by local governments, providing assistance and export incentives. Registration not only opens avenues for support but also becomes mandatory for accessing government incentives. For instance, in India, possessing an RCMC is a prerequisite for obtaining local government incentives, highlighting the importance of these registrations.

Figure: Registrations for Getting Support and Export Assistance

Moreover, these organizations often offer online services, providing exporters with instant access to crucial business intelligence. Platforms like the Indian Trade Portal exemplify the potential of government and non-government services, offering a wealth of online resources to facilitate informed decision-making.

2. Industry Bodies: Leveraging Networking and Intelligence

Another avenue for trade assistance lies in registrations with industry bodies, such as chambers of commerce, industry associations, and trade networking groups. Organizations like FICCI (Federation of Indian Chambers of Commerce and Industries) in India provide valuable business intelligence and trade leads. Networking groups like the Federation of Indian Export Organizations (FIEO) play a crucial role in connecting exporters with foreign clients, offering both online and offline services.

These industry bodies become essential platforms for gathering intelligence on market trends, potential clients, and industry-specific information. By becoming a registered member, exporters gain access to a network of professionals and resources that can significantly enhance their export endeavors.

3. Product-Specific Registrations: Meeting Standards for Market Access

Certain products may necessitate registrations beyond legal requirements, often related to quality standards, environmental considerations, or specific industry norms. Obtaining certifications from international organizations attesting to environmentally friendly practices can be critical, especially in markets that prioritize sustainability.

For instance, seafood exporters may seek certifications from organizations endorsing sustainable fishing practices, enhancing their appeal in premium markets. Additionally, product-specific registrations may be required to meet local labor laws, food safety standards, or international management standards like ISO. These registrations not only enhance the marketability of products but also address concerns related to environmental sustainability and public health.

In the complex world of international trade, strategic registrations with diverse organizations empower exporters with the knowledge, support, and incentives necessary for a successful global venture. In the subsequent sections, we will delve into further steps in the export procedure, unraveling the intricacies of each stage.

Topics 82-83: Step 3: Generating Export Business

Moving forward in our exploration of the export procedure, the third crucial step is the generation of export business. Successfully securing overseas clients demands a strategic blend of preparation, ingenuity, skills, hard work, and in-depth knowledge. In this section, we will unravel the intricate process of generating export sales, spanning three distinct stages.

1. Inquiry Generation: Initiating the Sales Process

The first stage in the sales generation process involves the initiation of inquiries. When prospective buyers express interest through letters of inquiry, exporters respond with quotations, typically presented in a specialized format known as the proforma invoice. This document, which we will delve into further in the next Topic on export documentation, serves as a crucial tool to facilitate the swift finalization of sales. Negotiations with foreign buyers often commence after the submission of the proforma invoice.

2. Due Diligence: Assessing Buyers and Markets

Following the initial interaction, the second stage necessitates thorough due diligence on both the buyer and the country of origin. This involves obtaining crucial business intelligence about the market and the prospective buyer. Screening processes, depending on the exporter's country, can range from specialized screening software to services provided by entities like the Export Credit Guarantee Corporation (ECGC). The goal is to assess the credibility of the buyer and evaluate the market feasibility before proceeding further. This due diligence is crucial for minimizing risks and ensuring a secure and successful export transaction.

3. Finalizing the Contract: Navigating Terms and Conditions

The third and final stage of sales generation involves the formalization of the export contract. As discussed in earlier Topics, exporters need comprehensive knowledge of international commercial terms, various options for receiving international payments, and different delivery terms. Armed with this understanding gained throughout the course, exporters can navigate negotiations with international buyers and agree on terms and conditions that form the basis of a robust and sustainable export contract.

By mastering these three pivotal stages, exporters can not only secure business from overseas clients but also establish a foundation for long-term and successful international trade relationships. In the subsequent sections, we will delve deeper into the subsequent steps in the export procedure, providing insights and practical guidance at each juncture.

Topics 84-85: Step 4: Appointing Freight Forwarder

As we delve deeper into the export procedure, the fourth critical step involves appointing a Clearing and Forwarding Agent, commonly known as a freight forwarder. These 3rd party logistics providers play a pivotal role in facilitating the smooth movement of goods internationally. The careful appointment of such intermediaries is essential, and due diligence must guide the selection process.

1. Role of a Freight Forwarder: Navigating International Logistics

Freight forwarders, also known as Clearing and Forwarding (CnF) Agents, are instrumental in managing various aspects of the export procedure. They play a multifaceted role that includes negotiating with shipping companies, handling customs clearance, and overseeing the movement of goods across borders. By outsourcing these responsibilities to a freight forwarder, exporters can streamline the logistics process and focus on other crucial aspects of their business.

2. Booking Shipping Space: Key Step After Contract Finalization

Once the export contract has been finalized, including payment terms and, if applicable, the acceptance of a letter of credit, the next crucial step is to book shipping space. This is where the appointment of a CnF agent comes into play. The freight forwarder, armed with expertise and industry connections, negotiates terms and conditions with shipping companies to secure space for the exporter's goods. This step is particularly vital to ensure timely and cost-effective international transportation.

3. Shipper's Letter of Instruction (SLI): Empowering the Freight Forwarder

The process of appointing a freight forwarder involves providing a document known as the Shipper's Letter of Instruction (SLI). This document serves multiple purposes, acting as an authorization letter and a limited power of attorney. By issuing the SLI, the exporter grants the freight forwarder the authority to carry out various local formalities, including dealings with customs and border control, on their behalf.

The SLI also delineates the scope of work for the freight forwarder. This includes defining the responsibilities based on product specifications, contract terms, payment terms, and the chosen method and mode of transportation. The SLI ensures a transparent understanding between the exporter and the freight forwarder, outlining the specific tasks and expectations for the international movement of goods.

By carefully navigating through this step, exporters can leverage the expertise of freight forwarders to optimize logistics, reduce risks, and ensure the efficient transportation of their products to international markets. In the subsequent sections, we will unravel further steps in the export procedure, guiding exporters through the intricacies of global trade.

Topics 86-87: Step 5: Managing Export Risks

In the intricate landscape of international trade, managing export risks is a specialized area that demands a comprehensive understanding of various risks inherent in export transactions. As we progress through the export procedure, step number five is dedicated to export risk management, a parallel and crucial aspect that runs concurrently with all other activities.

1. Export Risk Management: Navigating Various Risks

Export risk management is a nuanced discipline aimed at effectively navigating the diverse risks associated with export transactions. It is an ongoing process that involves implementing strategies and measures to minimize potential risks at various stages of the export journey.

2. Major Risks in Export Transactions: Identifying Key Challenges

In a typical export transaction, several risks must be addressed to ensure a smooth and secure process. These include:

Transportation Risk: This pertains to the potential risks during the transportation of goods. Cargo insurance is a common tool to mitigate this risk, providing coverage for potential damages or losses during transit.

Foreign Exchange Risk: Fluctuations in foreign exchange rates can pose a significant challenge. The disparity between the currency of the contract and the currency of the exporter's home country may lead to financial uncertainties. Strategies such as hedging and other financial instruments can be employed to minimize the impact of foreign exchange fluctuations.

Nonpayment Risk (Commercial Risk): The risk of nonpayment, often referred to as the commercial risk, is a critical concern. Factors such as the buyer's financial stability or the reputation of the bank involved in the transaction can influence the risk of nonpayment. Situations like buyer bankruptcy or difficulties in obtaining local confirmation for a letter of credit can pose challenges.

3. Mitigating Nonpayment Risk: The Role of ECGC

To address the nonpayment risk, organizations like the Export Credit Guarantee Corporation (ECGC) play a pivotal role. Typically sponsored by local governments, these entities provide commercial risk cover to exporters. By securing coverage through ECGC or similar organizations, exporters can protect themselves against the potential financial losses arising from nonpayment situations.

Step number five, therefore, involves a proactive approach to managing these major risks. Exporters must engage in continuous risk assessment and adopt appropriate strategies to safeguard their interests throughout the export transaction.

As we progress through the subsequent sections, we will unravel additional steps in the export procedure, providing insights and practical guidance to exporters navigating the complexities of global trade.

Topics 88-89: Step 6: Obtaining and Preparing Export Documents

In the intricate dance of international trade, step number six involves a critical process: obtaining and preparing export documents. These documents serve as the lifeblood of the export transaction, essential not only for compliance but also to facilitate payments. Let's delve into the significance of these documents and the meticulous preparation required.

1. Importance of Export Documents: Ensuring Quality and Compliance

The preparation of export documents is not just a procedural step; it is a fundamental necessity to facilitate payments and assure the quality of the shipment. The buyer relies on these documents, and their specifics are often outlined in the sales contract. One of the primary concerns of the buyer is the quality of the shipped goods, and a quality certificate becomes a crucial document in this regard.

Additionally, various documents are required for compliance purposes, both at the buyer's and the seller's ends. For instance, Letter of Credit (LC) documents, as stipulated in the letter of credit issued by the issuing bank, include commercial principal documents such as:

I. Commercial Invoice

II. Packing List

III. Certificate of Origin

IV. Transport Documents (confirming the shipment has been made)

2. LC Documents and Bank Requirements: Ensuring Financial Security

LC documents serve as a guarantee for payment, and the bank, as a third-party intermediary, may have specific requirements. Some of the documents required by the bank include:

Bank Draft or Bill of Exchange

I.   Covering Letter

II.   Additional requirements such as a Packing List for a clearer understanding of the shipment's nature.

The bank's involvement emphasizes the need for meticulous adherence to documentation requirements, as banks deal solely with documents, not physical shipments.

3. Local Regulatory Documents: Compliance with Local Governments

Beyond the buyer, seller, and the bank, local regulatory bodies play a crucial role. Sellers must comply with local government departments, including Customs and Excise or Sales Tax departments. These regulatory documents ensure that the export transaction aligns with local laws and regulations.

4. Auxiliary Documents: Supporting the Main Commercial Documents

In addition to the principal commercial documents required by the buyer and the letter of credit, exporters often need auxiliary documents. These auxiliary documents are submitted to local authorities or international organizations to obtain the primary commercial documents. While not directly involved in the export transaction, these supporting documents are vital in securing the necessary approvals and clearances.

Understanding the nuances of each type of document and the intricacies of compliance is paramount in this step of the export procedure. In the following sections, we will explore these documents in more detail, providing exporters with insights and guidance to navigate the complex realm of export documentation.

Topic 90: Step 7: Preparing and Packing the Goods for Exports

As we advance through the intricate steps of the export procedure, step number seven takes center stage, focusing on the crucial task of preparing and packing the goods for exports. This step involves a meticulous process, from securing financing to ensuring quality control and adhering to packing standards suitable for the chosen mode of transportation.

1. Financing for Goods Preparation: Pre and Post Shipment Credit

Before delving into the intricacies of preparing goods, it's imperative to secure the necessary financing. In many countries, governments offer support in the form of interest subsidies for exporters seeking pre-shipment credit. This credit, obtained before the shipment, assists in the purchase or manufacturing of goods. Post shipment credit, with favorable interest rates, may also be availed after the goods have been shipped. These financial mechanisms aim to provide exporters with competitive rates aligned with international market standards.

2. In-Process Quality Inspection and Manufacturing Oversight

For exporters engaged in manufacturing goods, in-process quality inspection becomes a critical checkpoint. Depending on the product and buyer's requirements, quality certification may be necessary. The exporter must ensure that the manufacturing process aligns with the agreed-upon standards, and in-process inspections may be required to maintain quality control.

3. Export Packing: Sea Worthy and Airworthy Standards

The mode of transportation dictates the packing standards for the goods. Sea-worthy packing is essential for goods shipped by sea, ensuring they withstand the rigors of maritime transport. Similarly, airworthy packing is required for goods transported by air. Exporters, whether manufacturers or merchant exporters procuring goods, must arrange packing that complies with the specific transportation mode to safeguard the integrity of the shipment.

4. Quality Control for Purchased Goods: Responsibilities of Merchant Exporter

In cases where the exporter acts as a merchant and procures goods from the market, stringent quality control measures are paramount. The merchant exporter bears the responsibility of ensuring that the purchased goods meet the buyer's specifications. This includes monitoring quality, both in-process and post-manufacture, to guarantee compliance with agreed-upon norms.

5. Dual Inspection: Buyer's Requirement and Local Government Standards

Goods destined for export undergo two types of inspections. The first, initiated by the buyer, ensures that the quality meets specified standards. Internationally recognized third-party inspection agencies, such as SGS, often carry out this inspection. The second type involves inspections mandated by the local government to uphold the country's reputation for exporting high-quality goods. Depending on product categories and exporter profiles, local governments categorize items and exporters for inspection requirements.

In essence, step number seven encapsulates the comprehensive process of preparing goods for export, encompassing financing, quality control, and adherence to packing standards. The exporter's diligence at this stage contributes significantly to the success and integrity of the export transaction. The subsequent sections will unfold additional layers of the export procedure, shedding light on further intricacies and considerations for exporters navigating the global trade landscape.

Topics 91-92: Step 8: Carrying Out Customs and Port Formalities

Embarking on step number eight, exporters find themselves navigating the intricacies of customs and port formalities. This phase of the export procedure is crucial, demanding precision and adherence to protocols for the timely clearance of export goods at customs areas and ports.

1. Export Declaration: Initiating the Customs Process

The initiation of customs procedures begins with the filing of an export declaration. This declaration serves as an intimation to customs authorities that the goods are ready for shipment. Typically filed electronically through systems like EDI (Electronic Data Interface) or AES (Automated Export System), the export declaration is a prelude to the subsequent processes involved in customs clearance.

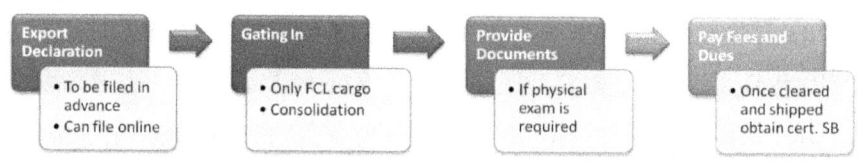

Figure: Customs Clearance Process: Step by Step

2. Gating In Process: Entry of Full Container Load (FCL)

Following the export declaration, the gating-in process comes into play, particularly for full container loads (FCL). This involves the entry of the entire container into the designated container yard or port area where customs clearance will occur. The completion of this process sets the stage for customs authorities to assess and clear the export.

3. LET EXPORT Order: Customs Clearance Approval

Upon satisfying the customs requirements, which include providing necessary export documents, the customs authorities issue a LET EXPORT order. This signifies the official approval for the export clearance process. It is at this juncture that any outstanding dues to customs or port authorities must be settled.

4. Payment of Fees and Taxes: Fulfilling Financial Obligations

Payment of fees and taxes is a critical component of the customs and port formalities. Exporters must fulfill any financial obligations owed to customs or port authorities promptly. This includes settling fees associated with customs clearance and port usage.

5. Shipping Bill: Culmination of Export Declaration

The issuance of the shipping bill marks the culmination of the export declaration process. This document, filed for export declaration, is a vital record that encapsulates key details of the shipment. Certified copies of the shipping bill, issued by customs authorities, become essential for post-shipment formalities.

In essence, step number eight in the export procedure revolves around the meticulous execution of customs and port formalities. From the electronic filing of export declarations to the culmination with the issuance of the shipping bill, exporters must navigate this phase with precision and compliance. The subsequent sections will unravel additional facets of the export journey, shedding light on the post-shipment processes awaiting exporters.

Topic 93: Step 9: Shipping and Documentation

Having successfully received the LET EXPORT order from customs, the exporter proceeds to the crucial step of shipping the goods. This involves transporting the goods to their destination, either by sea or air. The mode of transport dictates the subsequent procedures.

1. Loading onto Carrier:

Sea Shipment: Goods are transported to the ship, and upon arrival at the port of discharge, they are unloaded. For sea shipments, the primary document required at this stage is the Mate's Receipt (MR), issued by the ship's captain. The MR acts as an interim document necessary for obtaining the transport document.

Air Shipment: Goods are transported to the aircraft, and due to the rapid nature of air shipments, there's no need for the intermediate step of obtaining a receipt from the captain.

2. Mate's Receipt (MR) and NOC:

In sea shipments, the exporter must obtain the Mate's Receipt (MR) from the ship's captain.

The MR, however, does not serve as the final transport document; the exporter needs to acquire the Bill of Lading issued by the shipping company.

The captain can't issue the transport document directly; it requires a No Objection Certificate (NOC) from customs and port authorities, indicating that all dues and fees have been settled.

3. Transport Documents:

The shipping company issues the transport document, which is the Bill of Lading for sea shipments.

For air shipments, the Airway Bill is automatically issued by the airline.

These documents are crucial for receiving payment through a Letter of Credit.

4. Export General Manifest (EGM):

In parallel, the exporter should consider obtaining the Export General Manifest (EGM) for sea shipments. This document is issued once the ship has left the port of loading.

EGM provides proof of shipment, enabling the customs to issue certified copies of the shipping bill.

5. Documentation for Further Steps:

The exporter gathers the Bill of Lading (or Airway Bill), Mate's Receipt,

NOC from customs, NOC from port authorities, EGM, and certified copies of shipping bills.

These documents are crucial for subsequent steps in the export process and are often required for customs clearance at the destination.

Understanding these shipping and documentation procedures is vital for exporters, especially in the context of sea shipments, which constitute the majority of export transactions. These steps ensure a smooth transition of goods from the port of loading to the port of discharge, facilitating the subsequent stages of the export process.

Topics 94-95: Step 10: Shipment Advice and Communication with the Importer

In the continuum of export procedures, the tenth step is a pivotal moment for the exporter – intimating the buyer about the shipment. Author emphasizes the significance of preparing a Shipment Advice, a document that serves as a formal communication to the overseas buyer regarding the shipment status. This step is crucial not just for procedural adherence but also for maintaining transparency and fostering trust between the exporter and the importer.

1. Shipment Advice:

Format and Content: The exporter is obliged to prepare a Shipment Advice in a standard format. This document should include crucial details such as the vessel name, expected time of arrival at the port of destination, and the tracking number provided by the shipping company.

Electronic Communication: The Shipment Advice is sent electronically, typically through fax or email. This ensures quick and efficient communication with the buyer.

Proof of Sending: The exporter must retain proof of sending the Shipment Advice electronically, as this proof is required when submitting documents to the bank for payment under the Letter of Credit (LC).

2. Safeguarding Buyer's Interest:

The primary objective of sending the Shipment Advice is to inform the buyer promptly after the goods have been loaded on the ship and the ship has departed from the port of loading.

This proactive communication is vital in safeguarding the buyer's interests and maintaining transparency in the transaction.

3. Inclusions with Shipment Advice:

Along with the Shipment Advice, non-negotiable documents, such as a commercial invoice, packing list, certificate of origin, or transport documents, are also enclosed.

These non-negotiable copies are sent electronically to the buyer. It is a comprehensive approach to keep the buyer informed about various aspects of the shipment.

4. Physical Copies:

While non-negotiable documents are sent electronically, a physical copy of the Shipment Advice can be sent by airmail or courier to the buyer.

The physical copy serves as an additional formal record of communication and can be included for the buyer's reference.

5. Handling Negotiable Documents:

Notably, negotiable documents are not sent directly to the buyer. These documents, crucial in typical transactions, are submitted to the bank for obtaining payment against the Letter of Credit.

In conclusion, Step Ten underscores the exporter's responsibility to promptly inform the buyer about the shipment. The Shipment Advice, coupled with the electronic transmission of non-negotiable documents, contributes to a transparent and efficient export process. This proactive communication not only meets procedural requirements but also aligns with the mutual interests of the exporter and the importer in the pursuit of a successful transaction.

Topic 96: Step 11: Document Submission and Bank Formalities

As the export journey progresses, Step Eleven delves into the critical phase of bank and payment-related formalities. Dr. Jain emphasizes the importance of adhering to the terms stipulated in the Letter of Credit (LC) and the sales contract. This step involves the submission of meticulously prepared documents to the negotiating bank, marking a significant milestone in the exporter's financial transactions.

1. Document Preparation:

The exporter, having obtained all required commercial and LC documents, including the Bill of Exchange and covering letter, is ready for the next phase.

Documents should adhere to the agreed-upon conditions with the buyer, ensuring compliance with the terms of the sales contract and the Letter of Credit.

2. Submission to Negotiating Bank:

Documents are submitted to the negotiating bank, which is typically the local bank of the exporter.

The negotiating bank meticulously examines the documents, performing due diligence. If any discrepancies are identified, the exporter is notified and requested to rectify them promptly.

3. Negotiation Process:

Upon satisfactory verification of the documents, the negotiating bank proceeds to negotiate them. This involves the bank's endorsement of the documents and forwarding them to the LC issuing bank, which is the overseas bank of the buyer.

4. Covering Letter Instructions:

The exporter includes a covering letter along with the documents. This letter serves as a communication channel between the exporter and the banks involved in the transaction.

Any specific instructions, conditions, or information necessary for negotiating the documents are explicitly stated in the covering letter.

These instructions must align with the terms and conditions specified in the sales contract and the Letter of Credit.

5. Compliance with Agreed Terms:

The exporter's instructions in the covering letter should strictly adhere to the agreed terms in both the sales contract and the Letter of Credit. This ensures a smooth and compliant negotiation process.

6. Bank Collection Considerations:

If the payment method is bank collection, the exporter may need to include specific conditions in the covering letter. Unlike Letter of Credit transactions, these conditions need to be explicitly outlined in the letter for the intermediary banks to follow.

7. Focus on Covering Letter:

Emphasis is placed on the covering letter as it serves as a key document for instructions, especially for intermediary banks involved in the transaction.

In conclusion, Step Eleven underscores the significance of meticulous document preparation and submission to the negotiating bank. This step marks the initiation of the financial transactions, requiring careful adherence to the terms and conditions set forth in the Letter of Credit and the sales contract. The covering letter plays a crucial role in conveying specific instructions, ensuring a seamless negotiation process and paving the way for successful payment transactions.

Topic 97: Step 12: Settling Credits, Bond Reconciliation, and Export Incentives

As the export process unfolds, Step Twelve focuses on the crucial post-shipment formalities that exporters must navigate. Dr. Jain sheds light on key actions required to conclude the transaction successfully and obtain necessary certifications and incentives.

1. Settling Pre-shipment Credit:

If pre-shipment credit was availed, it must be settled immediately after the shipment. Post-shipment credit eligibility hinges on settling any outstanding pre-shipment credit.

Settling pre-shipment credit is essential for availing benefits such as favorable interest rates under interest subvention schemes.

2. Reconciling Bonds and LUTs:

Any bonds or Letters of Undertaking (LUTs) submitted to local authorities to avoid local taxes, including sales tax, GST, VAT, or excise duty, must be reconciled and settled in this phase.

3. Bank Remittance Certificate (BRC):

Obtaining the Bank Remittance Certificate (BRC) is crucial. This certificate certifies that the foreign exchange has been received by the exporter against the shipment.

Commercial banks electronically inform the central bank of the received payment. The BRC plays a pivotal role in central bank reconciliation, preventing the exporter from being blacklisted.

4. Export Incentive Claims:

Exporters need to file claims for export incentives available in their country. This involves using documents received from customs, such as a certified copy of the shipping bill, eBRC, or non-negotiable copies of the bill of lading.

Export incentives, common in various countries, contribute to profit calculations and pricing strategies. Timely filing ensures the exporter receives the monetary benefits.

5. Export Incentive Varieties:

Export incentives can include duty drawback, duty remission schemes, duty refund schemes, or other country-specific benefits.

Filing claims for these incentives is critical for the exporter's financial well-being and facilitates future exports.

6. Importance of Timely Actions:

Swift action in settling credits, reconciling bonds, obtaining BRC, and claiming export incentives is imperative. Delays in these post-shipment formalities can impact financial benefits and the exporter's standing with central banks.

In conclusion, Step Twelve encapsulates the critical post-shipment formalities that exporters need to undertake for a seamless conclusion of the export transaction. From settling financial credits and bonds to obtaining essential certificates and claiming export incentives, these activities contribute to the exporter's financial health and the success of future exports. Adherence to timelines is crucial, ensuring that all necessary documentation is in place and financial benefits are realized without any setbacks.

Topics 98-99: Step 13: Ensuring Comprehensive Record Keeping

In the final step of the export process, Step Thirteen underscores the critical importance of meticulous record keeping for exporters. Dr. Jain highlights the necessity of organized archiving of all documents, information, and contact details associated with a particular export transaction. This step is not just a good practice; it is often mandatory as per the laws and regulations of local governments.

1. Documents Archiving:

Inclusion of All Documents: All documents utilized throughout the export transaction must be included. This encompasses a broad range, including but not limited to, the sales contract, Letter of Credit (LC), commercial invoices, packing lists, transport documents, and the electronic Bank Remittance Certificate (eBRC).

Proper Filing: Copies of these documents should be filed meticulously, assigned file numbers, and organized systematically. This ensures easy retrieval when needed in the future.

2. Essential Documents for Archiving:

eBRC and Customs Certifications: The electronic Bank Remittance Certificate (eBRC) and certified copies of customs documentation are particularly crucial. These serve as official proof of payment receipt and shipment certification.

Order, File, and LC Numbers: Information such as order numbers, file numbers, LC numbers, and sales contract details must be recorded. This comprehensive record ensures that all relevant details are readily available for future reference.

3. Compliance and Future Requirements:

Legal Compliance: Adequate record keeping is not only good practice but often mandatory to comply with local laws and regulations.

Customs Requirements: Local customs authorities may require the exporter to furnish this information at a later date, making comprehensive records essential for continued legal compliance.

4. Contact Details:

Buyers and Intermediaries: Contact details of buyers and intermediaries involved in the shipment should be part of the record. This information is valuable for maintaining business relationships and for any future communication or transactions.

5. Future Reference and Analysis:

Readiness for Audits: Comprehensive records ensure that the exporter is well-prepared for audits or inquiries by regulatory authorities.

Future Business Decisions: The recorded information serves as a valuable resource for future business decisions, strategy planning, and financial analysis.

6. Compliance with Step Thirteen:

Critical Significance: Step Thirteen is emphasized for its critical significance. It is the culmination of the export process and lays the foundation for future endeavors.

In conclusion, Step Thirteen, the final step in the export process, highlights the paramount importance of comprehensive record keeping. By systematically archiving all relevant documents, information, and contact details, exporters not only ensure compliance with local regulations but also create a valuable resource for future business activities. This step is not just about legal adherence; it is a strategic investment in the exporter's future success and resilience in the dynamic world of international trade.

Topics 100: Chapter Conclusion: Navigating the Export Journey

As we conclude this chapter, the aim has been to provide you with a comprehensive overview of the export procedure, guiding you through the intricacies of each step involved. These 13 steps serve as a roadmap, helping you understand the sequential nature, timings, and significance of each activity in the export process.

1. Understanding Sequences:

The presented steps offer a clear sequence of activities, providing a systematic approach to export procedures. From market exploration to post-shipment formalities, each step plays a pivotal role in the overall success of the export transaction.

2. Timing Considerations:

The importance of timing has been emphasized throughout. From obtaining necessary licenses to submitting documents to banks, the timely execution of activities is crucial for a smooth export journey.

3. Why Each Step Matters:

An understanding of why each step is essential has been woven into the discussion. Whether it's complying with legal regulations, adhering to the terms of a Letter of Credit, or maintaining transparent communication, each step contributes to the overall success of the export endeavor.

4. Knowledge for Document Understanding:

This chapter serves as a foundation for the upcoming section on export documents. The knowledge gained here will be instrumental in comprehending the intricacies of various export documents discussed in the next section.

5. Looking Ahead:

As we transition to the exploration of export documents in the next section, the insights gained from these export procedures will serve as a valuable reference. The journey continues, and the knowledge acquired here will enhance your understanding of the practical aspects of international trade.

6. Keep Reading:

Stay engaged as we delve deeper into the specifics of export documents. The knowledge and insights acquired in this chapter will be applied to unravel the intricacies of paperwork involved in international trade.

In the dynamic landscape of global commerce, a thorough understanding of export procedures is a key asset. The journey from market analysis to record-keeping is a multifaceted process, and your continued exploration will unveil the nuances that make each export transaction unique. Keep watching as we navigate the intricate world of international trade together.

Chapter 12: Understanding Export Documents

Topic 101: Overview

Building on our comprehensive exploration of the end-to-end export procedure in the previous chapter, we are now embarking on a dedicated journey into the realm of export documentation. This chapter is designed to provide a nuanced understanding of both pre-shipment and post-shipment documents, unraveling their significance and role in international trade.

1. Logical Progression:

Following the logical progression of our previous discussions on export procedures, this chapter delves into the intricate world of export documents. The knowledge gained in the previous section serves as a solid foundation for comprehending the complexities of various export paperwork.

2. Pre-shipment and Post-shipment Documents:

The focus of this chapter is on two primary categories of export documents: pre-shipment and post-shipment. These documents play crucial roles in facilitating smooth transactions, dealing with customs, banks, port authorities, local governments, and buyers.

3. Categorization for Different Authorities:

Understanding the nature and functionality of each document is essential. These documents are meticulously categorized based on their purpose and the authorities they interact with, ensuring a systematic and organized approach to international trade.

4. Scope and Approach:

While delving into the specifics of each document, it's important to note that the scope of this section doesn't permit an exhaustive exploration of every detail. Instead, the focus is on providing a conceptual understanding of the logical functions and significance of each document.

5. Universality and Applicability:

The approach taken in this section ensures that the information is universally applicable to exporters from any country. By grasping the fundamental functions and roles of these documents, exporters can navigate the complexities of international trade with confidence.

As we progress through this chapter, I invite you to explore the intricacies of export documentation, recognizing the pivotal role each document plays in the broader landscape of global commerce. Let's unravel the logical functions, significance, and categorization of pre-shipment and post-shipment documents, equipping ourselves with knowledge that transcends geographical boundaries. Stay tuned for an enlightening journey into the world of export documentation.

Topic 102: Types of Export Documents

Friends, let's delve into the world of export documents and categorize them logically. Understanding the different types of export documents is crucial for a smooth and compliant international trade transaction. These documents can be broadly categorized into two main types: pre-shipment documents and post-shipment documents.

1. Pre-Shipment Documents:

a. Commercial Documents:

Nature: Commercial documents directly pertain to the buyer, the shipment, and the transaction between the seller and the buyer.

Examples: Commercial invoices, packing lists, bills of lading, and any other document directly associated with the commercial aspect of the transaction.

b. Regulatory Documents:

Nature: Regulatory documents relate to the regulations of the seller's home country.

Examples: Documents related to border control, foreign exchange management, compliance with import-export licenses, and membership in local trade bodies.

2. Post-Shipment Documents:

a. Shipment Confirmation Documents:

Purpose: These documents inform the buyer that the shipment has been made, providing key details.

Examples: Shipment advice, advising the buyer of the shipment details immediately after it has been dispatched.

b. Negotiation Documents:

Purpose: Pertinent for negotiating the commercial principal documents, especially in transactions involving a Letter of Credit (LC).

Examples: Documents necessary for negotiation with the LC issuing bank, ensuring compliance with documentary conditions.

c. Incentives Claim Documents:

Purpose: Pertaining to the claim of incentives related to tax implications, duties, and other financial benefits.

Examples: Documents supporting claims for avoiding or refunding import duties, sales tax, GST, VAT, or other incentives offered by the exporting country.

Understanding these categories provides a structured approach to handling the various documents involved in the export process. Each type of document serves a specific purpose, whether it's facilitating the shipment, complying with regulations, notifying the buyer, or claiming incentives. As we progress through this chapter, we will explore the nuances of each document type, unraveling their roles and significance in international trade. Stay tuned for a deeper dive into the world of export documentation.

Topic 103: Understanding Pre-Shipment Documents

In the realm of international trade, pre-shipment documents play a pivotal role in ensuring the smooth flow of goods from the seller to the buyer. Broadly categorized into commercial and regulatory documents, pre-shipment documents set the stage for a well-orchestrated export transaction.

Commercial Documents:

1. Principal Documents:

Nature: These are the core commercial documents directly associated with the shipment, buyer requirements, and often specified in the Letter of Credit (LC).

Examples: Commercial invoices, packing lists, bills of lading, and any document crucial for the buyer or required by the LC.

2. Auxiliary Documents:

Nature: Auxiliary documents are supplementary paperwork required to obtain the principal documents. They support the process of securing the main commercial documents.

Examples: Documents necessary for obtaining principal documents, such as certificates, inspection reports, or specific attestations.

Regulatory Documents:

3. Compliance Documents:

Nature: Essential for adhering to legal requirements, compliance documents include obtaining import-export licenses to conduct export activities lawfully.

Examples: Import-export licenses, certificates of origin, and membership documentation in local trade bodies.

4. Customs-related Documents:

Nature: Documents required for compliance with border control regulations and facilitating customs clearance for exported goods.

Examples: Shipping bills, export declarations, and any customs-specific paperwork ensuring the legal export of goods.

5. Port-related Documents:

Nature: Necessary for effective communication with port authorities, ensuring the seamless movement of goods from the port of origin.

Examples: Port clearance documents, dock receipts, and any paperwork required for interactions with the chosen port.

6. Foreign Exchange Management Documents:

Nature: Documents related to monitoring and managing foreign exchange transactions, particularly regarding payments received for exported goods.

Examples: Documents confirming foreign exchange transactions, bank certificates, and any paperwork associated with the central bank's oversight.

Understanding the distinct nature and purpose of each pre-shipment document is essential for exporters. The meticulous preparation and submission of these documents facilitate compliance with regulations, ensure smooth customs clearance, and contribute to the successful execution of international trade transactions. As we delve into the specific details of each document in subsequent Topics, you will gain a deeper appreciation for their individual roles in the pre-shipment phase of the export process. Stay tuned for a comprehensive exploration of these documents and their significance in international trade.

Topics 104-105: Principal Commercial Export Documents

In the intricate landscape of pre-shipment commercial documents, principal documents take center stage. These documents are not only vital for the smooth progression of the shipment but are also crucial elements stipulated in the Letter of Credit (LC), ensuring the buyer's interests are protected. Let's explore the key principal commercial export documents:

1. Commercial Invoice:

Nature: A comprehensive summary of the entire transaction and sales contract.

Information: Shipper and consignee details, ports of loading and destination, mode of transport, payment and commercial terms (Incoterms), and a detailed description of goods with unit and total prices.

2. Packing List:

Nature: Similar to the commercial invoice but focuses on the physical aspects of the shipment.

Information: Gross weight, net weight, dimensions, type of packing, and details about marks and labeling for export.

3. Certificate of Origin:

Purpose: Required by the buyer's local customs to determine the origin of the goods, impacting import duties and taxes.

Varieties: Can be of different types, and the buyer may demand a specific form of the certificate.

4. Certificate of Inspection:

Purpose: Ensures the quality of the shipped goods, serving as proof that the delivered goods match the agreed-upon quality.

Significance: Particularly crucial due to the geographical distance between the buyer and seller, making physical inspection challenging.

5. Transport Documents:

Options: Depend on the mode of shipment.

For Sea Shipment: Bill of Lading or Combined Transport Document.

For Air Shipment: Air Waybill.

Importance: Essential components of the principal documents, often required by the Letter of Credit.

Other Documents (Dependent on Incoterms agreed):

Freight Certificate: Required when the seller is responsible for freight charges.

Insurance Certificate: Demanded if the seller is responsible for insurance costs.

Phytosanitary Certificate: Necessary for shipments involving plants or agricultural products, including cases where wood is used for packing.

Understanding the role and significance of each principal commercial document is fundamental for exporters. These documents not only facilitate the transaction but also ensure compliance with the terms of the sales contract and the requirements of the Letter of Credit. As we delve deeper into the world of export documentation, each document will be examined in detail, unraveling their unique roles in the pre-shipment phase of international trade. Stay tuned for a comprehensive exploration of each document type and its practical implications in the export process.

Topics 106-107: Auxiliary Commercial Export Documents

In the realm of export documentation, auxiliary documents play a crucial role, acting as instrumental prerequisites for obtaining the principal commercial documents. These documents serve varied purposes, from initiating the export process to ensuring compliance with regulatory authorities. Let's delve into the key auxiliary commercial export documents:

1. Proforma Invoice:

Purpose: Provided to the buyer based on a letter of inquiry, outlining preliminary details of the future sales contract.

Function: Serves as a preliminary document that aids in creating the commercial invoice once the order is finalized.

2. Shipping Instructions:

Significance: Directs the shipping line on aspects like space booking and issuance of a shipping order.

Creation: Can be prepared by the exporter, freight forwarder, or CNF agent.

3. Application for Certificate of Origin:

Critical Step: Essential for obtaining the Certificate of Origin.

Declaration: The application serves as a declaration by the exporter, specifying the origin of the goods.

4. Intimation for Inspection:

Timing: Filed well in advance to notify about the inspection, whether by a third party or local government agencies.

Purpose: Required for quality assurance and compliance.

5. Mate's Receipt:

Nature: Issued by the captain of the ship for sea shipments.

Role: A precursor to obtaining transport documents like the Bill of Lading.

6. Insurance Declaration:

Function: Submitted to the insurance company for obtaining an insurance certificate or policy.

Contents: Includes details of the shipment's value and other necessary information for insurance coverage.

7. Covering Letter:

Recipient: Addressed to the negotiating bank for the purpose of negotiating documents with the LC issuing bank.

Accompaniment: Presented alongside the complete set of documents for payment under the Letter of Credit.

Understanding the nature and significance of these auxiliary commercial documents is paramount for exporters. These documents not only facilitate the progression of the export transaction but also play a vital role in adhering to regulatory requirements. As exporters navigate through the complexities of international trade, a clear comprehension of these auxiliary documents becomes an invaluable asset. In the following segments of this course, we will further dissect each document, unraveling its intricacies and practical implications in the export documentation process. Stay engaged for a comprehensive exploration of each auxiliary document type and its indispensable role in international trade.

Topic 108: Regulatory Export Documents: Navigating Compliance and Control

In the intricate landscape of international trade, regulatory export documents play a pivotal role in ensuring compliance with the diverse requirements imposed by customs, foreign exchange authorities, and port authorities. Let's embark on a comprehensive exploration of these pre-shipment regulatory documents and their multifaceted purposes:

1. Compliance-Related Regulatory Documents:

Import-Export Licenses:

- Example: IEC Code (Importer-Exporter Code) in India.

- Significance: Essential for conducting export-import operations globally.

- Registration Cum Membership with Trade Development Bodies:

- Purpose: Validates the bona fide of exporters for local government benefits.

Importance: Mandatory for obtaining export incentives in specific countries.

2. Customs-Related Regulatory Documents:

Export Declaration (Shipping Bill in India):

- Function: Informs customs in advance about the forthcoming export shipment.

- Usage: Critical for claiming export incentives and managing foreign exchange.

Certified Copies of Export Declaration (Shipping Bill):

- Significance:

- Proof of export for claiming export incentives.

- Central bank assurance of payment receipt against the shipment.

- Essential for port authorities' records.

Customs-Demanded Documents for Examination and Clearance:

- Examples: Commercial invoice, packing list, LC copy, technical brochures.

- Usage: Required for physical examination and clearance of goods.

Port Authority Documents:

Export Declaration-Port Authority Copy (Port Trust Copy in India):

- Purpose: Declaration and intimation to port authorities.

- Functions:

I. Serves as proof of export for port authorities.

II. Facilitates reconciliation with foreign exchange receipts.

- Export Application to the Port:

I. Contents: Includes details like AD number (Authorized Dealer number).

II. Usage: Required for port authorities' registration and

reconciliation processes.

Dock Challan:

- Issued by: The specific port being used for export.

- Usage: Essential for the gating-in process in the container yard or wet port.

3. Foreign Exchange-Related Regulatory Documents:

Exchange Control Copy of Export Declaration (EP Copy of Shipping Bill in India):

- Purpose: Declares exporter's responsibility for foreign exchange receipt.

- Usage: Essential for central bank assurance and monitoring of payment.

Bank Intimation to Central Bank:

- Function: Informs the central bank about the payment receipt against the shipment.

4. Port-Related Regulatory Documents:

Export Application to the Port:

- Inclusion: Requires details like AD number.

- Usage: Supports reconciliation of the shipment with foreign exchange receipts.

Dock Challan:

- Issued by: The specific port being used for export.

- Function: Necessary for the gating-in process in container yards or wet ports.

Conclusion:

Understanding the nuances of each regulatory document is vital for exporters navigating the global trade landscape. These documents not only facilitate compliance but also play a crucial role in securing export incentives, managing foreign exchange, and ensuring smooth port operations. In the subsequent sections of this course, we will delve deeper into the specifics of each document, unraveling their complexities and practical applications in the export process. Stay tuned for an in-depth exploration of the regulatory export documents and their indispensable role in international trade compliance.

Topics 109-110: Post-Shipment Documents: Navigating Realization, Negotiation, and Incentives

As we delve into the realm of post-shipment documents, the dynamics shift from pre-shipment objectives to realization of international payments and securing home country governmental incentives. Let's explore the key objectives and documents associated with the post-shipment phase:

1. Shipment Advice: Keeping Buyers Informed

Objective:

- Update the buyer about the status of the shipment.

- Enable the buyer to plan subsequent actions (warehousing, reselling, etc.).

Key Document: Shipment Advice

Contents:

- Vessel details.

- Expected time of departure.

- Expected time of arrival at the destination port.

- Shipment tracking number.

Delivery Method:

- By fax or email.

- Proof of delivery is crucial for further processing.

2. Negotiation of Documents with the Bank: Obtaining Payment

Objective:

- Secure payment against the letter of credit (LC).

- Documents to be sent to the LC issuing bank through a negotiating bank (usually the local bank).

Documents to be Presented:

- Original LC documents.

- Bank draft or Bill of Exchange.

- Covering letter.

Negotiating Bank's Role:

Transmits documents to the LC issuing bank for negotiation.

3. Export Incentives Claim: Unlocking Governmental Benefits

Objective:

- Claim export benefits provided by the local government.

- Ensure the government's assurance that the shipment has been made and payment received.

Supporting Documents:

- Certified copy of the export declaration (shipping bill).

- Bank confirmation in the form of Bank Remittance Certificate (BRC) or Electronic Bank Remittance Certificate (eBRC).

Benefits and Claims:

- Refund of direct taxes (GST, VAT, excise).

- Release of any bank guarantee.

- Claiming indirect taxes paid through duty drawback schemes.

4. Conclusion: Maximizing Post-Shipment Efficiencies

- Integration of Objectives:

- Shipment-related communication to the buyer.

- LC document negotiation for payment.

- Governmental incentive claims for financial benefits.

Role of Post-Shipment Documents:

- Facilitate communication.

- Ensure smooth payment processes.

- Support claims for export incentives.

In essence, post-shipment documents serve as the bridge between the completion of the export process and the realization of benefits. From updating buyers to navigating the intricacies of LC negotiation and unlocking government incentives, these documents play a pivotal role in the entire export lifecycle.

As we conclude this course, remember that a robust understanding of both pre-shipment and post-shipment documents is essential for exporters navigating the complexities of international trade. May your future export endeavors be marked by seamless processes and successful transactions. Best wishes for your continued success in the world of global trade.

Topic 111: Chapter Conclusion: Navigating the Landscape of Export Documents

As we draw the curtains on this comprehensive exploration of export documents, the overarching goal was to furnish you with foundational insights into the intricacies of international trade. Every facet of export documents, from pre-shipment to post-shipment, transport to LC and bank documents, has been meticulously dissected. Let's encapsulate the key takeaways:

1. Holistic Understanding of Export Documents:

Explored pre-shipment documents, delving into commercial, auxiliary, and regulatory categories.

Unveiled the significance of post-shipment documents, focusing on realization, negotiation, and incentive claims.

Navigated transport documents, LC documents, and those required by Customs, Border Control, or port authorities.

2. Empowering Your Confidence:

The objective was to equip you with fundamental knowledge and instill confidence in comprehending and handling diverse export documents.

Covered all essential elements to enhance your grasp of the export documentation landscape.

3. Preparation for the Next Leg:

Building on this foundation, the journey continues into the next section.

Upcoming discussions will revolve around the transportation of goods, bridging the gap from the country of origin to the destination.

4. Looking Forward: The Transport Odyssey:

The subsequent section will unravel the intricacies of transporting goods across borders.

Topics will span logistics, regulations, and strategies for a seamless transition from origin to destination.

5. Course Milestone:

You've reached a milestone in your exploration of international trade processes.

A robust understanding of export documents sets the stage for informed and successful global transactions.

As we transition to the next chapter on the transportation of goods, I encourage you to carry forward the knowledge acquired. May your journey through the realm of international trade be marked by continuous learning, confidence, and triumphs. Thank you for your engagement in this section, and I eagerly anticipate our continued exploration in the chapters to come.

Chapter 13: Moving Goods Internationally - Navigating the Global Logistics Landscape

Topic 112: Overview

Greetings, dear learners! In this section, we embark on an exciting journey into the heart of international trade logistics. Our focus will be on the intricate art of moving goods across borders, from the birthplace to their destination.

What to Expect:

In this comprehensive exploration, you will gain foundational insights into the essential skills and knowledge required for the seamless movement of goods. Whether it's through sea or air, understanding the nuances of logistics, supply chain management, and the diverse types of vessels and ships used in international trade will be our compass.

Key Topics We'll Navigate:

Modes of Shipment:

Delve into the specifics of sea and air shipments, unraveling the unique aspects and considerations associated with each mode.

Vessels and Aircraft:

Explore the world of maritime transport, understanding different types of ships and vessels that play a pivotal role in international trade. Additionally, get acquainted with aircraft used in air shipments.

Logistics and Supply Chain Management:

Grasp the fundamentals of international logistics, unraveling the complexities of supply chain management, and gaining insights into strategies for efficient movement of goods.

Basic Terminology:

Familiarize yourself with the lexicon of international logistics. From INCO terms to Bill of Lading, understand the terminology crucial for effective communication in this dynamic field.

Our Objective:

My primary goal in this section is to provide you with the essential knowledge required to navigate the challenges of international trade logistics. Whether you are a budding exporter or looking to enhance your existing skills, this section aims to equip you with the tools for success.

Your Path to Success:

By the end of this section, you will not only have a foundational understanding of the logistics landscape but will also be better prepared to orchestrate the movement of goods on the global stage.

Let's set sail into the realm of international logistics, where each term, each concept, is a milestone on your path to becoming a proficient and successful player in the world of global trade. So, fasten your seatbelts, and let's explore the dynamic world of moving goods internationally!

Topics 113-114: Understanding International Logistics and Supply Chain Management

Unveiling the Essence of International Logistics and SCM

International logistics is more than just the movement of goods; it is an intricate dance of design and management aimed at orchestrating the optimal, cost-effective movement of goods on the global stage. Complemented by the broader canvas of supply chain management, international logistics encompasses the meticulous planning and coordination of goods, materials, services, and information within a multinational framework.

The Multidimensional Scope:

Inward and Outward Movement:

Encompassing both the inbound and outbound flow of goods, materials, and information within an organization.

External Infrastructure Management:

Extending its reach to external infrastructure like offshore warehouses, storage hubs, and special economic zones strategically employed by international companies.

Tools of the Trade:

The effective management of this vast network involves leveraging cutting-edge tools, notably Information and Communication Technology (ICT) and the Internet. Innovations such as smart sensors and technologies contribute to the efficient orchestration of the entire supply chain.

Incorporating Diverse Elements:

In the realm of international logistics and supply chain management, the design involves harmonizing various elements:

Logistics Infrastructure:

Specialized storage hubs, warehouses, and logistics infrastructure are intricately managed for efficiency, smooth operations, and cost-effectiveness.

Technological Innovations:

Integration of smart technologies and innovations, including smart sensors, to enhance the overall management of goods, information, and services.

Intermediary and Outsourced Services:

The design incorporates the services provided by intermediaries, internal actors of the organization, and those outsourced by the company.

Key Decision Factors:

The decisions within international logistics and supply chain management are rooted in fundamental factors:

Cost:

The paramount consideration is the cost of operations, as it significantly influences the overall product lifecycle cost.

Predictability:

Predictability ensures smooth planning and robust operations, with considerations for the availability and reliability of transportation modes.

Time:

Time is equated with cost in international trade, making transit time a critical factor in decision-making.

Navigating Non-Economic Factors:

Beyond economic considerations, non-economic factors wield substantial influence:

Regulatory Compliance:

Adherence to local and overseas governmental rules and regulations becomes a crucial determinant.

Environmental Concerns:

Environmental considerations further shape decision-making, reflecting the increasing importance of sustainability in international logistics.

Striking the Balance:

The crux lies in striking a delicate balance between these factors, weighing the trade-offs between cost, predictability, transit time, and non-economic considerations. Decisions are finely calibrated based on the situational significance of each factor, ensuring the harmonious flow of goods on the global logistical stage.

In our exploration, we will unravel the intricacies of international logistics and supply chain management, unveiling the artistry behind the seamless movement of goods in the global arena. So, fasten your seatbelts as we delve deeper into the dynamic world of international trade logistics!

Navigating the Dynamics of International Logistics and SCM

Defining the Landscape: International logistics and supply chain management transcend mere transportation; they encapsulate the intricate orchestration of a comprehensive program governing the movement of goods, materials, services, and information within a multinational paradigm. This extends beyond the boundaries of the organization, encompassing the outward and inward flow of goods and penetrating into external infrastructures strategically positioned in overseas markets.

External Infrastructure Dynamics:

In the realm of global logistics, international companies strategically utilize external infrastructure components such as special warehouses, storage hubs, and special economic zones. These components serve as instrumental tools for enhancing the efficiency, smoothness, and cost-effectiveness of goods movement.

The Symphony of Design and Management:

International logistics and supply chain management require meticulous design, seamlessly integrating various components. The spectrum includes the management of storage infrastructure, logistics operations, and the utilization of cutting-edge tools, with a spotlight on Information and Communication Technology (ICT), the internet, and innovative technologies like smart sensors.

Collaboration and Outsourcing:

Collaboration forms a key element, involving internal actors, intermediaries, and outsourced services. The intricacies of these interactions necessitate well-thought-out designs, ensuring a synchronized approach to managing the movement of goods, information, and services.

Decision-Making Factors:

In the intricate design and management of international logistics and supply chain, decisions hinge on fundamental factors:

Cost Implications:

The cost of operations takes precedence, considering that international logistics entails significant expenses throughout the product lifecycle, influencing the end price for consumers.

Predictability:

Predictability emerges as a critical factor, offering the smoothness and robustness needed for planning. The availability and reliability of transportation modes are crucial, prompting considerations for trade-offs between cost and predictability.

Time as a Currency:

Time assumes the role of currency in international trade. Transit time becomes pivotal, with its implications for costs to buyers or distributors. Negotiability of transit time is contextual, varying based on product requirements and logistic cycle dynamics.

Non-Economic Influencers:

Beyond economic considerations, non-economic factors wield significant influence in decision-making:

Regulatory Compliance:

Adherence to rules and regulations imposed by local and overseas governments becomes a cornerstone in navigating international logistics.

Environmental Considerations:

Environmental concerns shape decisions, underlining the increasing importance of sustainability in international logistics and supply chain management.

Striking Harmonious Equilibrium:

The essence lies in striking a delicate balance between cost considerations, predictability, transit time, and non-economic factors.

The complexity of decision-making arises from the situational significance of each factor, ensuring a harmonious flow of goods on the global logistical stage.

As we navigate the dynamic landscape of international logistics and supply chain management, we unravel the intricacies that govern the movement of goods in the global arena. Join us in exploring the art and science behind the seamless orchestration of international trade logistics!

Topic 115: Crafting the Backbone: The Crucial Role of Transport Infrastructure in International Logistics

Navigating the Logistics Landscape: Transportation as a Pillar

In the intricate tapestry of international logistics and supply chain management, the role of transportation infrastructure emerges as a pivotal pillar. This crucial aspect warrants astute consideration from logistics managers, who are tasked with discerning the most suitable transport infrastructure model based on a myriad of factors.

Deciphering the Terrain: In-House vs. Outsourced Transportation

The decision between in-house and outsourced transportation infrastructure hinges on a nuanced understanding of organizational dynamics. Logistics managers delve into the experiential reservoir to glean insights into the specific requirements of the logistics landscape.

Budgetary Ballet: Aligning Investments and Strategies

The dance of budgetary allocations and investments becomes a key choreography in determining the nature of transport infrastructure. The available investment potential, coupled with budget considerations, plays a defining role in sculpting the logistics strategy.

Geography as a Compass: Location and Reach Dynamics

The geographical footprint of the organization—spanning from the origin of goods to their ultimate destination—acts as a compass guiding decisions on transport infrastructure. Logistics managers embark on a strategic quest to identify locations that offer optimal reach while minimizing the cost implications of transport infrastructure.

Firm's Symphony: Harmonizing with Overall Strategy

At the core of these decisions lies the overarching strategy of the firm, especially its international strategy. The alignment of transport infrastructure with the firm's vision and mission charts the course for an integrated logistics approach.

Factors at Play: A Holistic Approach

Location and Reach:

Identifying strategic locations for transport hubs to enhance reach and minimize costs.

Firm Strategy:

Harmonizing transport infrastructure decisions with the broader international strategy of the firm.

Budgets and Investment:

Navigating the delicate balance between available budgets, investment capacity, and the demands of the logistics landscape.

The Transport Infrastructure Conundrum: A Symbiotic Connection

In essence, the nature and role of transport infrastructure are entwined with the intricate dance of international logistics and supply chain management. This is not merely a logistical consideration but a strategic symphony that orchestrates the movement of goods on the global stage.

As we unravel the layers of this transport infrastructure conundrum, we delve deeper into the strategic decisions that underpin the seamless flow of goods across international borders. Join us in exploring the dynamic interplay between organizational strategies, budgets, and the geographical canvas in crafting a robust transportation backbone for international logistics.

Topics 116-117: Navigating Global Pathways: Modes of International Transportation

Unveiling the Spectrum: Sea, Air, and Beyond

In the intricate web of international logistics, the choice of transportation mode emerges as a strategic linchpin. Understanding the dynamics of movement by sea and air, the types of cargo ships, and the diverse modes of international transportation becomes imperative for logistics managers.

Global Availability Mosaic: Modes Depending on Location

The availability of transportation modes is a dynamic puzzle, intricately woven into the geographical tapestry of each country. The landscape of available modes dictates the grand design and management of goods movement, crafting a unique logistical footprint for different regions.

Charting Vast Waters: Sea Transportation

Undoubtedly, the most widespread mode of international transportation is sea transportation. Seamlessly connecting continents on a long-term basis, sea transport emerges as the backbone for long-distance movements, offering an economically viable solution.

Aerial Soar: Air Transportation

Air transportation takes the stage as the second most crucial international mode. Despite its higher cost, air transport is a swift and reliable option, making it within reach for most global locations. The need for speed often outweighs the cost considerations for time-sensitive cargo.

Land and Inland Waterways: Grounded Movements

Beyond the vast expanses of oceans and the heights of the skies, land transportation via trains and trucks comes into play. Inland waterways, navigated by cargo boats, carve their niche in certain countries, facilitating the internal movement of goods from production points to port terminals.

Varied Infrastructural Palettes: Country-Specific Considerations

Different countries exhibit diverse infrastructural landscapes, influencing the array of transportation modes available. Logistics managers adeptly navigate these variations to optimize the movement of goods.

Multimodal Symphony: Interplay of Transportation Modes

Enter the realm of multimodal transportation, where logistics managers orchestrate a symphony of modes in a single journey. From trucks and trains to sea and air, intermodal transportation caters to the evolving landscape of warehouse-to-warehouse movements, offering flexibility and efficiency.

Adapting to Complex Routes: The Logistics Manager's Dilemma

In the intricate ballet of logistics, the exporter often finds the need for complex routing. This necessitates a dance across various modes— trucks, trains, sea vessels, and airplanes—blurring the lines between modes in a seamless intermodal tapestry.

Conclusion: Deciphering the Logistics Mosaic

As we unravel the diverse modes of international transportation, we embark on a journey where logistics managers wield these options judiciously. The sea's tranquility, the skies' swiftness, the grounded reliability of roads and railways—all contribute to the symphony of global logistics. Join us as we delve deeper into the nuances of each mode, unraveling the secrets of successful international goods movement.

Topics 118-119: Sailing the Blue Highways: Transportation by Sea

An Oceanic Odyssey: Sea Transportation Dominance

Transportation by sea stands tall as the reigning champion in the global movement of merchandise, boasting dominance in both quantity and value. Nearly 99% of the world's cargo, measured by quantity, navigates the seas, while a staggering 95% by value embraces the maritime route.

Historical Tapestry and Infrastructure Prowess

The maritime triumph is rooted in history, with sea transportation emerging as the time-tested method for international goods movement. The centuries-old infrastructure, coupled with recent technological advancements, has cultivated an ecosystem making sea transportation the epitome of reliability.

Affordability at Sea: A Maritime Advantage

The colossal sizes of modern ships, notably the behemoth mother ships capable of carrying up to 400,000 metric tons of goods in a single voyage, contribute to the affordability of sea transportation. The sheer volume handled in each journey makes it the most economical choice for moving goods across continents.

Widespread Connectivity: Oceans as Global Connectors

The vast network of seaports, dry ports, and inland ports makes sea transportation the most widely available mode. The global map is interwoven with maritime routes, connecting nations and facilitating trade on an unparalleled scale.

Capacity Unleashed: Handling Massive Volumes

Sea transportation's allure lies in its ability to transport immense quantities of goods. The mode accommodates large volumes of commodities and heavy goods, economically unfeasible for air transportation. Its capacity to move substantial cargo in a single venture makes it an attractive proposition.

The Ebb of Sea Transportation: Challenges Beneath the Waves

Despite its supremacy, sea transportation grapples with challenges that warrant scrutiny:

Leisurely Pace: The most glaring downside is its sluggish nature, with some journeys spanning months between ports. Logistics managers must carefully weigh the time-cost dynamics when opting for sea transportation.

Last Mile Connectivity: The port-to-port service model poses challenges for landlocked countries, introducing last-mile connectivity issues. Hinterland locations often face obstacles in seamlessly connecting to coastal ports.

Perils on High Seas: Sea transportation is inherently peril-prone. Extended transit times expose shipments to potential damage from storms, salty sea water, sea pirates, or conflicts. The risk of perils increases due to the prolonged presence of goods in transit.

Environmental Ripples: Environmental concerns cast a shadow over sea transportation. Studies highlight the damage inflicted on sea ecosystems, especially coral reefs, due to extensive dredging activities for constructing large ports.

Sailing into the Future: Navigating Sea Transportation Dynamics

In the grand tapestry of global logistics, sea transportation remains an unparalleled force. As we delve into the intricate nuances of maritime movement, understanding both its strengths and vulnerabilities is paramount. Join us as we navigate the seas of knowledge, unraveling the complexities that define successful international transportation.

Aeronautical Expeditions: Transportation by Air

Topic 120: Up in the Skies: Air Transportation Dynamics

Transportation by air, a marvel of speed and efficiency, unfolds a tapestry of advantages and challenges. Let's soar through the heights of this dynamic mode, exploring the skies where time is of the essence.

Flight on Wings: Advantages of Air Transportation

Velocity Unleashed: The most apparent advantage of air transportation is speed. With the inherent rapidity of air travel, goods traverse vast distances in remarkably shorter durations. It stands as one of the fastest means for intercontinental logistics.

Arm's Length Delivery: Airports, strategically dispersed globally, offer convenient and accessible delivery points. Whether situated along coastlines, in hinterlands, or in landlocked regions, airports provide an extensive network for efficient goods movement.

Widespread Availability: The increasing popularity of air transportation has expanded its reach. Passenger aircraft, moonlighting as cargo carriers, contribute to its widespread availability. This ubiquity makes air transportation an attractive option for swift deliveries.

Security in the Skies: Air transportation boasts heightened security levels owing to reduced transit times and stringent safety protocols. The controlled and monitored nature of air travel adds an extra layer of protection to the cargo in transit.

Eco-Friendly Ascent: Relative to sea transportation, air travel is considered more environmentally friendly. The carbon footprint is notably smaller, aligning with evolving concerns about sustainable and eco-conscious logistics.

Turbulence Below: Challenges of Air Transportation

Sky-High Costs: The primary deterrent for air transportation lies in its exorbitant costs. Whether for domestic or international endeavors, the expenses associated with airfreight, influenced by diverse regulations and economic statuses, make it a costly affair.

Capacity Constraints: The limited size of aircraft in comparison to colossal sea vessels restricts the volume of goods that can be transported in a single journey. While speed is an asset, the payload capacity is a limiting factor.

Navigating the Trade Winds: Sea vs. Air Transportation

Comparing sea and air transportation unveils a tale of trade-offs. While air transportation dazzles with speed and accessibility, it does so at a premium. In contrast, sea transportation, though slower, triumphs in cost-effectiveness and voluminous capacity. The choice between these modes hinges on the delicate balance between time sensitivity and financial considerations. Join us as we dissect the intricacies of these transport giants, charting a course through the boundless skies and across the expansive seas.

Topics 121-122: Nautical Symphony: Diverse Sea Transport Operations

Navigating the vast seas demands a spectrum of sea transport operations, each tailored to specific cargo needs and preferences. Let's dive into the maritime realm and explore the varied options available for shipping goods by sea.

Liner Services: Sailing with Precision

Liner services mirror the structured schedules of airlines, offering predictability and reliability in sea transport. Much like scheduled flights, these services operate on predetermined routes, complete with expected times of departure (ETD) and arrival (ETA). The cargo, depending on its nature, finds its place on different types of ships provided by liner services.

Containerized Ships: The game-changer in maritime logistics, containerized ships revolutionized shipping. Efficient, secure, and cost-effective, these vessels carry standardized containers, simplifying the loading and unloading processes. For exporters, container ships provide a streamlined approach to planning and executing shipments.

Break Bulk Services: Liner services also cater to non-containerized cargo through break bulk services. This option accommodates goods that don't fit the container mold, ensuring flexibility in transporting various types of cargo.

Specialized Ships: Liner services often include specialized vessels designed for specific cargo types. Roll-on, roll-off (RO-RO) ships, for instance, are tailored for transporting passenger cars, providing a dedicated solution for particular cargo requirements.

Tramp Services: Navigating Uncharted Waters

Tramp services, akin to chartering a flight, offer flexibility without fixed schedules. These services involve ships that can be chartered based on the exporter's needs, departing when and where required. This dynamic approach suits unique cargo specifications and diverse port-to-port connections.

Chartered Ships: Tramp services frequently involve chartered ships, negotiated with shipping companies to fulfill specific export needs. With no fixed schedules, these ships provide a bespoke solution for cargo movement, adapting to the exporter's requirements.

Bulk Services: Ocean Giants Carrying the Load

Bulk services specialize in transporting large quantities of goods, often in bulk form. These services cater to diverse cargo, from liquids to raw materials, and utilize vessels with varying sizes and capabilities.

Tankers: Tankers dominate bulk services, transporting liquids such as crude oil in large quantities. These vessels come in different sizes and dimensions, each tailored to specific routes and canal restrictions.

Tankers like SUEZMAX and Panamax navigate the seas, contributing to the bulk movement of liquids on a global scale.

In the symphony of sea transport, exporters orchestrate their choices based on cargo characteristics, timelines, and cost considerations. The diverse options provided by liner, tramp, and bulk services offer a sea of possibilities, allowing goods to traverse the oceans with precision and efficiency.

Topics 123-124: Navigating the Seas: Understanding Common Types of Ships

In the dynamic world of maritime logistics, understanding the diverse types of ships is crucial for efficient and cost-effective sea transportation. Let's delve into the common types of ships that play a pivotal role in the global movement of goods.

Figure: Different common types of cargo ships

1. HandyMax Ships: Versatile Cargo Carriers

HandyMax ships are versatile cargo carriers designed to handle a range of goods. These ships come in various sizes, adapting to different cargo requirements. Their flexibility makes them suitable for a multitude of industries, contributing to the efficient transport of goods across the seas.

2. Reefer Ships: Keeping Perishables Fresh

Reefer ships, equipped with refrigeration capabilities, specialize in transporting perishable goods. These vessels maintain controlled temperatures to ensure the freshness and quality of cargo such as fruits, vegetables, and other temperature-sensitive products.

3. Crude Carrier: Transporting Liquid Gold

Crude carriers, commonly known as oil tankers, specialize in transporting large quantities of crude oil across the seas. These vessels play a crucial role in the energy sector, facilitating the global movement of one of the world's most essential commodities.

4. LNG and LPG Carriers: Handling Gas with Precision

LNG (Liquefied Natural Gas) and LPG (Liquefied Petroleum Gas) carriers are designed for the safe and efficient transport of liquefied gases. These vessels adhere to strict safety standards, contributing to the global supply chain of natural gas and petroleum products.

5. Roro Ships: Effortless Vehicle Transport

Roll-on, roll-off (Roro) ships provide seamless transportation for vehicles, including passenger cars. These vessels feature ramps, allowing vehicles to be driven on and off the ship, streamlining the process of shipping automobiles across international waters.

6. Livestock Carriers: Ensuring Animal Welfare

Livestock carriers are designed to transport animals, ensuring their welfare during the sea journey. These vessels adhere to strict regulations to provide a safe and comfortable environment for the transportation of livestock.

7. Chemical Carriers: Safeguarding Hazardous Cargo

Chemical carriers are specialized vessels equipped to transport hazardous chemicals safely. These ships follow stringent safety protocols to prevent environmental risks and ensure the secure movement of chemical cargo.

8. Heavy Lift Cargo Ships: Managing Over-sized Goods

Heavy lift cargo ships are tailored for transporting oversized and heavy goods that may not fit conventional shipping parameters. These vessels offer unique solutions for industries requiring the transportation of large and cumbersome cargo.

As the variety of cargo demands specialized vessels, these ships, each with its unique capabilities, contribute to the intricate web of global trade. The continuous evolution in ship sizes, as witnessed in the progression of container ship capacities, reflects the industry's commitment to efficiency, predictability, and affordability in sea transportation.

Topic 125: Revolutionizing Sea Transportation: Standardization, Containerization, and Palletization

In the ever-evolving landscape of international logistics and supply chain management, three key innovations have played a transformative role: standardization, containerization, and palletization. These advancements are not merely procedural changes; they revolutionize the very core of how goods are handled, loaded, and transported by sea.

1. Standardization: Precision in Handling

Standardization, at its essence, aims to create uniform units for the mechanized handling, loading, and unloading of goods. The loading and unloading processes, traditionally time-consuming and prone to damage, are significantly streamlined through standardization. The focus is on creating standardized units that can be efficiently lifted and handled by mechanical means.

2. Containerization: The Metal Box Revolution

Containerization marks a paradigm shift in the handling of cargo. The introduction of standardized metal containers, such as the widely used 20-foot and 40-foot containers, has redefined the loading and unloading dynamics at ports. These containers provide a secure, enclosed space for goods, ensuring protection from external elements and enhancing safety during transportation.

Benefits of Containerization:

Mechanical Loading and Unloading: Enables rapid and efficient loading and unloading at ports.

Safety and Security: Protects goods from external factors like seawater, ensuring the integrity of the cargo.

Efficiency and Cost-Effectiveness: Speeds up operations, reducing turnaround time and costs.

3. Palletization: Streamlining Loading Processes

Palletization is the art of arranging cargo on wooden bases, known as pallets, in a standardized manner. These pallets, typically sized at 40 inches by 48 inches, facilitate easy handling and loading by forklifts. The use of pallets streamlines the stuffing process, making it more organized, efficient, and cost-effective.

Benefits of Palletization:

Easy Container Stuffing: Pallets can be lifted and loaded into containers with minimal manual effort.

Protection of Goods: Pallets are often shrink-wrapped or stretch-wrapped, providing an additional layer of protection.

Easy Handling and Identification: Streamlines cargo handling and identification processes, enhancing overall efficiency.

Seaworthiness: Ensures that goods are well-protected against the corrosive effects of seawater.

Overall Impact: Smarter, Faster, and Safer Operations

The amalgamation of standardization, containerization, and palletization has ushered in an era of smarter, faster, and safer sea transportation operations. The entire logistics chain benefits from these innovations, from the mechanical loading and unloading at ports to the protection and identification of goods. These advancements contribute significantly to the efficiency and cost-effectiveness of international logistics and supply chain management, making the global movement of goods a well-orchestrated symphony of precision and speed.

Topics 126-127: Ports Infrastructure: Catalysts of Global Trade

In the intricate web of international logistics and supply chain management, the backbone lies in the ports infrastructure, facilitating the movement of goods by sea. This network comprises various types of ports strategically located across coastal areas and inland regions, seamlessly connecting manufacturers to consumers worldwide.

1. Wet Sea Ports: Giants of Coastal Connectivity

Overview: Wet sea ports, situated on coastal areas, represent the pinnacle of port infrastructure.

Technology Integration: These advanced ports, notably in China, boast mechanical jetties for container handling and loading, employing cutting-edge technologies.

Logistic Integration: While their number might be limited, wet sea ports are vital hubs in global logistics networks.

2. Inland Container Depots (ICDs): Bridging the Inland Gap

Role and Significance: ICDs, located inland away from wet sea ports, fill the logistical needs of areas not directly served by coastal ports.

Container Handling: Equipped with the ability to load containers onto trains or trucks, ICDs play a crucial role in hinterland logistics.

Strategic Locations: Typically found in large industrial cities, these depots complement the capabilities of wet sea ports.

3. Container Freight Stations (CFS): Warehousing and Consolidation Hubs

Warehousing and Waiting: CFS, often overlooked but crucial, serve as warehousing and waiting points for containers.

Consolidation: They facilitate the consolidation of cargo, especially for less-than-container-load (LCL) shipments, optimizing container capacity.

Convenient Locations: Strategically situated away from wet ports and dry ports, CFS locations balance accessibility and congestion concerns.

Distinct Roles, Unified Purpose: A Holistic Network

These varied port infrastructures, including wet sea ports, ICDs, and CFS, collectively form a dynamic and interconnected network. Their roles differ, addressing specific logistical needs, yet they share a unified purpose: facilitating the efficient, secure, and cost-effective movement of goods across the globe.

Challenges and Implications: Dredging and Environmental Considerations

The construction and expansion of larger ports, catering to the demands of ever-growing ships, necessitate extensive dredging. While this ensures accessibility for larger vessels, it comes with implications for coastal ecosystems and environmental concerns. Striking a balance between maritime expansion and environmental conservation is a challenge that port authorities worldwide grapple with.

In conclusion, the evolving landscape of ports infrastructure reflects the adaptability and innovation required to sustain the complex demands of international trade. From colossal wet sea ports to strategically placed ICDs and CFS, each component plays a crucial role in ensuring the smooth flow of goods across continents, contributing to the ever-expanding realm of global commerce.

Topic 128: International Inventory Management: Strategies and Challenges

In the vast landscape of international supply chain management, the role of effective inventory management is pivotal. It acts as a linchpin in ensuring a seamless flow of goods across borders, and its strategic implementation is paramount for exporters of all sizes. Let's delve into the complexities, advantages, and challenges associated with international inventory management.

Strategic Inventory Policies: Navigating Global Markets

Delivery Pipeline Maintenance: International inventories strategically located across the globe play a crucial role in maintaining a robust delivery pipeline. Whether stored in in-house facilities or outsourced warehouses, the right products in the right locations facilitate efficient deliveries to diverse markets.

Demand Fluctuation Absorption: Different countries, cultures, and customer needs lead to demand fluctuations worldwide. International inventories act as a buffer, absorbing these fluctuations and ensuring a steady supply of goods to meet market demands.

Enhanced Distribution Efficiencies: The presence of overseas inventories significantly improves logistics and distribution efficiencies. Timely and quantity-appropriate deliveries to distributors worldwide become feasible with well-planned inventory strategies.

Challenges in International Inventory Management: Balancing Act

Corporate Funds Holdup: The primary challenge lies in the holdup of corporate funds in international inventories. Costs associated with warehousing, demurrage, and storage can tie up substantial financial resources. Prudent inventory policies are crucial to control and optimize these costs.

Investment and Risk: Establishing and maintaining international inventories require substantial investments, whether in-house or outsourced. This investment comes with inherent risks, and meticulous planning is essential to mitigate potential financial pitfalls.

Complexity of Storage Location Management: Managing storage locations across different countries poses a significant challenge. The nuanced understanding of ideal locations comes with experience. The logistics manager's expertise is instrumental in navigating the intricacies of international storage management.

Strategic Considerations: Balancing Efficiency and Financial Prudence

International inventory management is a delicate balancing act, requiring strategic considerations to ensure operational efficiency while minimizing financial burdens. Crafting well-thought-out policies is essential to harness the advantages while mitigating the challenges associated with global inventories.

In conclusion, international inventory management is a critical component of supply chain dynamics, influencing the efficiency, responsiveness, and financial health of global operations. As a logistics professional, navigating these complexities requires a blend of strategic foresight, financial acumen, and a nuanced understanding of diverse markets.

Topic 129: International Packaging: Ensuring Safety and Compliance

In the realm of international logistics and supply chain management, meticulous attention to packaging is indispensable, irrespective of whether goods are shipped by sea or air. Tailoring packaging to suit specific transportation modes is essential—seaworthy for sea shipments and airworthy for air transport. While packaging serves the fundamental purpose of ensuring goods reach their destination safely and in optimal condition, it becomes particularly challenging when dealing with delicate or hazardous items.

Key Considerations for International Packaging

1. Cost Efficiency:

Weight Management: The weight of packaging materials directly impacts costs. Lightweight yet durable materials strike a balance between protection and cost-effectiveness.

Material Cost: Selecting cost-efficient yet robust materials is a critical decision. The aim is to provide ample protection without inflating overall shipping expenses.

2. Protection:

Ensuring Goods Safety: The primary objective of packaging is to safeguard goods during transit. Evaluating the robustness of packaging materials and techniques is vital to prevent damage or loss.

Climate and Environmental Considerations: Understanding the climate and environmental conditions during transit is crucial. Packaging materials should shield goods from elements like moisture, temperature variations, and other environmental factors.

3. Multimodal Transportation Requirements:

Adaptability: Multimodal transportation involves various transshipment points, necessitating packaging that can endure handling transitions seamlessly. Packaging must be adaptable to different modes—trucks, trains, ships, and air transport.

Challenges in International Packaging

1. Hazardous Goods:

Regulatory Compliance: Exporting hazardous goods demands adherence to stringent regulations. Packaging must comply with international standards to ensure safety during transportation and handling.

Documentation: Proper documentation of hazardous goods, including clear labeling and compliance certificates, is essential to prevent legal and safety issues.

2. Delicate Goods:

Customized Packaging Solutions: Delicate items, especially those susceptible to breakage, require tailored packaging solutions. This may involve cushioning, padding, or specialized containers to protect against shocks and vibrations.

Conclusion: Strategic Approach to Packaging

In conclusion, international packaging is a multifaceted aspect of logistics management, demanding a strategic approach. Logistics managers must weigh cost considerations against the need for robust protection. Compliance with international regulations, especially for hazardous goods, is non-negotiable. Ultimately, effective packaging ensures not only the physical safety of goods but also adherence to legal and environmental standards throughout the journey from origin to destination.

Topic 130-131: Special Trade Zones: Catalysts for Global Trade Efficiency

In the realm of international logistics and supply chain management, the concept of Special Trade Zones has emerged as a pivotal force, offering a strategic advantage to countries and businesses alike. These zones, often referred to as Export Processing Zones (EPZ) or Special Economic Zones (SEZ), are designated areas where specific rules and regulations foster an environment conducive to free trade and seamless international transactions.

Key Features and Benefits of Special Trade Zones

1. Facilitating Free Trade:

Legal Framework: Special trade zones operate under a distinct legal framework that promotes free trade. This includes provisions for duty-free import and export of goods within the zone.

Raw Material Accessibility: Businesses operating within these zones enjoy unrestricted access to raw materials, facilitating streamlined production processes.

2. Storage and Inventory Management:

Storage Facilities: Special trade zones serve as strategic hubs for storage, accommodating both finished and semi-finished goods. The flexibility in storage options enhances overall inventory management.

Processing Capabilities: Some zones are equipped with processing facilities, allowing for value addition to raw materials or semi-finished products within the zone itself.

3. Re-export Opportunities:

Global Market Access: Leveraging the benefits of special trade zones, businesses can engage in re-export activities with minimal import duties and logistics costs. This opens up opportunities for businesses to cater to diverse markets worldwide.

4. Import Duty Management:

Transshipment Advantages: Special trade zones provide a platform for transshipment, allowing goods to move seamlessly from these zones without incurring import duties. This facilitates efficient import duty management for businesses.

5. Marketing Management:

Price Control: Special trade zones play a crucial role in marketing management by providing a mechanism to control regional prices. Businesses can strategically process, store, or re-export goods from these zones to meet specific pricing requirements.

6. Regional Economic Impact:

Economic Growth: Hosting countries earmark significant economic areas for special trade zones, contributing to overall economic growth. These zones attract foreign investments, fostering economic development and employment opportunities.

Conclusion: Navigating the Strategic Landscape

In essence, understanding the critical role of Special Trade Zones is imperative for logistics managers and international marketing professionals. These zones not only offer logistical advantages in terms of storage, processing, and transshipment but also serve as catalysts for economic development on a regional scale. Businesses that strategically leverage the benefits of special trade zones can enhance their global competitiveness and navigate the complexities of international trade with greater efficiency.

Topic 132: Approaches to International Supply Chain Management: Centralized, Decentralized, and Outsourcing

In the dynamic landscape of international logistics and supply chain management, businesses adopt various approaches to optimize their operations globally. The key strategies encompass centralized supply chain management, decentralized supply chain management, and the strategic use of outsourcing.

1. Centralized Supply Chain Management: Enhancing Coordination and Minimizing Conflicts

Benefits:

Enhanced Coordination: A centralized approach involves reporting to a single office or person, leading to improved coordination in decision-making.

Conflict Management: Centralized decision-making helps mitigate conflicts that may arise at regional or functional levels, fostering a harmonized supply chain.

Considerations:

Potential Drawbacks: While enhancing coordination, a centralized approach may encounter challenges in adapting to diverse markets, facing regional differences, and managing local complexities.

2. Decentralized Supply Chain Management: Tailoring Strategies for Diverse Markets

Benefits:

Local Adaptation: Decentralized management is advantageous when targeting diverse international markets, allowing for local adaptation based on distinct market conditions.

Efficiency in Diverse Markets: Decentralization brings efficiency by tailoring strategies to local requirements, reducing overall logistics costs.

Considerations:

Local Challenges: While promoting local adaptation, decentralized approaches may pose challenges in maintaining uniformity and centralized control over operations.

3. Outsourcing: Leveraging Specialized Expertise for Strategic Advantages

Benefits:

Focus on Core Business: Outsourcing allows businesses to focus on their core competencies, maximizing benefits in areas where they excel.

Access to Specialized Expertise: Third-party logistics providers bring specialized expertise, infrastructure, and experience, enhancing overall supply chain efficiencies.

Considerations:

Premium for Expert Services: While outsourcing offers specialized services, businesses should be prepared for associated costs. The value derived from expert services often justifies the premium.

Strategic Decision-Making: Tailoring Approaches to Business Needs

The choice between centralized and decentralized supply chain management hinges on various factors:

Product Line and Industry Nature: Certain industries may benefit from a centralized approach, while diverse product lines or industries may find decentralized strategies more effective.

Target Markets: The nature and diversity of target markets influence the choice between centralized and decentralized approaches.

International Business Strategy: The overall international business strategy guides decisions related to supply chain management approaches.

Conclusion: Crafting a Tailored Supply Chain Strategy

In navigating the complexities of international supply chain management, businesses must carefully evaluate their product lines, target markets, and overall business strategies. The choice between centralized, decentralized, or outsourced approaches is not one-size-fits-all but requires a nuanced understanding of business dynamics and global market intricacies. A strategic blend of these approaches can lead to a resilient and efficient international supply chain management system.

Topics 133-134: International Logistics in the Connected World: Navigating Global Connectivity Challenges

The integration of Information and Communication Technology (ICT) has ushered in a new era in international logistics and supply chain management, fostering transparency, real-time insights, and heightened efficiency. In this connected world, leveraging the power of the Internet plays a pivotal role in expanding global reach and ensuring seamless operations.

**1. Global Reach and Supplier Visibility:

Advantages: The connected world offers unparalleled global reach, providing businesses with a vast array of supplier options. Internet connectivity enables real-time exploration of potential partners, aiding in making informed decisions.

Benefits of Global Comparisons: The ability to compare suppliers and partners globally facilitates the adoption of best practices, cutting-edge technology, and proven logistics infrastructure from different regions.

**2. 24X7 Operations and Order Tracking:

Continuous Operations: The connected supply chain operates on a 24X7 basis, ensuring continuous and uninterrupted logistics and supply chain management activities.

Importance of Order Tracking: 24X7 order tracking becomes imperative for exporters. Ensuring the availability of robust infrastructure for tracking orders at any given time is crucial.

**3. Customer Services in a Global Village:

Infrastructure for Customer Services: In a global village facilitated by connected supply chain management, having systems for around-the-clock customer service is paramount. The infrastructure for chat-based interactions and global call centers across different time zones is vital.

Adaptation to Different Time Zones: Successful exporters need to adapt to various time zones and implement customer service strategies that cater to a global audience.

**4. Internet Penetration Challenges:

Understanding Internet Penetration: Challenges arise in markets with varying levels of development, where Internet penetration may be limited. Developing and least developed countries may face issues related to weak Internet backbone, slow speeds, and overall suboptimal Internet infrastructure.

Adaptation Strategies: Exporters need to be aware of these challenges and tailor their strategies to accommodate regions with lower Internet penetration. Implementing solutions that consider the connectivity limitations in certain markets is crucial for success.

Conclusion: Navigating Opportunities and Challenges

Embracing the connected world in international logistics provides unprecedented opportunities, but it also demands strategic adaptation to challenges. Exporters must not only leverage the benefits of global reach and continuous operations but also address issues like Internet penetration to ensure a seamless and successful international logistics journey. In this dynamic landscape, the ability to harness connectivity while mitigating challenges is key to becoming a resilient and prosperous exporter.

Topics 135-136: Understanding Security Challenges in International Logistics and Supply Chain Management

In the realm of international logistics and supply chain management, security is a paramount concern, encompassing both physical threats and emerging hi-tech challenges. Successful exporters must be vigilant and well-informed about potential risks in this interconnected global landscape.

1. Physical Security Threats:

Areas Prone to Attacks: Operating on an international level exposes logistics operations to physical threats, especially in grey areas. Regions with a history of piracy, such as Somalia, pose inherent dangers to sea shipments. Knowledge about routes prone to attacks is crucial.

Cybersecurity in a Connected World: With the increasing reliance on the Internet, Internet of Things (IoT), and smart sensors, the vulnerability to cyber attacks rises. Understanding cyber threats and implementing robust cybersecurity measures is essential for protecting online operations.

Smart Contracts and Blockchain: As the supply chain adopts smart contracts and blockchain technology, security risks and vulnerabilities may arise. Exporters need to comprehend these technologies and explore protective measures against potential cyber threats.

2. Fraud Prevention:

Types of Frauds: Fraudulent activities, whether through LC frauds, order frauds, or frauds by shipping lines, can jeopardize international shipments. Exporters should be aware of the various types of frauds that can occur in different stages of the supply chain.

Risk Management: A comprehensive understanding of export operations enables exporters to identify weak areas prone to fraud. Courses on risk management and frauds management can provide in-depth knowledge on managing these risks effectively.

3. Emerging Technologies and Safeguards:

Blockchain and Metaverse: The emergence of new technologies like blockchain and the metaverse introduces novel challenges to international trade. Exporters must stay abreast of these disruptions and proactively adopt safeguards against potential threats.

International Regulations: The evolving landscape calls for international regulations and guidelines to address new challenges. Exporters need to stay informed about these regulations to ensure compliance and safeguard their operations.

Conclusion: Navigating the Security Landscape

In the face of evolving security challenges, successful exporters must remain vigilant, adaptable, and well-informed. Combining a strong understanding of physical threats, cybersecurity measures, fraud prevention strategies, and awareness of emerging technologies will empower exporters to navigate the complexities of international logistics and supply chain security. Continuous learning and staying updated on international regulations and safeguards are crucial for ensuring the resilience and security of global operations.

Topics 137-138: Environmental Compliance and Green Logistics in International Trade

The growth in global shipping, facilitated by larger vessels and advanced ports, has undeniably improved the efficiency of international logistics. However, the environmental impact of this expansion raises crucial concerns. For successful exporters, understanding and navigating environmental compliance in international logistics has become increasingly significant.

1. Impact of Shipping on the Environment:

Sea Traffic and Climate Toll: The affordability of sea shipments, driven by larger ships, contributes to increased international water traffic. This has a discernible impact on the climate. The construction of advanced ports, accommodating mammoth ships, often involves dredging ecologically critical sea shores, affecting vital ecosystems like sea corals.

2. Emerging Environmental Regulations:

Diverse International Regulations: New and diverse international regulations are emerging, encompassing worldwide, country-specific, and process-specific guidelines. These regulations are designed to address the environmental impact of international logistics and ensure sustainable practices.

Mandatory Reverse Logistics: Some countries are instituting regulations mandating reverse logistics. Exporters now bear the responsibility not only to supply goods but also to manage the reverse logistics of used items after consumption. Understanding these regulations is essential for exporters to stay compliant.

3. Green Logistics Solutions:

Understanding Reverse Logistics: A specialized course on reverse logistics in the VJ Global MBA Knowledge series on Udemy delves into the nuances of reverse logistics. Exporters can explore this course to gain comprehensive insights into the environmental aspects of logistics.

Environmentally Friendly Solutions: Environmentally friendly solutions are emerging as viable and sometimes cost-effective alternatives. These solutions not only contribute to environmental conservation but also offer marketing advantages. Exporters can adopt such solutions to enhance their market position and appeal to eco-conscious consumers.

4. Green Marketing Opportunities:

Market Premium for Environmentally Friendly Products: Certain exporters are successfully marketing products at a premium by emphasizing their environmentally friendly attributes. For instance, the case study of organic tuna fish from Lakshadweep highlights how traditional fishing methods without modern trawlers or plastics have become a selling point in premium markets like Japan.

Green Marketing Strategies: Exploring green marketing strategies can open up new possibilities for exporters. Balancing environmental goals with economic objectives is essential, and exporters can leverage green initiatives to enhance their brand image.

Conclusion: Achieving Balance in Green Logistics

As the global community acknowledges the environmental impact of international logistics, successful exporters need to proactively engage with emerging regulations and green logistics solutions. The challenge lies in finding a balance between environmental goals and economic aspirations. By embracing environmentally friendly practices, understanding reverse logistics intricacies, and exploring green marketing opportunities, exporters can contribute to sustainable international trade while enhancing their competitiveness in the market.

Topic 139: Chapter Conclusion: Navigating the World of International Logistics and Supply Chain Management

In concluding this chapter on international logistics and supply chain management, our primary goal was to lay a foundational understanding for the intricate processes involved in moving goods from the country of origin to the country of destination. The key takeaways from this section aim to provide you with essential insights into the dynamic world of international trade logistics.

1. Foundational Understanding:

The section aimed to equip you with a basic yet crucial foundation for comprehending the complexities of international logistics and supply chain management.

2. Initial Steps in International Logistics:

By covering topics ranging from shipping and ports to inventory management and packaging, we addressed the initial steps that exporters need to navigate in the global logistics landscape.

3. Deep Dive Opportunities:

While this section serves as a starting point, recognizing that a deeper understanding is often necessary, we encourage you to explore the comprehensive course available in this series on "International Logistics Management." This course delves into the minutiae of various topics covered in this section.

4. Ongoing Learning:

International logistics is a dynamic field with constant updates, emerging trends, and evolving regulations. As you venture further into this realm, staying informed and engaging in ongoing learning will be instrumental.

5. Future Exploration:

The international logistics landscape is vast, and opportunities for exploration are abundant. Whether it's understanding the nuances of reverse logistics, embracing environmentally friendly practices, or leveraging the interconnected world of logistics, continuous exploration is key.

Closing Note:

We hope this section has sparked your interest in international logistics management and has set you on a path to deeper exploration. For more detailed insights, consider enrolling in the dedicated course. Keep watching this space for continued learning on diverse facets of international trade and logistics.

As the world of international logistics unfolds with new challenges and opportunities, we encourage you to stay curious, stay informed, and keep watching for more insights into the ever-evolving landscape of global trade logistics.

Chapter 14: Practical Tips for Successful Exporting

Topics 140-141: Overview

Greetings, and welcome back to the course! In this chapter, we embark on a journey into the realm of practical export insights, drawing directly from the author's wealth of experience. The aim is to arm you with invaluable tips and techniques that are grounded in the realities of international trade operations and marketing.

Navigating the Practical Landscape:

Exporting is not just about theories and strategies; it's a hands-on, dynamic venture. This section is designed to provide you with practical wisdom that comes from facing real-world challenges and finding effective solutions.

Experience-Driven Tips:

The tips and techniques shared here are not mere theoretical constructs but are born out of experiences—instances where exporters encountered complexities and navigated through them. These insights are rooted in the practicalities of international marketing and operations.

Categories of Practical Guidance:

The chapter covers various categories of practical guidance, including pricing strategies, communication nuances, insurance considerations, and the intricacies of documentation. Each category addresses critical aspects that can significantly impact your success in the exporting arena.

Logic Rooted in Experience:

Unlike direct logical constructs, these tips are grounded in the tangible outcomes of numerous situations. They offer a pragmatic approach, showcasing the importance of foresight and adaptability in the face of diverse challenges.

Building Confidence Through Knowledge:

By the end of this section, our goal is for you to feel more confident in your exporting endeavors. Practical insights, when applied judiciously, can make a substantial difference in your ability to navigate the complexities of the global market.

Let's Dive In:

Join us in delving into the practical export marketing and operations tips and techniques. From pricing strategies to effective communication and from insurance considerations to mastering documentation, each tip is a building block towards a more successful export journey.

As we unfold these practical insights, remember that the best strategies often emerge from the amalgamation of experience and a keen understanding of the intricacies of international trade. Let's explore, learn, and apply these practical tips to enhance your capabilities as a successful exporter.

Topic 142: Export Pricing: Practical Tips and Considerations

When delving into export pricing, it's essential to recognize that the dynamics can vary based on the industry, product, and market. However, there are foundational principles that can serve as a compass for decision-making. Let's explore some practical tips related to export pricing:

1. Setting Pricing Goals:

B2C Sales: For business-to-consumer sales facilitated by international digital channels like Amazon or Alibaba, aim for a net profit of at least 100%. Adjustments based on experience may follow.

B2B Sales: In business-to-business transactions, especially for substantial quantities, target a minimum profit of 50% to initiate pricing discussions.

2. Avoiding Deep Price Cuts:

In the realm of export business, the focus should not solely be on offering the lowest price. Experience suggests that good buyers seek a fair price, considering various dimensions of the landed cost.

Caution: Deep cuts should be avoided unless absolutely necessary. Buyers, especially in developed countries, prioritize fair pricing over the lowest cost.

3. Building Relationships Over Price Leadership:

Unlike domestic markets, the strategy of becoming a price leader may not yield the same results in export marketing.

Emphasize relationship-building as a primary goal. Aiming for a fair and sustainable pricing model encourages better services and fosters long-term partnerships.

4. Consideration of Incoterms:

EXW (Ex Works) Terms: Advising the buyer to consider Ex Works terms can be beneficial. This places more responsibility on the buyer for the shipment, potentially saving costs for both parties.

Research and Dialogue: Thoroughly research and discuss Incoterms with overseas buyers. Understand their preferences, concerns, and the responsibilities they are willing to undertake. Strive for Incoterms that create a mutually advantageous situation.

5. Flexibility and Customization:

Recognize the need for flexibility in pricing strategies. Customization based on the unique aspects of the product, market conditions, and buyer expectations is key.

Regularly assess and adjust pricing strategies based on evolving market dynamics and feedback from international buyers.

In essence, the art of export pricing involves a delicate balance between profitability, fairness, and relationship-building. While these tips provide a foundational understanding, the nuances of each situation should be carefully considered. Keep the channels of communication open, adapt to changing circumstances, and approach export pricing as a collaborative and dynamic process.

Topic 143: Tips for Effective Communication with Overseas Buyers

Communicating with overseas buyers is a critical aspect of international trade. To ensure a successful and smooth communication process, consider the following tips:

1. Professional and Thorough Communication:

- Maintain a high level of professionalism in all your interactions.

- Provide thorough and detailed information in response to various questions from international buyers.

2. Lead Time Discussion:

- Discuss lead time extensively with the overseas buyer.

- Understand the implications of lead time on cost and work collaboratively to find practical solutions.

3. Payment Terms Clarification:

- Navigate the complexities of international payment terms.

- Ensure payment terms are comfortable for both parties and comply with local regulations.

- Be aware of any payment terms restrictions in your home country.

4. Delivery Terms Explanation:

- Clearly define delivery terms, including the method (sea or air) and potential implications.

- Discuss the feasibility of partial shipments and the impact on overall delivery.

5. Patents and Certification Communication:

- Communicate information about patents and certifications related to your product in both your home country and the destination country.

- Clarify any legal implications and restrictions associated with patents and certifications.

6. Sample Pricing Transparency:

- Communicate the pricing strategy for product samples.

- Address any prohibitive costs associated with samples and discuss the viability of free samples.

7. ASIN and UPC Code Understanding:

- Discuss the importance of ASIN and UPC codes, especially when selling through platforms like Amazon Global Selling.

- Ensure clarity on how these codes align with international standards.

8. Timely and Professional Responses:

- Respond promptly and professionally to importer's queries.

- Aim for timely and efficient communication to build confidence in your reliability.

9. Brand Use Policy Awareness:

- Understand and communicate any brand use policy and restrictions imposed by the buyer.

- Discuss the implications of branding on your products and its impact on selling to other markets.

Continuing our discussion on effective communication with overseas buyers, let's focus on additional aspects that can strengthen your business relationships:

10. Documentation of Innovations and Patents:

- Maintain a comprehensive record of any innovations or special patents your company possesses.

- Ensure that the documentation of these innovations is readily available for communication with overseas buyers.

11. Brand Status and Differentiation:

- Clearly articulate your brand's status on international marketplaces.

- Differentiate your products from your own brand and

emphasize how they stand out compared to client brands.

12. Real-life Example - Haier:

- Learn from successful companies like Haier, which effectively communicates its brand status to OEM clients.

- Understand how such companies manage relationships with various brands they supply to.

13. Packing Details and Compliance:

- Collaborate with the buyer to determine the appropriate packing requirements.

- Discuss technical and scientific aspects of packing, especially for hazardous or dangerous goods.

14. Assistance and Information Provision:

- Be proactive in providing complete information about your products to overseas buyers.

- Offer assistance by understanding and addressing any concerns raised by the buyers.

15. Two-way Communication:

- Establish a two-way communication channel to address concerns from both parties.

- Discuss and resolve any conflicts or discrepancies in a transparent and constructive manner.

16. Legal Compliance and Certifications:

- Stay informed about legal aspects related to quality, sellability, and certifications in the buyer's country.

- Provide necessary documentation, such as certificates from local government, to facilitate the sale of your product in the buyer's country.

17. Product Features and Value Addition:

- Communicate the unique features of your products that set them apart from competitors.

- Emphasize how these features add value to overseas buyers, addressing their specific needs.

18. Product Reviews and Digital Presence:

- Showcase honest product reviews, especially on international and digital marketplaces.

- Maintain a strong digital presence, regardless of the sales channel, and communicate customer reviews to build trust.

19. Client References for Sophisticated Markets:

- Provide references from regular clients, especially those in sophisticated markets.

- Demonstrate your credibility by sharing testimonials and client names, fostering trust with potential buyers.

20. Sensitivity in Information Sharing:

- Exercise caution in sharing sensitive information about your business, innovations, and patents.

- Communicate strategically to enhance relationships without compromising vital business secrets.

21. Prompt and Honest Responses:

- Respond promptly and honestly to inquiries and concerns raised by overseas buyers.

- Build a reputation for reliability through transparent and open communication.

22. Continuous Improvement in Communication:

- Regularly evaluate and improve your communication strategies based on feedback and changing market dynamics.

- Adapt your communication style to meet the evolving needs and expectations of overseas buyers.

By incorporating these additional tips into your communication strategy, you can foster stronger relationships with overseas buyers, showcase the value of your products, and contribute to the success of your international business endeavors.

Topic 144: Tips for Finalizing Payment Terms in Export Contracts

When finalizing payment terms in export contracts, it's crucial to consider various factors to ensure a secure and mutually beneficial arrangement. Here are some tips to guide you through the process:

1. Digital Payment Systems for B2C Transactions:

For B2C transactions, especially through platforms like Amazon Global Selling or Shopify, insist on using the respective digital payment systems.

Opting for platform-based payments ensures safety for both parties and minimizes risks associated with direct transactions.

2. Confirmed Irrevocable Letter of Credit for B2B Transactions:

In B2B transactions, prioritize a confirmed irrevocable letter of credit (LC) issued by a reputable international bank.

Consider involving digital platforms for B2B transactions, if available and trustworthy.

3. Avoid Direct Payments in B2C, Unless Necessary:

In B2C dealings, generally avoid direct payments outside digital platforms to prevent bypassing commissions and ensure the safety of the transaction.

If large orders or specific reasons warrant bypassing the platform's payment system, consider utilizing International Trade financing through a confirmed letter of credit.

4. Concerns about Local Banks in Buyer's Country:

Exercise caution when dealing with local banks in the buyer's country, especially in developing or least developed countries.

Local banks may pose risks, and the buyer might have more influence, potentially putting the exporter at a disadvantage.

5. Preference for Local Currency in LC Payments:

When dealing with letter of credit payments, if feasible and agreeable to the buyer, prefer transactions in the local currency of your own country.

This choice helps mitigate foreign exchange risks and offers greater convenience.

6. Clarification on LC Amendment Charges:

Clearly define and clarify responsibility for LC amendment charges.

As LC amendments are common, understanding who bears the cost— buyer or exporter—is essential for effective payment strategies.

7. Nominate Your Own Local Bank:

Nominate your local bank as the advising and negotiating bank for international trade financing, especially in letter of credit payment systems.

Specify this preference in your LC opening instructions to the buyer.

8. Mitigating Foreign Exchange Risks:

When possible, deal in your local currency to avoid foreign exchange fluctuations.

Discuss with the buyer the benefits of using your local currency and gain agreement on this aspect of the payment.

9. LC Opening Instructions:

Clearly outline the details of your nominated bank in the LC opening instructions sent to the buyer.

Ensure that the buyer follows these instructions to streamline the payment process.

10. Regularly Review and Update Payment Strategies:

Stay proactive and regularly review your payment strategies based on changing market conditions.

Adapt to new opportunities or challenges and make necessary adjustments to enhance your payment processes.

By adhering to these tips, you can establish secure payment terms in your export contracts, minimizing risks and fostering smoother transactions with both B2B and B2C partners.

Topic 145: Considering Legal Points in Export Deals

Negotiating export deals involves careful consideration of various legal aspects to ensure a smooth and compliant process. Here are key points to smartly address legal considerations in export deals:

1. Product's Legal Validity:

Ensure your product complies with legal requirements in the buyer's country.

Discuss patents, certification issues, and any legal dimensions related to the sale of goods, especially in B2B transactions.

2. Certifications for Sale in Buyer's Country:

Obtain necessary certifications for selling goods in large quantities, particularly in B2B formats.

Certify that your products meet legal standards and regulations in the buyer's country.

3. Clarify Legal Unknowns:

Discuss all legal dimensions with the buyer, even aspects you may not be aware of.

Leverage the buyer's knowledge to ensure comprehensive legal clarity.

4. Choice of Law and Legal Jurisdiction:

Preferably, choose the exporter's country's law and legal jurisdiction.

If the buyer insists otherwise, opt for a choice of law and legal jurisdiction in a neutral third country.

Avoid accepting the buyer's country's law and jurisdiction, especially in significant B2B transactions.

5. Safety Measures for Large B2B Deals:

Exercise caution in large B2B deals and prioritize the exporter's legal safeguards.

Safeguard your interests by choosing legal frameworks that provide a fair and balanced perspective.

6. Insist on Clear Legal Terms:

Ensure legal terms are explicit and leave no room for ambiguity.

Clearly outline legal responsibilities and expectations to prevent misunderstandings.

7. Legal Expertise Engagement:

Consider engaging legal experts to navigate complex legal nuances.

Legal professionals can offer valuable insights and help structure agreements in a legally sound manner.

8. International Legal Standards:

Familiarize yourself with international legal standards applicable to your industry.

Align your export deals with recognized legal norms to enhance credibility and compliance.

9. Review and Update Legal Terms:

Regularly review and update legal terms based on evolving regulations.

Stay informed about legal changes in your industry and adapt your agreements accordingly.

10. Documentation and Compliance:

Ensure meticulous documentation to meet legal compliance requirements.

Uphold transparency in transactions, providing a legal foundation for your export deals.

11. Legal Dispute Resolution Mechanisms:

Include clear mechanisms for legal dispute resolution in export contracts.

Define procedures for arbitration or mediation to resolve disputes efficiently.

12. Ethical Considerations:

Uphold ethical standards in all legal dealings.

Prioritize fair and lawful practices, reinforcing trust in your business relationships.

By navigating these legal considerations intelligently, exporters can establish a solid legal framework, fostering confidence and compliance in their export deals. It's essential to prioritize legal clarity and mitigate potential risks through strategic choices in law and jurisdiction.

Topic 146: Negotiating Delivery Terms in Export Contracts

When negotiating delivery terms in export contracts, it's crucial to clarify and explain the commercial terms, especially when using Incoterms. Here are key considerations to ensure a clear understanding between you and the foreign buyer:

1. Understanding Incoterms:

Clearly explain Incoterms to the foreign buyer, emphasizing points of transfer of ownership and responsibility.

Despite the clarity in Incoterms, provide written clarification based on the specific circumstances of the deal.

2. FOB Contracts - Shipping Details:

In FOB (Free On Board) contracts, discuss shipping details with the buyer.

Clarify whether the exporter is required to load the goods on the ship, considering that, in some cases, buyers may prefer delivering the goods 'alongside the ship' to streamline processes and reduce costs.

3. EXW Terms - Delivery Policy Clarification:

For EXW (Ex Works) terms, clearly define the delivery policy.

Specify whether it is at the factory gate, a specific location in your city, or a designated terminal.

Clearly communicate the point at which the title transfer occurs, providing additional clarity beyond the standard Incoterms definition.

4. Loading of Goods in EXW Terms:

In EXW terms, where Incoterms state that loading is the buyer's responsibility, explicitly clarify the loading process.

Clearly define who is responsible for loading the goods onto the first carrier, addressing any potential misunderstandings.

5. Place to Place Delivery Terms:

In place to place delivery terms, consider requesting the acceptance of a Combined Transport Document (CTD) as the main transport document in the letter of credit.

Acknowledge the time gap between loading the goods on the first carrier and the actual loading on the ship in sea shipments.

Insist on practical solutions, such as accepting a CTD, to streamline the documentation process and avoid inconvenience.

6. Written Clarifications:

Emphasize the importance of written clarifications for specific terms and conditions beyond what Incoterms outline.

Document extensions or modifications to Incoterms to avoid misunderstandings and ensure a smooth transaction.

7. Consideration of Buyer Preferences:

Be open to accommodating buyer preferences within the framework of legal and logistical feasibility.

Engage in transparent communication to align expectations and reach mutually beneficial agreements.

8. Bank Acceptance of Transport Documents:

If applicable, negotiate with the overseas buyer to accept a Combined Transport Document in the letter of credit.

Address the time gap concern in place to place delivery terms to enhance the efficiency of the transaction.

9. Regular Review and Adaptation:

Regularly review and adapt delivery terms based on evolving circumstances and feedback.

Stay proactive in addressing potential issues and maintaining clarity in contractual agreements.

By proactively addressing these considerations and maintaining open communication, exporters can navigate the complexities of negotiating delivery terms, ensuring a clear and mutually beneficial understanding with foreign buyers.

Topic 147: Ensuring Clarity in Packing Details

In the realm of export, paying attention to packing details is crucial for a smooth and successful transaction. Here are some tips to ensure you don't miss important packing details:

1. Define Standard Packing:

Clearly communicate your standard packing procedures for exports to regions similar to where your buyer operates.

Specify the typical packaging used for your products unless customization is requested by the buyer.

2. Customization and Buyer's Insistence:

If the buyer insists on customized packing, discuss and clarify the specific requirements.

Clearly outline any additional costs associated with customized packing and include them in your price quote.

3. Incorporate Extra Costs:

When offering a price quote, include any extra costs related to customized packing.

Transparently communicate these costs to the buyer to avoid misunderstandings.

4. Special Retail Packing:

In scenarios where specialized retail packing is required, such as for fashion garments, address the buyer's preferences.

Clearly define the specifications and any associated costs for such packing.

5. Request for Buyer's Marks:

Ask the buyer for specified marks on export boxes, including primary, secondary, and tertiary packaging.

Clarify whether there are specific requirements for marking each level of packaging.

6. Shipment Marks for Identification:

Work closely with the buyer to identify and specify shipment marks, especially for tertiary packing.

Discuss the details of shipping marks, including color preferences (e.g., black or red), to ensure alignment with buyer expectations.

7. Clarify Marking Requirements:

Clarify with the buyer the necessary marking requirements on the packing list.

Ensure consistency between the shipping marks on the boxes and the information provided in the packing list.

8. Detailed Communication:

Engage in detailed communication with the buyer regarding packaging expectations.

Discuss specifics such as color, size, and placement of marks to meet the buyer's preferences.

9. Critical for Large Quantities:

Recognize the critical nature of clear shipping marks, especially when dealing with large quantities.

Ensure that the buyer's requirements are understood and implemented accurately.

10. Identification in a Sea of Goods:

Acknowledge the importance of unique shipping marks for product identification.

Emphasize the significance of clear markings, particularly in B2B sales where products need to stand out in a large volume of goods.

11. Consistent Follow-Up:

Maintain consistent follow-up with the buyer to address any evolving packaging requirements.

Adapt your packing procedures based on changing needs and preferences.

By following these tips, exporters can navigate the complexities of packing details, ensuring a harmonious collaboration with buyers and minimizing the risk of misunderstandings in the shipping and delivery process.

Topic 148: Navigating Export Documentation Essentials

In the realm of export documentation, attention to detail is paramount. Here are crucial considerations to ensure a smooth documentation process:

1. EX Works Terms and Document Clarity:

In EX Works terms, where customs clearance is the buyer's responsibility, seek exact details on the required documents.

Collaborate with the buyer to compile a comprehensive list to facilitate seamless customs clearance in the buyer's home country.

2. Study Letter of Credit (LC) Terms:

Thoroughly study all documentary credit (LC) terms before accepting the letter of credit.

Understand the required documents for payment and ensure alignment with your ability to provide them.

3. Pre-Emptive Clarification on LC Amendments:

Request clarity on potential LC amendments before accepting the letter of credit.

Be prepared to address any genuine difficulties in procuring specific documents and discuss the possibility of amendments with the buyer.

4. Special Documentary Requirements:

Inquire about any special documentary requirements in the buyer's country.

Acknowledge that the buyer may have specific needs for customs clearance, and proactively address these requirements.

5. Exact Goods Description:

Request the buyer to provide an exact and detailed description of the goods, especially for the commercial invoice.

Clarity in goods description is vital for accurate documentation and compliance with customs regulations.

6. Clarify ITC HS Classifications:

Ensure alignment on ITC HS classifications with the buyer, addressing any potential variations in the 10- and 12-digit codes.

Understand the approved codes by the buyer's customs and border control for precise documentation.

7. Adapt Documents to Home and Host Country:

Adapt document preparation to suit both the home country (exporter) and the host country (buyer).

Be aware of specific requirements in each country and prepare documents accordingly for a seamless cross-border transaction.

8. Proactive Approach to LC Amendments:

Maintain a proactive stance in anticipating and addressing potential issues related to LC amendments.

Keep communication channels open with the buyer to discuss and resolve any challenges in the documentation process.

9. Collaborative Approach:

Foster a collaborative approach with the buyer to ensure that all required documents meet the standards of both the exporter and the buyer.

Facilitate transparency and open communication throughout the documentation process.

10. Continuous Communication:

Establish continuous communication channels with the buyer to stay informed about any evolving documentary requirements.

This allows for timely adjustments and prevents last-minute challenges in the documentation process.

By adhering to these considerations, exporters can navigate the complexities of export documentation, ensuring compliance, smooth customs clearance, and timely payments through letter of credit transactions.

Topic 149: Navigating Insurance Terms in Export Negotiations

Ensuring clarity on insurance terms is crucial in export negotiations. Here are key considerations and tips when negotiating insurance terms:

1. Transit Insurance for Inland Transportation:

Depending on the agreed Incoterms, the responsibility for Inland Transportation Insurance may lie with the exporter.

It is essential to clarify whether the exporter or the buyer will be responsible for obtaining transit insurance for inland transportation.

2. Comprehensive Door-to-Door Insurance:

International buyers often opt for comprehensive door-to-door insurance coverage.

This coverage spans from the exporter's factory gate to the designated warehouse or receiving address of the buyer.

3. Clarification on Transit Insurance Responsibility:

Engage in open communication with the buyer to determine who will bear the responsibility for transit insurance.

Clearly outline whether the buyer intends to procure comprehensive insurance or if the exporter is expected to arrange transit insurance.

4. Verification of Buyer's Insurance Policies:

Verify and understand the insurance policies opted for by the buyer.

In cases where buyers secure door-to-door coverage, the exporter may not need to separately obtain transit insurance.

5. Insurance Cost Considerations:

Discuss and clarify any cost implications associated with insurance.

Understand whether the insurance costs are included in the overall pricing or if they are separate and borne by the buyer.

6. Documentation and Policy Details:

Request and review documentation related to the insurance policies chosen by the buyer.

Ensure that policy details, coverage extent, and relevant terms are transparent and align with the agreed-upon Incoterms.

7. Collaborative Decision-Making:

Foster collaboration with the buyer in deciding the most suitable insurance arrangement.

Ensure that both parties are comfortable with the chosen insurance approach and that it aligns with the overall export agreement.

8. Timely Confirmation of Insurance Arrangements:

Seek timely confirmation of insurance arrangements to avoid last-minute discrepancies.

Ensure that insurance-related details are confirmed well in advance to facilitate a smooth and secure transportation process.

9. Customization of Insurance Coverage:

If required, discuss the customization of insurance coverage based on specific needs or concerns.

Be open to tailoring insurance arrangements to address the unique requirements of the export transaction.

10. Continual Communication on Insurance Matters:

Maintain ongoing communication regarding insurance matters throughout the export process.

Address any changes or additional requirements promptly to prevent disruptions in the transportation and delivery of goods.

By proactively addressing these considerations, exporters can navigate insurance terms effectively, ensuring a secure and well-protected export process. Open communication and clarity on responsibilities contribute to a successful and risk-mitigated international trade transaction.

Topic 150: Chapter Conclusion: Navigating the Dynamics of Export Operations

In concluding this chapter, I trust that the insights shared have proven beneficial for your understanding of international marketing and export operations. Drawing from practical experiences, we delved into critical aspects that contribute to a successful export venture.

Recap of Key Topics Explored:

Export Pricing Strategies:

- Unveiled effective strategies to determine competitive yet profitable pricing.

- Emphasized the significance of market research and flexibility in pricing models.

Effective Communication with Overseas Buyers:

- Highlighted the importance of comprehensive product information.

- Explored strategies to communicate innovations, patents, and brand status without compromising confidentiality.

- Emphasized two-way communication to address concerns and build robust relationships.

Payment Terms Negotiation:

- Discussed the significance of utilizing secure digital payment platforms.

- Advocated for confirmed, irrevocable letters of credit for B2B transactions.

- Cautioned against direct payments outside digital platforms, especially in B2C, unless justified.

Legal Considerations in Export Deals:

- Stressed the importance of ensuring the legal validity of products in the buyer's country.

- Advised on the strategic selection of choice of law and legal jurisdiction.

Navigating Delivery Terms:

- Clarified Incoterms, highlighting the importance of specifying ownership transfer points.

- Examined nuances in FOB and EXW contracts, urging clear communication on loading responsibilities.

Packing Details and Implications:

- Underlined the significance of standard packing details and customization when required.

- Explored the need for clarity on shipping marks and their specifications.

Export Documentation Insights:

- Emphasized the necessity of understanding buyer requirements for custom clearance.

- Urged thorough study of documentary credit terms to avoid potential issues.

Negotiating Insurance Terms:

- Advised on clarifying responsibilities for transit insurance, especially in comprehensive door-to-door coverage.

- Encouraged verification and understanding of the buyer's chosen insurance policies.

Future Updates and Continued Learning:

I commit to keeping you informed with additional tips and techniques as they come to my attention. The world of international trade is dynamic, and staying updated is essential. Your newfound knowledge from this section is designed to enhance your confidence in navigating the intricacies of export marketing and operations.

I trust this section has equipped you with valuable insights, empowering you to engage in successful and secure international business ventures. If you have any further questions or seek additional guidance, feel free to reach out. Here's to your continued success in the realm of international trade!

Chapter 15: Concluding Case Study

Topic 151: Overview

Greetings, esteemed readers,

As we draw the curtains on this comprehensive course, we embark on an enlightening journey through our concluding case study—CopyTron India Going Overseas. This case study serves as a culmination of the concepts and principles meticulously explored throughout this course.

Unveiling Real Events for Educational Insight:

While the narrative is rooted in genuine events, it is important to note that identities have been shielded, and details such as names, company affiliations, and locations have undergone alterations. The primary intent is to leverage these real-world occurrences for educational purposes, creating a practical and immersive learning experience.

A Gateway to Practical Application:

Titled with precision, CopyTron India Going Overseas offers a glimpse into the intricacies and challenges a company faces when venturing into international markets. It encapsulates the essence of our discussions, providing you with a tangible application of the principles elucidated throughout the course.

Your Learning Companion:

This case study is not merely a conclusion but an extension of your learning journey. It is designed to reinforce your understanding, allowing you to witness how theoretical concepts manifest in real-world scenarios. The experiences and decisions of CopyTron India become a canvas upon which we can apply and validate the insights garnered from our study.

So, without further ado, let's delve into the dynamic narrative of CopyTron India Going Overseas. Explore, analyze, and extract the invaluable lessons that await within the folds of this case study. Your comprehension and application of these lessons will undoubtedly enhance your prowess in the realm of international business.

Let the exploration commence!

Topic 152: Background and Introduction to CopyTron India

In the realm of entrepreneurial ventures, CopyTron India emerges as a distinctive player with an intriguing origin story. Founded by Mr. Jimmy Shah, a seasoned professional based in Gujarat, the inception of CopyTron India took shape amid the global turbulence of the COVID-19 pandemic.

Entrepreneurial Aspirations Amidst the Pandemic:

Mr. Jimmy Shah, a former professional in the US, seized the unique opportunity presented by the pandemic to fulfill his entrepreneurial dream. Fueled by a vision of establishing a manufacturing venture with a global reach, he returned to India in early 2020, leaving his MNC job behind.

Inception and Vision:

CopyTron India was officially established on January 1, 2022, following meticulous research and groundwork during the pandemic. With financial support from the Indian government, Mr. Shah set up a state-of-the-art manufacturing unit in Gujarat. The focus of CopyTron India's production centered on toners and related chemicals—specifically dry black and color inks essential for photocopier machines and laser printers.

Product Range and Market Segments:

The product line included toners and developers, available in bulk quantities (20 Kg or 10 Kg drums) and cartridges (both OEM and refill cartridges). The manufacturing plant, equipped with imported machines and know-how from leading global companies, ensured world-class quality.

In the Indian market, CopyTron India targeted large wholesalers, distributors, stockists, OEM clients, government clients, and significant stationers. However, our case study will predominantly focus on the overseas markets, where the identified target segments were importers, wholesalers, large users, and OEM clients.

Strategic Orientation:

Driven by a B2B approach for the international market, Mr. Shah conducted extensive research to identify potential buyers. The emphasis on product quality, backed by supplier collaboration and performance evaluations, formed the cornerstone of CopyTron India's strategic orientation.

Challenges and Technical Considerations:

While CopyTron India embarked on its global journey, certain technical challenges surfaced in the manufacturing process. These intricacies will be explored in detail within the context of this case study, offering valuable insights into the complexities faced by an aspiring global player.

As we delve into the dynamics of CopyTron India Going Overseas, the background and introduction set the stage for a deeper understanding of the company's aspirations, challenges, and strategic decisions. Let's navigate the complexities and unveil the lessons embedded in this real-world business scenario.

Topic 153: Overseas Market Business Plan of CopyTron India

In formulating the overseas market business plan for CopyTron India, Jimmy Shah employed a strategic approach that encompassed essential research and meticulous planning. The following key elements constituted the foundation of his plan:

1. Desk Research:

Market Dynamics: Understanding the models and brands most popular in significant markets was a primary focus. Identifying major markets and prevalent models/brands was crucial for aligning production with international demand.

Technical Considerations: Recognizing the technical limitations and requirements of the product, particularly the variations in manufacturing formulas for different models and brands, was imperative.

2. Product Research:

Technical Specifications: Conducting deep product research to comprehend the specific requirements and technical nuances associated with manufacturing dry ink for various photocopier and laser printer models.

Quality Assurance: Ensuring that the production process met international quality standards, considering magnetic properties, fusion properties, and other technical intricacies.

3. Overseas Visits:

Target Markets: Planning personal visits to major markets and engaging with large importers and distributors to establish strong business connections.

Trade Leads: Leveraging the advantage of limited global manufacturers for the product to generate promising trade leads through face-to-face interactions.

4. Trade Show Participation:

Identification: Identifying international trade shows related to stationery products, office supplies, and consumables with high potential for attracting major importers and distributors.

Strategic Presence: Actively participating in trade shows to showcase products, build relationships, and create a strong presence in the international market.

5. Lead Generation:

Resource Utilization: Employing a multi-faceted approach to lead generation, incorporating desk research, overseas visits, and participation in trade shows.

Support Agencies: Collaborating with trade promotion bodies, both in India and internationally, and utilizing online resources for comprehensive market insights.

6. Market-Specific Plans:

Customization: Recognizing diverse market requirements, including preferences for bulk quantities or retail packs, and tailoring specific plans for each market.

Flexibility: Adapting to variations in model numbers, brands, and unique market demands by crafting specific strategies for different regions.

7. Implementation and Execution:

Confidence in Trade Leads: Banking on the confidence derived from robust trade leads generated through visits, research, and trade show participation.

Strategic Selling: Anticipating substantial sales by strategically aligning production with the identified markets and effectively catering to their specific needs.

Conclusion:

CopyTron India's overseas market business plan showcased a methodical and comprehensive approach. By combining research, direct engagement, and strategic planning, Jimmy Shah aimed to position the company as a significant player in the global market. The success of the plan hinged on its adaptability to diverse market dynamics and the meticulous execution of market-specific strategies. As CopyTron India ventured into overseas marketing, the effectiveness of these strategies would unfold in the competitive landscape of international trade.

Topic 154: Critical Operations Areas Identified by Jimmy Shah

In navigating the complexities of international business, Jimmy Shah, the founder of CopyTron India, strategically identified and addressed several critical operational areas to ensure the success of his venture. The following key operational challenges were recognized and effectively managed:

1. International Logistics for Raw Materials:

Challenge: Procuring specialized and technically complex raw materials.

Considerations: Quantities, stock management, and handling import taxes.

Strategic Focus: Ensuring duty-free documentation for imported raw materials to align with government export schemes.

2. International Logistics for Finished Products:

Challenge: Timely and efficient delivery of finished products, often requiring air freight.

Considerations: Cost implications, delivery timelines, and avoiding delays.

Strategic Focus: Ensuring a reliable and swift supply chain for finished goods to meet international market demands.

3. Documentation and Compliances:

Challenge: Navigating complex documentation and compliance requirements for a relatively new product in the Indian market.

Considerations: Import duty-free documentation, understanding and complying with government export schemes.

Strategic Focus: Expertise in fulfilling compliance requirements to streamline the importation process.

4. Intellectual Property Rights (IPR) Issues:

Challenge: Mitigating risks associated with potential infringements, especially competing with OEM office supplies.

Considerations: Vigilance from major international companies in litigating against IPR infringements.

Strategic Focus: Crafting a guerrilla marketing strategy, avoiding conflicts with OEM clients, and entering markets with less OEM activity to minimize IPR-related risks.

5. Product Matching:

Challenge: Producing a product that matches the diverse requirements of different photocopier and printer models in various target markets.

Considerations: Technical intricacies related to magnetic properties, fusion properties, and climate-specific demands.

Strategic Focus: High-level technical production to match product specifications, creating a competitive edge in the market.

6. Maintaining Production Plans:

Challenge: Managing diverse demands from OEM clients, stockists, distributors, and large wholesalers.

Considerations: Procuring the right cartridges for retail packing, filling cartridges, and handling wholesale pack demands.

Strategic Focus: Efficient inventory management, raw material procurement, and meeting various demand patterns with tailored production plans.

7. Quality Control and Certification:

Challenge: Ensuring quality control in a sophisticated production process and obtaining the right certifications.

Considerations: Adhering to product standards, specifications, and certifications.

Strategic Focus: Rigorous quality control measures and obtaining certifications to establish the credibility and reliability of the products.

Jimmy Shah's adept management of these critical operational areas reflects a holistic understanding of the challenges associated with international business. His strategic focus on compliance, intellectual property protection, and technical production contributed to the success of CopyTron India in the competitive global market.

Topic 155: Critical Marketing Issues Identified by Jimmy Shah

In navigating the intricate landscape of international marketing, Jimmy Shah, the founder of CopyTron India, adeptly identified and addressed several critical marketing issues. These key marketing challenges were strategically managed to ensure the success and sustainability of CopyTron India in the global market:

1. Direct Selling Challenges:

Issue: Servicing smaller orders directly to wholesalers and individual importers.

Advantages: Direct selling allows for better pricing and direct engagement with target markets.

Complexities: Managing small orders, especially with the intricate retail packing requirements for individual end-users.

Strategic Focus: Balancing advantages with complexities, ensuring efficient direct selling operations.

2. Indirect Selling Considerations:

Issue: Dealing with large traders in hub locations like Singapore and Dubai.

Advantages: Bulk orders streamline operations, but profitability becomes a concern due to competitive pricing.

Complexities: The need for an overseas presence and potential challenges in profitability.

Strategic Focus: Establishing a balance between servicing bulk orders and maintaining profitability in the indirect selling channel.

3. Institutional Selling Complexities:

Issue: Supplying toners to OEM clients such as HP, Canon, and Ricoh.

Advantages: Lucrative market with good price realization and regular business.

Complexities: Gaining entry into the supply chain of OEM clients, meeting stringent quality standards.

Strategic Focus: Building trust with OEM clients, navigating complexities in institutional selling.

4. After-Sales Service Challenges:

Issue: Providing satisfactory after-sales service in the overseas market.

Complexities: Complicated processes for returning goods, technical corrections, and handling client complaints.

Strategic Focus: Compensating for issues through future orders, offering better pricing to offset past losses, and relying on local partners for on-site issues.

5. Compensatory Strategies for After-Sales:

Strategic Approach: Using compensation methods, such as providing better prices for subsequent orders, to address client complaints and losses.

Effectiveness: Compensation strategies proved successful in managing client expectations and maintaining satisfaction.

Long-Term Consideration: Continuous assessment and adaptation of compensatory strategies based on the nature of client issues.

Jimmy Shah's astute management of these critical marketing issues reflects a comprehensive understanding of the complexities associated with different sales channels and the importance of customer satisfaction in the global market. The strategic approaches employed demonstrate a proactive stance in overcoming challenges and sustaining a competitive edge in the industry.

Topic 156: Current Status of CopyTron India (January 2022 to January 2023)

After delving into the company's background, initial challenges, and critical areas of operation, let's assess CopyTron India's current status as of January 2023:

Financial Overview:

Total Sales: The company has achieved a significant milestone with total sales reaching approximately 200 million Indian rupees in the year 2022 to 2023.

Overseas-to-Domestic Sales Ratio: CopyTron India has displayed a robust international presence, as the overseas-to-domestic sales ratio stands at around 1.5. This indicates that the company is performing better in the international market compared to the domestic market.

Target Markets:

CopyTron India strategically serves several countries, each with its unique market dynamics:

Singapore: Primarily engaged in indirect selling, targeting traders who, in turn, sell to customers worldwide.

Dubai: Similar to Singapore, focusing on bulk sales to traders who distribute globally.

Russia: Directly dealing with importers and significant organizations in the market.

Bangladesh: Supplying goods to distributors, importers, and large stationers through road transportation.

Other Markets (Malaysia and Thailand): While not currently major buyers, these markets hold future potential, and the company aims to expand its presence.

OEM Brands and Clients:

OEM Brands Served: CopyTron India caters to the "FOR USE IN" brands, with a focus on Canon, HP, Ricoh, and Xerox. These brands have diverse models and specifications, varying across countries.

Main Clients: The primary clients include importers, wholesalers, and OEM clients, with a notable presence among traders in Singapore and Dubai. These clients are crucial to CopyTron India's international operations.

Future Growth Prospects:

Potential Markets: While Malaysia and Thailand are currently not significant markets, the company recognizes their future potential and aims to enlarge its target market base.

Diversified Clientele: By serving a range of clients, including importers, wholesalers, and OEM clients, CopyTron India has strategically positioned itself for sustained growth.

In summary, CopyTron India has made substantial strides in its third year of operations, achieving noteworthy sales figures and establishing a robust international presence. The company's focus on diverse markets and clientele, coupled with its strategic approach to serving OEM brands, positions it for continued success in the competitive landscape of office consumables.

Topic 157: Future Plans of CopyTron India

Given the current status and achievements, CopyTron India, under the leadership of Jimmy Shah, has outlined strategic future plans to further enhance its position in the global market. Let's delve into the key future initiatives:

1. Establishment of Overseas Marketing Offices:

Focus Area: Primarily in Singapore.

Rationale: To better serve international clients and major buyers in different countries.

Advantages: Enhances proximity to significant markets, facilitates direct engagement with clients, and strengthens the company's international presence.

2. Air Logistics Partnership with DHL:

Partnership Scope: Advanced negotiations for a long-term partnership with DHL, the largest air transport management company.

Objective: Improve logistics management and enhance the delivery of goods globally.

Benefits:

Faster Deliveries: Meeting client expectations with prompt shipments.

Cost Savings: Potential for better prices by offering faster and more reliable services.

Damage Reduction: Minimizing damages and losses associated with air transportation.

3. Establishment of Overseas Warehouses:

Countries Considered: Singapore, Bangladesh, and Dubai.

Warehouse Purpose: Stock and sale of both bulk toner and retail packs.

Advantages:

International Logistics Management: Facilitating faster deliveries to clients.

Operational Efficiency: Streamlining stock and sale processes.

Enhanced Client Satisfaction: Ensuring product availability and timely deliveries.

4. Financial Stability and Operational Success:

Current Status: The company has maintained financial stability and operational success.

Operational Challenges: Addressed critical areas in operations, including international logistics, raw material procurement, and compliance.

Market Position: No significant difficulties faced, and the company continues to progress in the global market.

5. Client-Centric Approach:

Client Engagement: The company aims to offer better prices and improved services based on client feedback and expectations.

Market Research: Insights gathered from discussions with clients in different countries contribute to refining future strategies.

6. Damage Reduction and Improved International Sales:

Objective: Address damages in air transportation and reduce losses.

Expected Outcome: A formal partnership with DHL is anticipated to minimize damages, ensuring efficient air transportation and boosting international sales.

CopyTron India's future plans reflect a proactive approach to international expansion, logistics optimization, and client satisfaction. The envisioned overseas offices, logistics partnership, and warehouses align with the company's commitment to delivering high-quality products and services in the global market. These strategic initiatives position CopyTron India for sustained growth and competitiveness in the evolving landscape of office consumables.

Topic 158: Summary of the closing case study

The case study of CopyTron India Going Overseas serves as an illuminating exploration into the complexities and triumphs of a company's foray into the international business landscape. From its inception amid the challenges of the COVID-19 pandemic, CopyTron India, led by the visionary Jimmy Shah, exemplifies a strategic and resilient approach to entrepreneurial endeavors.

The narrative unfolds with the establishment of CopyTron India in January 2022, focusing on the production of toners and related chemicals essential for photocopier machines and laser printers. The company strategically targets both the domestic and international markets, with a meticulous business plan that includes extensive desk research, product research, overseas visits, and active participation in trade shows.

As CopyTron India navigates the complexities of international operations, Jimmy Shah adeptly identifies and addresses critical areas, from operational challenges such as international logistics, documentation, and quality control to nuanced marketing issues in direct and indirect selling, institutional selling, and after-sales service. The compensatory strategies employed by the company, such as providing better prices for subsequent orders, emerge as effective measures to manage client expectations and ensure satisfaction.

Examining the current status of CopyTron India from January 2022 to January 2023 reveals significant milestones, with total sales reaching approximately 200 million Indian rupees. The overseas-to-domestic sales ratio of 1.5 underscores the company's robust international presence, particularly in markets like Singapore, Dubai, Russia, Bangladesh, Malaysia, and Thailand. CopyTron India's strategic focus on serving "FOR USE IN" brands, including Canon, HP, Ricoh, and Xerox, positions it favorably among importers, wholesalers, and OEM clients.

Looking ahead, the future plans of CopyTron India underpin a commitment to sustained growth and competitiveness. Initiatives such as establishing overseas marketing offices, forging an air logistics partnership with DHL, and setting up overseas warehouses in strategic locations signify a proactive approach to international expansion and client satisfaction. The company's dedication to financial stability, operational success, and a client-centric approach underscores its resilience in the dynamic landscape of office consumables.

In conclusion, the CopyTron India case study encapsulates not only the challenges and triumphs of an individual company but also provides a rich tapestry of lessons for those venturing into the realm of international business. From strategic decision-making to operational excellence and client-focused strategies, the narrative of CopyTron India offers valuable insights and practical applications for aspiring entrepreneurs and international business practitioners alike. The concluding case study, titled with precision, is indeed a fitting culmination of a comprehensive course on becoming a successful exporter.

Discussion Questions:

1. Strategic Decision-Making: How did Jimmy Shah's strategic decision to establish CopyTron India during the COVID-19 pandemic reflect a visionary approach to entrepreneurial opportunities? What challenges and opportunities arise when venturing into international markets during a global crisis?

2. International Market Entry: In formulating the overseas market business plan, what key elements did Jimmy Shah consider, and how did these elements contribute to the success of CopyTron India's entry into global markets? Discuss the significance of desk research, product research, overseas visits, and trade show participation in international market penetration.

3. Operational Challenges: Considering the critical operational areas identified by Jimmy Shah, how did CopyTron India effectively address international logistics, documentation and compliances, intellectual property rights, product matching, maintaining production plans, and quality control? What lessons can other aspiring global players draw from these operational

strategies?

4. Marketing Strategies: Analyze the critical marketing issues identified by Jimmy Shah, such as challenges in direct selling, complexities in indirect selling, institutional selling nuances, and after-sales service complications. How did CopyTron India's compensatory strategies contribute to client satisfaction, and what implications do these strategies have for long-term client relationships?

5. Current Status and Future Plans: With a focus on the current status and future plans of CopyTron India, discuss the significance of achieving a sales milestone, the overseas-to-domestic sales ratio, target markets, OEM brand focus, and the company's resilience and growth potential. How do the outlined future plans align with industry trends, and what risks or opportunities might the company face in executing these plans?

These discussion questions aim to explore various aspects of CopyTron India's journey, encouraging a deeper understanding of the challenges and strategic decisions involved in international business operations.

Chapter 16: Book Conclusion:

Topics 159-160: Concluding Remarks

The journey through the pages of "All About How To Become A Successful Exporter | Any Origin" has been a comprehensive exploration into the intricate world of international business. As we draw the curtains on this enlightening odyssey, the concluding chapter aims to distill the essence of the key learnings and principles that have unfolded throughout the book.

A Holistic Learning Experience: This book has served as a versatile companion for readers seeking to delve into the nuances of becoming a successful exporter. The journey commenced with foundational concepts, progressed through strategic planning, and culminated in a real-world application through the detailed case study of CopyTron India Going Overseas.

Practical Application of Theoretical Concepts: The concluding case study, featuring CopyTron India, provided a tangible application of the theoretical concepts elucidated earlier in the book. By grounding the narrative in real-world events, the aim was to offer readers an immersive learning experience, bridging the gap between theory and practice.

Entrepreneurial Resilience Amidst Challenges: The entrepreneurial journey of Mr. Jimmy Shah and CopyTron India serves as a testament to the resilience required to navigate challenges, especially during the unprecedented times of the COVID-19 pandemic. From seizing unique opportunities to strategic decision-making, the case study illustrates how resilience and adaptability are pivotal traits for success.

Strategic Elements for Successful Exporting: Throughout the book, strategic elements critical to successful exporting have been systematically explored. This includes meticulous market research, product development, overseas visits, participation in trade shows, and a client-centric approach. The emphasis on adaptability to diverse market dynamics, as evidenced in CopyTron India's approach, underscores the book's commitment to providing actionable insights.

Operational Excellence and Risk Mitigation: CopyTron India's adept management of critical operational areas, including logistics, documentation, intellectual property rights, and quality control, sheds light on the importance of operational excellence and risk mitigation in the global business landscape. The case study demonstrates how proactive approaches to these challenges contribute to sustained success.

Client Satisfaction and After-Sales Strategies: The significance of client satisfaction is a recurring theme, especially in the dynamic field of international business. CopyTron India's compensatory strategies for after-sales services, such as providing better prices for subsequent orders, highlight the importance of fostering long-term relationships and addressing client concerns.

Looking Ahead: As we conclude this journey, the future plans outlined by CopyTron India, including overseas marketing offices, logistics partnerships, and strategic warehouses, serve as a forward-looking guide. The commitment to continuous improvement, financial stability, and a client-centric approach positions the company for sustained growth in the evolving landscape of office consumables.

Empowering Success in International Business: In essence, "All About How To Become A Successful Exporter | Any Origin" has sought to empower aspiring exporters with a comprehensive toolkit. Whether embarking on entrepreneurial ventures or contributing to established organizations, the principles and insights presented aim to fortify individuals in the pursuit of success in the dynamic and global arena of exporting.

As readers absorb the final words of this book, it is our sincere hope that the knowledge imparted here serves as a catalyst for informed decision-making, strategic planning, and entrepreneurial endeavors in the exciting realm of international business. May your path as an exporter be marked by resilience, innovation, and enduring success. Safe travels on your journey to becoming a successful exporter, irrespective of your origin.

Bonus Chapter 1: Understanding Foreign Trade Policy - Example: India's FT Policy

Topics 161-162: Overview

Greetings, Esteemed Readers,

As we embark on the first installment of our bonus chapters, we delve into a pivotal aspect crucial for any successful exporter: Understanding Foreign Trade Policy. In this chapter, we will use India's Latest Foreign Trade Policy as an example to unravel the intricate web of regulations, opportunities, and strategies that shape international trade.

The Strategic Importance of Foreign Trade Policy: Foreign trade policies are intricately woven frameworks influenced by a myriad of external and internal factors. The role of organizations like the World Trade Organization (WTO) is pivotal in shaping and aligning the foreign trade policies of democratic nations. Factors such as per capita GDP, unemployment rates, and internal political dynamics contribute to the nuanced crafting of these policies.

Now, as we have delved into various aspects crucial for exporters, it's time to shine a spotlight on a cornerstone of international business - understanding the foreign trade policy of a country.

The Blueprint for a Robust Export Plan: Why is it indispensable to comprehend the foreign trade policy of a country? Simply put, it serves as the blueprint for creating a robust export plan. The local government's foreign trade policy provides a comprehensive set of rules and regulations that dictate how exporters formulate their strategies and operations.

Understanding foreign trade policy is not just a legal requirement; it's a strategic imperative. Without this understanding, creating a plan that complies with the law of the land becomes inappropriate and impractical.

Boosting Sales Through Policy Support: One of the remarkable aspects of foreign trade policies is their potential to increase sales. These policies often provide demand-side support through initiatives like market development assistance. For instance, in India, the government subsidizes the marketing costs of new exporters exploring overseas markets, fostering global participation.

Such demand-side support, present in various forms across different countries, holds significant potential for boosting export sales.

Reducing Costs via Supply-Side Initiatives: Foreign trade policies also offer supply-side support, aiming to reduce production costs. Initiatives such as special economic zones, subsidized utility services, and access to government-funded warehouses are common elements. By strategically leveraging these initiatives, exporters can streamline operations and cut down on production costs.

Navigating Geopolitical Changes: In the ever-changing landscape of international business, geopolitical events can have profound impacts. A well-structured foreign trade policy acts as a shield, helping absorb the impact of sudden changes in the global environment. Governments can provide support to exporters, minimizing the repercussions of geopolitical shifts.

Classification and Compliance Simplified: Foreign trade policies play a crucial role in classifying goods and categorizing exporters and importers. This classification ensures that different types of treatment align with trade and tariff regulations. Understanding these provisions aids exporters in making informed decisions, aligning with the categorization that benefits their specific circumstances.

Compliance with Local and Overseas Regulations: Rule of law is paramount for the efficient functioning of any society. Foreign trade policies facilitate compliance with local and overseas regulations. They provide a template for exporters and importers to navigate the intricate web of rules and regulations governing external trade. This compliance is essential for the overall well-being of societies, ensuring economic development and employment generation.

As we unravel the layers of India's Foreign Trade Policy in this bonus chapter, remember that a nuanced understanding of foreign trade policies is not just a legal necessity; it's a strategic advantage. It empowers exporters to navigate the complexities of international trade, capitalize on support initiatives, and position themselves for sustained success.

Let the exploration of India's Foreign Trade Policy commence, providing valuable insights for exporters seeking a deeper understanding of the regulatory landscape in one of the world's dynamic markets.

Topic 163: Who Formulates Foreign Trade Policy?

Understanding the dynamics of foreign trade policy requires clarity on the entities responsible for its formulation. In every country, the onus of shaping foreign trade policies lies squarely on the shoulders of the local government. It is a strategic undertaking that involves meticulous planning and coordination among various ministries.

In the context of India, the responsibility for formulating foreign trade policies rests with the Government of India. This crucial task is delegated to specific ministries, each playing a unique role in crafting policies that align with the nation's economic objectives.

Ministry of Commerce and Industries: The primary custodian of India's foreign trade policies is the Ministry of Commerce and Industries. This ministry spearheads the formulation and implementation of trade-related strategies, ensuring they align with the broader economic agenda. Within the ministry, there exists a dedicated department exclusively focused on the nuances of foreign trade policy.

Department of Commerce (DOC): At the heart of foreign trade policy formulation in India is the Department of Commerce (DOC). This department operates as the driving force behind the creation and execution of policies that govern international trade. With a specialized focus on commerce, the DOC is instrumental in shaping regulations, incentives, and initiatives that impact exporters and importers.

In essence, every country designates a specific ministry, often with a dedicated department, to take charge of foreign trade policy formulation. This strategic approach ensures that policies are crafted with precision, addressing the unique needs of the nation's businesses and aligning with global economic trends.

As exporters navigate the complexities of international trade, understanding the pivotal role played by government ministries, such as the Ministry of Commerce and Industries in India, becomes crucial. These entities not only formulate policies but also serve as key partners in fostering a conducive environment for businesses to thrive in the global market. Let's delve deeper into the mechanisms and considerations that shape foreign trade policies, unraveling the intricate threads that connect governmental strategies with the aspirations of exporters.

Topic 164: Stakeholders of Foreign Trade Policy

In dissecting the intricate landscape of foreign trade policy, it becomes imperative to identify and comprehend the diverse stakeholders who wield influence over its formulation and impact. These stakeholders, encompassing various segments of society, play pivotal roles in shaping the trajectory of international trade policies.

Provincial Governments:

In large and diverse countries like India, where multiple states contribute to the nation's economic fabric, provincial governments emerge as significant stakeholders. These state governments operate in tandem with the central government, aligning their policies with the overarching foreign trade strategies formulated at the national level.

Industry:

At the heart of foreign trade policy lies the vast tapestry of the industry, representing a spectrum of players. Key stakeholders within the industry include exporters, importers, manufacturers, and various traders. Additionally, industry bodies such as associations and Chambers of Commerce, which serve as collective voices for businesses, actively participate in influencing and shaping foreign trade policies.

Society:

The broader canvas of society, encompassing citizens and their collective interests, stands as a crucial stakeholder in foreign trade policy. The impact of these policies ripples through various aspects of societal well-being. Employment generation, availability of imported goods, and the requisites of foreign exchange for diverse purposes, including education and medical needs, significantly shape the societal perspective on foreign trade policies.

Understanding the dynamics among these three primary stakeholders provides a comprehensive view of the intricate web of relationships that foreign trade policies navigate. The delicate balance between the aspirations of provincial governments, the dynamism of the industry, and the broader societal interests forms the crucible in which foreign trade policies are forged.

As we delve deeper into the interplay of these stakeholders, we unravel the nuanced considerations that policymakers must navigate to strike a harmonious equilibrium. The collaboration and alignment of interests among provincial governments, industry players, and society become integral to crafting policies that not only foster economic growth but also uphold the collective welfare of the nation. Let's explore how these stakeholders interact and influence the contours of foreign trade policy, shaping the landscape of international business.

Topic 165: Implementation of Foreign Trade Policy

Having grasped the nuances of who formulates and who the stakeholders are in the realm of foreign trade policy, the logical progression leads us to a crucial question: who takes on the mantle of implementing these intricate policies? Unraveling this aspect reveals the dedicated bodies and institutions tasked with executing the strategic vision outlined in foreign trade policies.

Directorate General of Foreign Trade (DGFT):

In most nations, the responsibility for implementing foreign trade policies is entrusted to specialized government bodies. A prime example is India, where the Directorate General of Foreign Trade (DGFT) assumes a pivotal role. The DGFT serves as a dedicated entity with the expertise and knowledge required for the effective implementation of foreign trade policies. This organization acts as the linchpin in translating policy provisions into tangible actions, ensuring alignment with the broader economic goals.

Central Banks:

Central banks emerge as another critical constituent in the

implementation infrastructure of foreign trade policies. The overarching responsibility of central banks, such as the Reserve Bank of India (RBI) in India, extends to monitoring the inflow and outflow of capital. This entails meticulous oversight of diverse foreign exchange transactions, including investments and trade-related financial movements. The synergy between central banks and specialized trade bodies is fundamental to maintaining financial equilibrium and aligning with the tenets of foreign trade policies.

Customs and Border Control Authorities:

At the forefront of the implementation architecture stands the indispensable role of border control and customs authorities. For instance, in India, the Customs and Excise Department assumes the pivotal task of guarding borders and overseeing the smooth flow of goods through various ports, be they seaports, airports, or dry ports. These departments are entrusted with a comprehensive understanding of the latest provisions within foreign trade policies. Their role encompasses enforcing regulations, ensuring compliance, and facilitating the seamless movement of goods across international borders.

In essence, the triad of the DGFT, central banks, and customs and border control authorities forms the robust foundation of the machinery that brings foreign trade policies to life. The synergy among these entities is paramount in navigating the complexities of international trade, fostering economic growth, and safeguarding the interests of the nation.

As we delve deeper into the dynamics of implementation, we unravel the intricate processes that these bodies orchestrate to translate policy frameworks into actionable initiatives on the ground. The meticulous coordination among these pillars ensures that the aspirations encapsulated in foreign trade policies materialize into tangible outcomes, contributing to the nation's economic vibrancy. Let's explore the collaborative efforts and challenges faced by these implementers as they navigate the ever-evolving landscape of global commerce.

Topic 166-167: Role of Independent Industry Bodies in Foreign Trade Policy

In the intricate tapestry of formulating and implementing a country's Foreign Trade Policy (FTP), the role of independent industry bodies emerges as a linchpin. These entities, ranging from export promotion councils to industry associations and chambers of commerce, play a pivotal role in facilitating a seamless exchange of information between the grassroots and the higher echelons of policy formulation and implementation.

Export Promotion Councils (EPCs):

Grassroots Feedback Mechanism:

EPCs, such as those in India, function as catalysts in developing the exports of specific product categories. Crucially, they maintain a direct line of communication with significant exporters, collecting invaluable feedback on challenges, aspirations, and necessary provisions within the FTP. This grassroots-level engagement becomes a cornerstone in understanding the industry's pulse and tailoring policies accordingly.

Bridge to Policy Formulation Bodies:

Acting as intermediaries, EPCs bridge the gap between exporters and policy formulation bodies like the Department of Commerce. By relaying the collected feedback, these councils ensure that the concerns and expectations of exporters are not only heard but also incorporated into the evolving foreign trade policies. This collaborative approach enhances the effectiveness and acceptance of the policies at the ground level.

Industry Bodies (CII, FIEO):

Comprehensive Feedback Channels:

Industry bodies, exemplified by entities like the Confederation of Indian Industries (CII) and the Federation of Indian Export Organizations (FIEO), serve as conduits for a diverse range of stakeholders. They engage with exporters, manufacturers, and corporate bodies, gathering multifaceted feedback on the industry's evolving landscape. This comprehensive understanding is pivotal in crafting policies that are adaptable and responsive to the dynamic business environment.

Facilitating Information Flow:

Industry bodies act as proactive agents, providing a channel for the flow of information from the industry to the government. The feedback they furnish to policy formulation bodies, such as the Ministry of Commerce, ensures that the policies are not only aligned with industry needs but are also nimble enough to navigate changing circumstances.

Chambers of Commerce (FICCI):

Bridging Industry Requirements and Policy Formation:

Chambers of Commerce, like the Federation of Indian Chambers of Commerce and Industries (FICCI), serve as vital intermediaries that bridge the gap between industry requirements and the intricacies of policy formulation. By acting as facilitators, these chambers ensure that the nuanced needs of the business community are translated into actionable policy measures.

In essence, these independent industry bodies act as guardians of the symbiotic relationship between the government and the business community. Their role extends beyond mere representation; they are dynamic conduits of information, ensuring that the FTP remains a living document that is both reflective of industry dynamics and responsive to the evolving global trade landscape. The collaborative synergy between these bodies and the government is indispensable in shaping foreign trade policies that resonate with the diverse needs of the business ecosystem. As we delve deeper, we will explore the challenges, successes, and ongoing evolution of this collaborative paradigm.

Topics 168-169: Factors Influencing Foreign Trade Policy Formulation

Understanding the intricacies of foreign trade policy necessitates a keen awareness of the myriad factors that shape its formulation and implementation. These factors, both external and internal, coalesce to create a dynamic framework that governs a nation's approach to international trade.

External Factors:

World Trade Organization (WTO):

The WTO, with its membership exceeding 180 states, serves as a linchpin in the global trade architecture. Member states align their foreign trade policies with WTO rules and regulations, which are derived from multilateral and bilateral agreements. The principles of the WTO, emphasizing free and fair trade, exert a profound influence on the formulation of foreign trade policies worldwide. Regular monitoring ensures compliance, and deviations trigger scrutiny.

Free Trade Agreements (FTAs):

Countries engaged in FTAs, whether on a bilateral or regional basis, shape their foreign trade policies based on the terms negotiated. These agreements directly impact policy provisions, dictating the inclusion or exclusion of certain elements. The evolving landscape of FTAs contributes to the dynamism of foreign trade policies, creating a complex interplay between global and regional trade dynamics.

International Business and Geopolitical Environment:

The current global business and geopolitical landscape significantly influences foreign trade policies. Ongoing geopolitical shifts, trade tensions, and international events reshape the priorities and strategies embedded in these policies. Nations must navigate this ever-changing environment to ensure their policies remain adaptive and responsive to global developments.

Internal Factors:

Pressing National Issues:

Each country grapples with unique national issues driven by its distinct geography, culture, and socio-economic conditions. Foreign trade policies must address these pressing concerns, aligning with broader national priorities. Whether it's economic development, resource management, or cultural preservation, policies need to be tailored to resolve these internal challenges.

Economic Status:

The economic standing of a country, whether classified as developed, developing, or least developed, profoundly influences foreign trade policy. Economic considerations such as the level of industrialization, GDP per capita, and trade balance inform the strategic choices made in the policy formulation process.

Internal Political Environment:

The political landscape within a country shapes the contours of its foreign trade policy. The government's ideology, approach to international relations, and domestic political dynamics play a pivotal role. The alignment of foreign trade policies with the prevailing political climate ensures coherence and consistency in the pursuit of national interests.

In essence, the formulation and implementation of foreign trade policies are intricate processes that involve a delicate balancing act between external obligations and internal imperatives. Navigating the interplay of these factors requires a nuanced understanding of global trade dynamics, a keen awareness of national challenges, and an adept response to the evolving geopolitical milieu. As we delve deeper into this chapter, we will unravel the complexities and nuances that characterize the interplay of these factors in shaping foreign trade policies.

Topic 170: Objectives of a Typical Foreign Trade Policy

As we delve into the intricacies of foreign trade policy, it is paramount to elucidate the key objectives that underpin its formulation and execution. A typical foreign trade policy is designed with multifaceted goals aimed at ensuring regulatory compliance, fostering international trade, and managing the economic well-being of a nation. Let's dissect these fundamental objectives:

1. Rule Framing and Compliance:

The cardinal objective of any foreign trade policy is to establish rules and regulations in alignment with the local laws. These regulations serve as the bedrock, mandating compliance from all participants in international trade, be it exporters, importers, or manufacturers. The sanctity of the law of the land remains sacrosanct, forming the cornerstone of a robust foreign trade policy.

2. Information Dissemination:

A crucial facet involves disseminating comprehensive information regarding rules, regulations, restrictions, and procedures governing external trade. Clarity on these aspects is imperative for all stakeholders. The dissemination extends to outlining procedures that must be adhered to for the seamless conduct of exports and imports, in harmony with the regulations set by the World Trade Organization (WTO).

3. Boost International Trade:

Foreign trade policies are crafted with the goal of introducing innovative schemes that provide support to exporters and importers. These schemes are strategically designed to address local and international challenges. By offering both demand-side and supply-side support, these policies aim to boost the competitiveness of businesses on the global stage.

4. Prohibitions and Restrictions:

The foreign trade policy explicitly outlines prohibitions and restrictions on certain goods and services. These restrictions, influenced by local culture, religion, and prevailing conditions, are presented in compliance with international norms. The policy serves as a comprehensive guide, delineating what is restricted or prohibited in the international trade arena.

5. Taxation and Tariff Structure:

Another pivotal objective is to elucidate the local taxation structure, import duties, tariffs, and non-tariff restrictions. The policy meticulously categorizes products and goods, detailing the applicable local taxes, duties, and any barriers—tariff or non-tariff—that might impede the flow of international trade.

6. Foreign Exchange Management:

The foreign trade policy assumes a critical role in managing the inflow and outflow of foreign exchange. It delineates the responsibilities and strategies for central banks to monitor and regulate the movement of capital. The policy ensures the maintenance of adequate foreign exchange reserves, essential for addressing normal demands, emergencies, and future economic needs.

In essence, a well-crafted foreign trade policy serves as a guiding framework that not only fosters international trade but also safeguards the economic interests of a nation. By addressing legal, procedural, and economic aspects, these policies contribute to the creation of a conducive environment for businesses to thrive in the global marketplace. As we proceed, we will unravel the nuanced layers of these objectives, delving deeper into their implications and applications in the realm of international trade.

Topic 171: Most Common Acts and Regulations Impacting Foreign Trade Policies

Understanding the legal landscape surrounding foreign trade policies involves a keen awareness of the various acts and regulations that shape this dynamic arena. These acts, often specific to each nation, play a pivotal role in defining the rules and regulations governing international trade. Here are some of the most common acts and regulations that exert a direct influence on foreign trade policies:

1. Foreign Trade Development and Regulation Act:

Example: Foreign Trade Development and Regulation Act of 1992 (India)

This act serves as a linchpin, defining the foundational framework for the rules and regulations embedded within local foreign trade policies. It intricately shapes the architecture of policies that guide international trade practices.

2. Foreign Exchange Management Act (FEMA):

Example: FEMA, 1999 (India)

Crucial to foreign trade policy formulation, FEMA is dedicated to managing foreign exchange. It outlines the regulations governing the inflow and outflow of capital, contributing significantly to the overarching strategy for foreign trade policies.

3. Foreign Contribution Regulation Act (FCRA):

Example: Foreign Contribution Regulation Act of 2010 (India)

While not directly tied to trade, the FCRA is instrumental in regulating foreign contributions to non-governmental organizations (NGOs), charities, and societal causes within a country. It addresses the inflow of foreign funds for purposes beyond commerce.

4. Customs Act:

Varied Examples: Customs Acts in different countries

The Customs Act is a cornerstone for countries in regulating imports and exports. It delineates the procedures, duties, and tariffs associated with cross-border trade, ensuring compliance with foreign trade policies.

5. Export Control Laws:

Varied Examples: Export Control Laws in different countries

Nations often have specific laws governing the export of certain goods and technologies. These laws, integral to foreign trade policies, aim to control the export of sensitive items that could have strategic implications.

6. Trade Barriers and Tariffs:

Varied Examples: Tariff laws in different countries

Tariff laws and trade barrier regulations directly impact foreign trade policies. They define the taxes and barriers imposed on imported and exported goods, influencing the cost and accessibility of products in the international market.

7. Competition Laws:

Varied Examples: Competition Laws in different countries

Competition laws address anti-competitive practices, promoting fair trade. They play a role in shaping foreign trade policies by ensuring a level playing field for businesses engaged in international commerce.

8. Intellectual Property Laws:

Varied Examples: Intellectual Property Laws in different countries

Protection of intellectual property is paramount in international trade.

Laws governing patents, trademarks, and copyrights influence foreign trade policies by safeguarding the rights of innovators and creators.

Understanding these acts and regulations provides a comprehensive view of the legal underpinnings that guide and govern foreign trade policies. While names and specific provisions may vary, the overarching purpose and nature of these legal frameworks align globally, contributing to the harmonization of international trade practices. As we navigate through the intricacies of foreign trade, these legal foundations become indispensable for businesses, policymakers, and stakeholders engaged in the global marketplace.

Topic 172: Impact of Foreign Trade Policies on Trade

Understanding the impact of foreign trade policies on trade is crucial for businesses and nations alike. The nature of these policies, whether open or narrow, and their approach to international trade barriers and investment regulations directly shape the dynamics of global commerce. Let's delve into the key facets that delineate the impact of typical foreign trade policies (FTPs) on trade:

1. Nature of Foreign Trade Policy:

The openness or narrowness of an FTP significantly influences its impact on trade. An open policy, fostering a liberal approach, encourages trade by facilitating exports and imports. Conversely, a narrow policy may impose restrictions, hindering the free flow of goods and services. The nature of the policy is often aligned with a country's strategies, political environment, and pressing national needs.

2. International Trade Barriers:

FTPs guide the adoption of international trade barriers, which can be high, medium, or low. Countries, even within the framework of the World Trade Organization (WTO), have the flexibility to set these barriers. Non-tariff barriers, such as quotas or quality standards, may also be employed. The choice made by local governments impacts the accessibility and cost-effectiveness of traded goods.

3. Investment Barriers:

The approach towards investment barriers is a crucial aspect of FTPs. Governments decide the level of restrictions on foreign investments based on their assessment of local business and political environments. For example, restrictions on multi-brand retailing, as seen in India, showcase how countries regulate foreign investments to align with national priorities and cultural considerations.

4. Realization of Interconnectedness:

Governments increasingly recognize the interdependence of exports and imports. The realization that a robust export sector often requires a well-supported import ecosystem has led to shifts in FTPs. Post-1990, countries like India transitioned from a control-oriented approach to a development-oriented one, acknowledging the importance of a balanced approach for sustainable economic growth.

5. Quality of Implementation:

The impact of FTPs on trade is intrinsically tied to the quality of their implementation. While policies may be well-crafted, their effectiveness relies on diligent execution. Disparities in implementation across countries can lead to varied outcomes. A lack of structural reforms or failures in adapting to changing global environments, as seen in some instances, can compromise the benefits envisioned by foreign trade policies.

6. Structural Reforms and Adaptability:

The ability of a country to undertake necessary structural reforms, coupled with its adaptability to changing global scenarios, plays a pivotal role. Countries that succeed in implementing reforms aligned with their FTPs navigate challenges more effectively. Conversely, those that fall short in making required adjustments may face economic consequences, especially during unexpected events like the global pandemic.

In conclusion, the impact of FTPs on trade is multifaceted, encompassing the nature of the policy, its stance on international trade and investment barriers, and the quality of implementation. The interconnectedness of global trade necessitates a strategic and adaptable approach in crafting and executing foreign trade policies. Governments that strike a balance between fostering a conducive trade environment and addressing national priorities are better positioned to harness the full potential of international commerce.

Topics 173-174: Using India Trade Portal to Access Policy Resources - A Case Study

In the realm of foreign trade, staying updated on policy resources is vital for businesses and individuals involved in international commerce. The Indian Trade Portal serves as a comprehensive and organized platform offering valuable insights into India's foreign trade policies. Let's explore how this portal can be leveraged, using it as a case study.

1. Navigation to Foreign Trade Policy Section:

On the Indian Trade Portal website, users can access pertinent information related to foreign trade policies. The portal provides sections dedicated to policy provisions, policy statements, policy highlights, schemes, incentives, tariffs, and more.

2. Example Demonstration:

To illustrate how users can obtain critical information, a case study is presented. The demonstration focuses on the initiative by the Government of India, particularly the India Trade Portal.

3. Accessing Foreign Trade Policy Documents:

Users navigate to the designated section by clicking on "Foreign Trade Policy / Export Promotion Schemes" on the sidebar. This section serves as a repository for various documents and information related to India's foreign trade policy.

4. Available Resources:

Within the Foreign Trade Policy section, users find a wealth of resources:

Policy Documents: Core documents outlining the foreign trade policy.

Procedure Documents: Detailed guidelines and procedures related to foreign trade.

Amendments and Appendices: Information on policy updates and additional documents.

Policy Statements: Official statements outlining the current foreign trade policy.

Highlights: Key features and focal points of the existing foreign trade policy.

5. User-Friendly Interface:

The portal's interface is designed to facilitate easy navigation and quick access to the desired information. Users can seamlessly download policy documents, amendments, and other essential resources.

6. Accessibility and Privileged Information:

The Indian Trade Portal provides most of its critical information free of cost. While members of organizations like the Federation of Indian Exporters (FIEO) may enjoy privileged access to certain sections, the majority of policy-related documents are available for download to all users.

7. Resourceful for the Exporting and Importing Community:

The portal caters specifically to the needs of the exporting and importing communities in India. It serves as a centralized hub for accessing up-to-date and relevant information crucial for making informed decisions in the realm of foreign trade.

8. Conclusion:

In conclusion, the Indian Trade Portal stands as a valuable resource for those engaged in foreign trade. Its user-friendly interface, comprehensive sections, and the availability of critical documents make it an indispensable tool for staying abreast of India's foreign trade policies. Whether accessing core policy documents or seeking the latest amendments, users can rely on this portal for accurate and timely information.

Topic 175: Chapter Conclusion: Navigating Foreign Trade Policies for Export Success

In this section, we delved into the pivotal role foreign trade policies play in shaping the landscape for global business endeavors. The primary objective was to equip you with the essential knowledge required to navigate the intricacies of these policies and emerge as a successful exporter. Let's recap the key takeaways:

1. Significance of Understanding Foreign Trade Policies:

Recognizing the impact of foreign trade policies on your journey to becoming a successful exporter is crucial. A comprehensive understanding of these policies is indispensable for navigating the global business arena.

2. Key Aspects Explored:

We explored various critical aspects related to foreign trade policies. From the formulation process, stakeholders involved, implementation structures, to the role of independent industry bodies – each element contributes to the intricate tapestry of global trade dynamics.

3. Stakeholder Awareness:

Acknowledging the key stakeholders, including local governments, industry bodies, and societal elements, is paramount. Their roles and interests intersect with foreign trade policies, significantly influencing the overall trade environment.

4. Implementation Architecture:

Understanding the entities responsible for implementing foreign trade policies, such as specialized government bodies, central banks, and customs departments, is crucial. This knowledge ensures a seamless execution of policy provisions.

5. Role of Independent Bodies:

Independent bodies, including export promotion councils, industry associations, and chambers of commerce, play a vital role in bridging the gap between the industry and policy formulation. Their feedback mechanisms contribute to the effectiveness of foreign trade policies.

6. Factors Influencing Formulation:

External and internal factors, such as international agreements, free trade agreements, geopolitical situations, national issues, economic status, and political environments, significantly influence the formulation and execution of foreign trade policies.

7. Objectives of Foreign Trade Policy:

We outlined the primary objectives of foreign trade policies, emphasizing the importance of framing rules, disseminating information, devising support schemes, and managing foreign exchange to foster a conducive environment for international trade.

8. Acts and Regulations:

Highlighting the role of acts and regulations, we emphasized the need to be aware of key legislations governing foreign trade. Acts like the Foreign Trade Development and Regulation Act, Foreign Exchange Management Act, and Foreign Contribution Act were discussed as crucial components.

9. Impact on Trade:

Foreign trade policies have a direct impact on trade dynamics. Whether open or narrow, these policies influence trade barriers, investment regulations, and overall trade quality. The quality of policy implementation is a critical determinant of its effectiveness.

10. Case Study: India Trade Portal:

A practical example illustrated how online portals, like the India Trade Portal, serve as valuable resources for accessing policy documents, amendments, and relevant information. Such platforms facilitate informed decision-making for exporters and importers.

11. Conclusion:

In conclusion, a robust understanding of foreign trade policies is indispensable for navigating the global business landscape. Whether you are an aspiring exporter or an established global player, staying informed about these policies is key to ensuring success in international trade.

12. Future Exploration:

The knowledge acquired in this section serves as a foundation for your ongoing exploration of foreign trade policies. As you venture into specific markets, leverage similar resources and platforms to stay abreast of policy changes and optimize your global trade strategies.

Keep this knowledge in your arsenal as you embark on your journey as a global business professional. Stay informed, stay proactive, and continue watching for further insights into the dynamic world of international trade.

Bonus Chapter 2: Understanding All About International Business Environment

Topic 176: Overview

Welcome back to the course! In this second bonus chapter, we're delving into the intricate realm of the international business environment. As promised, we'll unravel the significance of comprehending this multifaceted landscape and explore various dimensions, issues, and tools associated with it. This knowledge is indispensable for anyone aspiring to thrive as a successful exporter in today's global marketplace.

What to Expect:

Components of International Business Environment: We'll dissect the components that collectively shape the international business environment. Understanding these elements is pivotal for formulating effective strategies.

Tools for Analysis: Learn about the tools and methodologies used to analyze the international business environment. These analytical insights are key to making informed decisions and navigating the complexities of global trade.

Benefits of International Business Environment: Uncover the advantages that a nuanced understanding of the international business environment can bring to your ventures. From risk mitigation to strategic planning, these benefits are crucial for sustained success.

Foundations of International Business Environment: Explore the foundational principles that underpin the international business environment. A solid understanding of these principles lays the groundwork for navigating the dynamic global business landscape.

Recent Trends: Stay updated on the latest trends shaping the world of international business. Recognizing and adapting to these trends is essential for staying competitive and seizing emerging opportunities.

What's Ahead:

While this course provides a comprehensive overview, do note that a dedicated course on the international business environment is in the pipeline for those seeking an in-depth exploration. In this section, we aim to cover the highlights, giving you a solid foundation and a clear understanding of how the international business environment can significantly impact your success in global trade.

Get ready for an insightful journey into the intricate dynamics of the international business environment, providing you with the knowledge and insights needed to excel in the realm of international trade. Let's dive into this enriching exploration in the following bonus chapters.

Topics 177-178: Foundations of International Business Environment

Understanding the foundations of the international business environment is pivotal for any business entity venturing into the global marketplace. These foundations are dynamic, shaped by various factors that influence how a business operates on an international scale. Let's delve into the key elements that constitute the bedrock of the international business environment:

Political Environment:

The political landscape of a country significantly impacts international business. It encompasses government policies, regulations, stability, and the prevalence of corruption. It's crucial for businesses to navigate these political factors adeptly.

Economic Environment:

Economic conditions, including inflation, exchange rates, interest rates, and overall economic growth, play a vital role in shaping the international business environment. Businesses need to adapt to varying economic landscapes across different countries.

Cultural Environment:

Culture is a cornerstone in international business. Understanding the attitudes, values, and beliefs of people in a country is essential for successful business dealings. Cultural differences require nuanced approaches to ensure effective communication and collaboration.

Legal Environment:

The legal framework of a country dictates various aspects of international business, from contracts to intellectual property, labor laws, and environmental regulations. Navigating these legal landscapes is crucial for compliance and risk management.

Technological Environment:

Technological factors, including infrastructure, research and development capabilities, and access to new technologies, influence international business. Adapting to technological advancements is key for staying competitive in global markets.

Competitive Environment:

The competitive landscape varies across countries, impacting international business through factors such as the strength of domestic and foreign competitors, market saturation, and entry barriers. Strategic positioning is essential to thrive in diverse competitive environments.

Natural Environment:

The natural factors of a country, such as the availability of resources, climate, and environmental regulations, can influence international business operations. Adapting to and respecting the natural environment is crucial for sustainable business practices.

Geographic Advantage:

The physical infrastructure and logistical capabilities of a region constitute its geographic advantage. Businesses operating in areas with efficient logistics benefit from cost-effective and streamlined operations.

Geopolitical Factors:

Geopolitics, a fusion of politics and geography, forms a critical aspect of the international business environment. Understanding geopolitical factors is essential as they can shape new business environments and introduce complexities.

Tailoring Strategies to Individual Perspectives:

It's essential to recognize that each business entity perceives and interacts with the international business environment uniquely. Factors such as the company's origin, nationality, and operational areas contribute to its distinct perspective. Adapting strategies to these individual perspectives is crucial for success.

In the upcoming Topics, we'll delve into geopolitical factors, exploring how politics and geography intersect to create a unique business landscape – the geopolitical environment. Stay tuned for a deeper exploration of these dynamic facets of the international business environment.

Topic 179: Benefits of Understanding the International Business Environment

Comprehensive knowledge of the international business environment offers several key advantages, shaping the success and growth of businesses in the global arena. Let's explore the benefits derived from a profound understanding of the international business environment:

1. Business Growth and Expansion:

Understanding the international business environment is a catalyst for business growth and expansion. The vast international playground provides opportunities for companies to strategically select areas for expansion. This knowledge empowers organizations to navigate the global landscape, making it possible to realize international ambitions.

2. Exposure to Diverse Markets:

The international business environment exposes businesses to a diverse and expansive market. Dealing with customers from various cultures, backgrounds, and nationalities broadens the scope of doing business. This exposure not only brings advantages in terms of customer diversity but also enhances a company's competitive edge, leading to improved positions in existing markets.

3. Effective Management of Product Lifecycle:

Proper management of the product lifecycle is a crucial aspect of international trade. Understanding the international business environment aids in strategically navigating the different stages of a product's life. This is particularly significant in the context of the international product lifecycle, allowing companies to extend the lifecycle of innovations and new products.

4. Mutual Growth:

Understanding the international business environment facilitates mutual growth, fostering collaboration between business entities and their partners abroad. This concept of mutual growth extends to various stakeholders, both internal and external. It involves not only achieving growth for the business entity itself but also ensuring that stakeholders, including local governments abroad, reap the benefits of collaborative and mutually beneficial business activities.

In essence, a comprehensive understanding of the international business environment empowers key managers involved in international trade. It equips them with the knowledge to navigate the complexities of global markets, seize expansion opportunities, and foster mutually beneficial relationships with diverse stakeholders. As we delve further into this section, we will uncover additional dimensions of the international business environment, providing insights that are instrumental for success in the global business landscape. Stay tuned for a deeper exploration of these critical aspects.

Topic 180: Elements and Components of International Business Environment

In the vast landscape of the international business environment (IBE), several key elements and components shape the dynamics of global commerce. Let's delve into these fundamental aspects to understand the intricate plays that unfold in this dynamic environment.

1. International Trade - The Primary Element:

The most visible and fundamental activity in the international business environment is international trade. Whether it's the export or import of goods, this activity forms the core of the global business landscape. With the rise of globalization, there has been a significant surge in the movement of goods across borders. This surge has transformed the nature and scale of international trade, making it a pivotal element of the IBE.

2. Capital Flows and Investments:

Another critical element of the IBE is the flow of capital and investments across borders. Money moves globally in various forms, including foreign direct investments, foreign institutional investments, and government-led investments. For instance, the infrastructure development in India benefits from substantial investments flowing from countries like Japan. These diverse forms of capital flows constitute a crucial component of the international business environment.

3. Collaborations and Strategic Partnerships:

Strategic collaborations and partnerships between business entities located in different countries define the third major element of the IBE. These collaborations take shape as joint ventures, franchising agreements, or other mutually beneficial partnerships. Such strategic alliances contribute to mutual growth, not only for the involved companies but also for the local governments. The visible activities of collaboration on the international stage form a vital component of the complex international business landscape.

4. Dynamic Spectrum of Activities:

Beyond these primary elements, the international business environment encompasses a spectrum of diverse activities. These activities, ranging from joint ventures to collaborative partnerships, form the components that collectively shape the global business scenario. The international playground witnesses an array of activities, and understanding these elements provides insights into the multifaceted nature of international business dealings.

In essence, the elements and components of the international business environment illuminate the varied plays that unfold in this global playground. As businesses engage in international trade, capital flows, and strategic collaborations, they navigate the intricacies of a dynamic and interconnected global market. Understanding these elements is essential for successfully navigating the complexities and leveraging opportunities in the international business landscape. Stay tuned for further exploration into the tools and dimensions crucial for analyzing and thriving in this dynamic environment.

Topic 181: Analyzing the International Business Environment: Tools and Techniques

Understanding the international business environment (IBE) is a strategic imperative for business entities seeking to thrive in the global marketplace. To make informed decisions and navigate the complexities of international trade, companies utilize a set of powerful analytical tools. Let's explore some of the most common and effective tools employed for analyzing the IBE.

1. Porter's Five Forces Model:

Developed by Michael Porter, this model assesses the competitive forces within an industry to determine the attractiveness and profitability of a market. The five forces include the threat of new entrants, bargaining power of buyers, bargaining power of suppliers, the threat of substitute products or services, and the intensity of competitive rivalry. By evaluating these forces, businesses can gauge the competitive landscape and position themselves strategically in the international market.

2. PESTEL Analysis:

PESTEL, an acronym for Political, Economic, Social, Technological, Environmental, and Legal factors, provides a comprehensive framework for analyzing the macro-environmental factors impacting business operations. This tool helps businesses assess the external forces that can influence their performance in the international arena. By examining these diverse factors, organizations gain insights into potential risks, opportunities, and challenges in different markets.

3. SWOT Analysis:

SWOT analysis involves evaluating an organization's internal Strengths and Weaknesses, along with external Opportunities and Threats. This tool provides a holistic view of the business environment, enabling companies to identify key areas for improvement and capitalize on their competitive advantages. SWOT analysis is valuable for strategic planning and decision-making, guiding businesses in aligning their capabilities with the demands and opportunities present in the international market.

4. Competitor Analysis:

Understanding competitors is crucial in the global business landscape. Analyzing the strategies, strengths, and weaknesses of competitors allows businesses to fine-tune their own strategies, identify gaps in the market, and uncover potential niches. This analysis aids in formulating effective market entry and expansion plans, ensuring a competitive edge in the international business environment.

5. Market Research and Intelligence:

While not a specific model, continuous market research and intelligence form an indispensable tool for analyzing the IBE. Staying abreast of market trends, consumer behavior, and emerging technologies helps businesses make informed decisions. This ongoing process of gathering, analyzing, and interpreting data is vital for adapting strategies to the ever-evolving dynamics of the international market.

In essence, these tools empower business entities to delve deep into the nuances of the international business environment. By leveraging these analytical frameworks, companies can strategically position themselves, mitigate risks, and capitalize on opportunities in the global marketplace. The choice of tools depends on the specific needs and goals of the organization, allowing for a customized and effective analysis of the international business landscape.

Topic 182-183: Porter's Five Forces Model: Analyzing the International Business Environment

In our exploration of tools for analyzing the international business environment (IBE), one of the cornerstones is Porter's Five Forces model. This widely used model, developed by Michael Porter, provides a structured framework to assess the competitive forces shaping an industry. Let's delve into the key components of Porter's Five Forces and understand how it aids organizations in strategic decision-making for their international ventures.

Figure: Porter's Five Forces Model

1. Threat of New Entrants:

The first force in Porter's model scrutinizes the potential threat posed by new entrants into the market. Organizations must assess the ease or difficulty for new players to enter the industry and compete. Factors such as barriers to entry, economies of scale, and brand loyalty influence this force. A high threat of new entrants may intensify competition and impact profitability.

2. Bargaining Power of Customers:

Understanding the bargaining power of customers is crucial for businesses operating in the international arena. This force assesses the ability of customers to influence prices, demand better quality, or seek alternatives. Organizations must gauge customer loyalty, the availability of substitute products, and the impact of switching costs to formulate effective strategies.

3. Bargaining Power of Suppliers:

The third force evaluates the bargaining power held by suppliers providing inputs to the business. Organizations need to analyze the influence suppliers have on prices, quality, or availability of crucial resources. A strong bargaining position for suppliers could affect the cost structure and profitability of the business. Supplier power is influenced by factors like the uniqueness of inputs and the concentration of suppliers.

4. Threat of Substitutes:

The fourth force focuses on the threat posed by substitute products or services. Organizations need to assess the availability of alternatives that can fulfill the same need as their core offering. Factors such as customer propensity to switch, the uniqueness of products, and the availability of comparable alternatives impact the level of threat substitutes pose.

5. Intensity of Competitive Rivalry:

The fifth force explores the level of competition within the industry, both domestically and internationally. High competitive intensity may lead to price wars, reduced profitability, and increased marketing efforts. Understanding the competitive landscape helps organizations devise strategies to differentiate their offerings, enhance product features, or focus on niche markets.

Benefits and Applications:

Profitability Analysis: Porter's Five Forces aids in assessing the potential profitability of international ventures by considering all competitive forces at play.

Strategic Positioning: The model assists in formulating strategies to navigate the international market, considering factors such as entry barriers, buyer power, and competitive dynamics.

Industry Environment Analysis: Organizations can gain insights into the overall industry environment on a global scale, helping them tailor their approach based on international market conditions.

In conclusion, Porter's Five Forces model serves as a powerful tool for businesses seeking to understand and analyze the intricacies of the international business environment. By systematically evaluating these forces, organizations can make informed decisions, formulate effective strategies, and enhance their competitive position in the global marketplace.

Topic 184: PEST Analysis: Decoding External Factors in International Business Environment

In our exploration of tools for dissecting the international business environment (IBE), the second powerful instrument in focus is the PEST analysis. This widely embraced tool predominantly delves into external factors shaping the macro-level landscape of business operations. Let's dissect the four pivotal categories encapsulated in the PEST analysis and understand how it aids organizations in comprehending market dynamics on a broader scale.

1. Political Factors:

The first facet of the PEST analysis delves into political factors, scrutinizing the impact of government policies, regulations, and political stability on international business. Organizations must assess how political conditions in the target markets can influence their operations. This includes evaluating trade policies, taxation, government stability, and any geopolitical risks that might affect the business landscape.

2. Economic Factors:

Economic considerations form the second pillar of the PEST analysis. Organizations need to gauge the economic conditions of the countries they are entering. This involves analyzing factors such as inflation rates, exchange rates, economic growth, and overall stability. Understanding the economic backdrop helps organizations anticipate the financial landscape and potential challenges or opportunities in international markets.

3. Social Factors:

The third dimension explores social factors that can impact international business operations. This encompasses the study of cultural norms, demographics, social trends, and consumer behaviors. Organizations must adapt their strategies to align with the social fabric of the target market, ensuring their products or services resonate with the local population.

4. Technological Factors:

Technological considerations constitute the fourth element of the PEST analysis. Organizations need to assess the technological landscape in their target markets, understanding factors such as innovation, infrastructure, and the adoption of emerging technologies. This analysis helps businesses align their technological strategies with the prevailing trends in international markets.

Macro-Level Analysis:

Market Trends: PEST analysis provides insights into market trends, enabling organizations to discern whether the industry they are entering is in a growth or decline stage. This macro-level perspective aids in strategic decision-making.

Comparative Business Positioning: The tool facilitates a comparative analysis of business positions based on external factors. Organizations can understand where they stand in relation to market conditions and competitors.

Operational Direction: PEST analysis assists in gauging the potential and direction of international business operations. Organizations can anticipate challenges and opportunities, aligning their strategies with the prevailing external environment.

In essence, PEST analysis serves as a compass for organizations navigating the international business landscape. By comprehensively evaluating political, economic, social, and technological factors, businesses can strategically position themselves and make informed decisions as they embark on international ventures.

Topic 185: PESTEL Analysis: A Comprehensive Lens on International Business Environment

In our exploration of tools for dissecting the international business environment (IBE), we delve into the PESTEL analysis—a more comprehensive sibling of the PEST analysis. This tool surpasses the PEST analysis by encompassing both external and internal factors, offering a deeper understanding for business entities venturing into international markets.

Factors Encompassed:

The PESTEL analysis incorporates a broader spectrum of factors, spanning political, economic, social, and technological dimensions—akin to PEST analysis. However, it extends its reach to delve into environmental and legal factors. This depth is crucial for businesses navigating international waters, where environmental impact and legal considerations can significantly shape the operational landscape.

Internal Factors:

A distinctive feature of PESTEL lies in its incorporation of internal factors within the analysis. This includes an introspective look at how the internal workings of a business entity, such as production techniques and processes, may impact the environment or attract legal implications in international markets.

Analytical Objectives:

The overarching objectives of PESTEL analysis mirror those of its predecessor:

Market Trends Understanding: PESTEL aids in discerning prevailing market trends, allowing organizations to gauge whether the international market is witnessing growth or decline.

Comparative Business Positioning: Similar to PEST analysis, PESTEL facilitates a comparative analysis of business positions. Businesses can align themselves with market conditions and benchmark against competitors.

Operational Status Assessment: PESTEL helps in comprehending the status of international business operations, offering insights into potential challenges, opportunities, and the direction of operations.

Internal Dynamics and Challenges:

The inclusion of internal factors in PESTEL analysis introduces a nuanced perspective. Organizations must evaluate how their internal processes, production methods, and product nature might trigger legal consequences or environmental concerns. This introspection becomes particularly vital in industries where the product lines and internal processes have a significant environmental or legal footprint.

Addressing Legal and Environmental Concerns:

PESTEL analysis proves indispensable in cases where legal and environmental issues can impact business sustainability. By anticipating potential legal barriers and gauging environmental concerns, organizations can proactively address challenges, ensuring both regulatory compliance and environmental sustainability.

Specialized Cases:

While PEST analysis serves as a general framework, PESTEL comes to the fore in specialized cases. Products or industries with inherent environmental implications, or those susceptible to legal scrutiny, benefit from the nuanced analysis provided by PESTEL.

In essence, PESTEL analysis equips businesses with a comprehensive tool to navigate the multifaceted landscape of the international business environment. By embracing a holistic view that spans external and internal dimensions, organizations can make informed decisions, align with market trends, and proactively address challenges in the dynamic world of international business.

Topic 186: SWOT Analysis: Navigating the Dynamics of International Business

Moving forward in our exploration of tools for dissecting the international business environment (IBE), we delve into the SWOT analysis—a robust framework that strategically evaluates a business entity's Strengths, Weaknesses, Opportunities, and Threats.

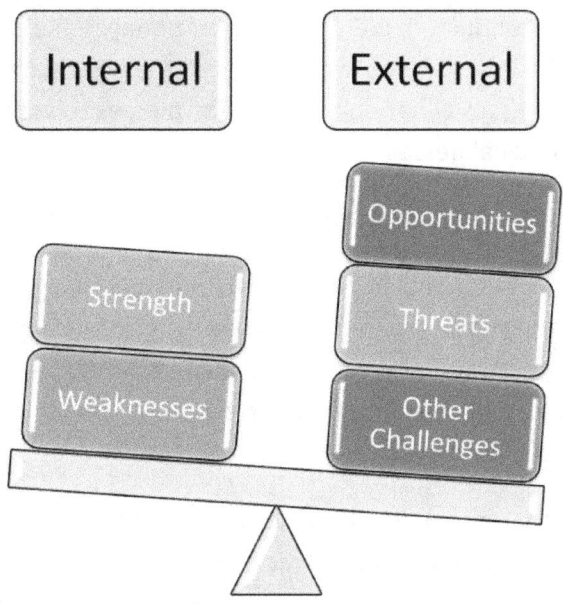

Figure: SWOT Analysis

Comprehensive Self-Reflection:

SWOT analysis involves an in-depth exploration of both internal and external factors shaping the landscape of international business. The objective is to conduct a comprehensive self-reflection, aligning internal capabilities with external opportunities and fortifying against potential threats.

Internal Dynamics - Strengths and Weaknesses:

Strengths: Organizations scrutinize their internal strengths, encompassing core competencies, market advantages, and unique selling propositions. This introspection allows businesses to leverage inherent capabilities for competitive advantage in the international arena.

Weaknesses: Simultaneously, a critical examination of internal weaknesses is conducted. Identifying operational inefficiencies, resource limitations, or gaps in competencies is essential for strategic planning. Businesses can then formulate strategies to address or mitigate these weaknesses.

External Factors - Opportunities and Threats:

Opportunities: SWOT analysis extends its purview to external opportunities in the international market. This involves identifying emerging trends, untapped markets, and areas where the organization can expand or excel. Recognizing opportunities is pivotal for crafting growth-oriented strategies.

Threats: External threats, such as market competition, regulatory challenges, or economic uncertainties, are rigorously assessed. Understanding potential threats helps organizations proactively devise risk mitigation strategies and fortify their position in the global marketplace.

Strategic Planning:

The crux of SWOT analysis lies in converting insights into actionable strategies. By aligning internal strengths with external opportunities, organizations can formulate growth strategies. Similarly, weaknesses are addressed to better capitalize on opportunities, while threats are navigated with strategic resilience.

Dynamic Adaptation:

Given the dynamic nature of the international business environment, SWOT analysis proves invaluable. It empowers organizations to adapt dynamically, foresee immediate opportunities, and preempt challenges that may arise in the ever-evolving global market.

Navigating International Dynamics:

For businesses venturing into international markets, SWOT analysis serves as a compass. It guides organizations through the intricacies of the global landscape, offering a nuanced understanding of their position and influencing strategic decisions.

Holistic Perspective:

In concert with other tools like Porter's Five Forces, PESTEL, and PEST analysis, SWOT analysis completes the arsenal of tools essential for a holistic perspective on the international business environment. By integrating these analyses, businesses can craft robust strategies, ensuring sustainable growth and competitiveness on the global stage.

In essence, SWOT analysis emerges as a cornerstone tool for businesses eyeing international expansion, providing a strategic roadmap to navigate the complexities and capitalize on opportunities in the global business arena.

Topics 187-188: Recent Trends in International Business Environment: Navigating the Evolving Landscape

As we delve deeper into the dynamics of the international business environment (IBE), it's crucial to explore the recent trends that have reshaped the global landscape. These emerging trends signify transformative shifts, presenting both challenges and opportunities for business entities navigating the intricate world of international trade.

1. Crowdfunding Revolution:

Concept: Crowdfunding has emerged as a revolutionary financing method, where businesses secure funding online from a global crowd. Impact: This democratization of funding has opened up new avenues for businesses, allowing them to gather support and resources from diverse corners of the world.

2. Metaverse and NFTs:

Concept: Metaverse and Non-Fungible Tokens (NFTs) are at the forefront, enabling the pledging and financing of ideas and products.

Impact: Utilizing blockchain and Internet 4.0, businesses can explore innovative funding mechanisms, potentially transforming the future of project financing.

3. Remote Employment Wave:

Concept: Enabled by internet technologies, remote employment has gained prominence, allowing individuals to work for companies irrespective of geographical distances. Impact: This shift in employment dynamics offers benefits to both organizations and employees, fostering flexibility and global collaboration.

4. Virtual and Augmented Marketing:

Concept: Leveraging 3D, virtual reality, and augmented reality, businesses are adopting innovative marketing strategies for enhanced customer engagement. Impact: Virtual and augmented marketing provides a novel way to communicate messages, creating immersive experiences for customers in the digital realm.

5. Live Advertising on Digital Platforms:

Concept: Live videos on major digital platforms, such as YouTube, Instagram, and Facebook, have become powerful tools for conveying marketing messages. Impact: Live advertising taps into the vast audiences present on these platforms, offering real-time interactions and a personalized approach to brand communication.

6. Digital Communities and Social Media Dynamics:

Concept: The emergence of large digital communities on social media platforms has redefined audience segmentation and engagement strategies. Impact: Businesses can leverage the expansive reach and segmented audiences on digital platforms for targeted communication, enhancing their global visibility.

Strategic Considerations:

These trends reflect the ongoing transformation of IBE. Businesses need to strategically align themselves with these developments to stay competitive and innovative in the global market. Understanding the nuances of crowdfunding, remote employment, virtual marketing, and live advertising is paramount for organizations eyeing international expansion.

Future Outlook:

The landscape of IBE is dynamic, and these trends signal a promising future. As technologies continue to evolve, businesses must stay agile, adapt to changing consumer behaviors, and embrace innovative approaches to thrive in the ever-evolving international business environment.

In essence, these recent trends showcase the profound impact of technological advancements on the way businesses operate globally, heralding a new era of possibilities and challenges in the realm of international trade.

Topics 189-190: Geopolitics: Navigating the Dynamic Landscape of International Business Environment

In the realm of international business environment (IBE), understanding the concept of geopolitics becomes imperative. Geopolitics is the intricate interplay between political factors and geographic influences that significantly shape power relationships in international relations. This dynamic concept is pivotal in comprehending the ever-changing landscape of global affairs and its profound impact on businesses worldwide.

Origins of Geopolitics:

Coined by Rudolf Kjellen in the early 19th century, geopolitics gained prominence as a theoretical framework. Social and political thinkers associated it with the geographic factors that influenced the dominating power of nations. Advancements in sea transportation, railroads, and later air transport marked different eras, each leading to shifts in geopolitical power dynamics.

Tri-Factor Dynamics:

Geopolitics evolved beyond the interplay of politics and geography, incorporating military capabilities. Today, it encompasses the complex dynamics between political decisions, geographical considerations, and military power. This tri-factor nature of geopolitics is vital for understanding the aggressive moves and strategic decisions made by nations on the global stage.

Impact on International Business:

The changing face of geopolitics has a profound impact on international trade and businesses. Recent events, such as the Russian-Ukrainian war and China's assertive stance on Taiwan, exemplify the evolving geopolitical equations. The pandemic further accelerated these changes, challenging established geopolitical theories and prompting a reevaluation of global power dynamics.

Strategic Considerations for Businesses:

For businesses engaged in international trade, the shifting geopolitics demand strategic foresight. Companies need to navigate the complexities and uncertainties arising from geopolitical events. The ability to adapt to changing circumstances and capitalize on geopolitical shifts becomes a key determinant of success in the global marketplace.

Examples of Geopolitical Adaptation:

Countries like Singapore, leveraging their strategic geographical location on international sea highways, showcase how smaller nations can benefit from geopolitical changes. Remaining neutral and strategically positioning their businesses, these countries demonstrate resilience in the face of evolving geopolitical landscapes.

Future Outlook:

As the geopolitical landscape continues to evolve, businesses must stay vigilant and proactive. Geopolitical considerations are no longer confined to major powers; even smaller nations can strategically position themselves to capitalize on changing global dynamics.

In conclusion, geopolitics emerges as a critical area of understanding in the IBE. Its tri-factor nature – combining politics, geography, and military capabilities – shapes the world order and influences the strategies of nations and businesses alike. Navigating this dynamic landscape requires a nuanced understanding of geopolitical shifts and the agility to adapt to emerging challenges and opportunities in the global arena.

Topic 191: Impacts of Changing Geopolitical Scenarios on Business

The ever-changing geopolitical landscape casts a profound impact on global businesses, shaping their strategies, operations, and overall resilience. Recent events, including the ongoing COVID-19 pandemic, the Russian-Ukrainian war, and shifts in China's stance towards Taiwan, have triggered seismic changes with far-reaching consequences for businesses worldwide.

**1. Global Recession and Economic Shifts:

The world is grappling with a significant economic downturn, influenced by geopolitical events and exacerbated by the enduring COVID-19 pandemic. The repercussions of this global recession are felt across industries, leading to varying degrees of economic impact on different countries.

**2. Disruption of Global Supply Chains:

Geopolitical tensions, especially evident in the Russian-Ukrainian war, are causing disruptions to global supply chains. Businesses are reevaluating their reliance on traditional supply lines and reassessing the risks associated with geopolitical uncertainties. This reconfiguration is altering the dynamics of global value chains, impacting the movement of investments and resources.

**3. Shifting Investments and Supply Lines:

In response to geopolitical changes, businesses are reconsidering their investment destinations and supply chain configurations. The geopolitical stance of a country significantly influences its attractiveness for investments. Companies are now diversifying their operations to mitigate risks associated with geopolitical tensions and ensure a more resilient business model.

**4. Political Stability and Business Confidence:

The democratic world is witnessing shifts in political stability, notably exemplified by events in the United States. These political dynamics can impact the confidence of businesses in the stability of their operating environments. The perceived reliability of political leadership, especially in major economies, plays a pivotal role in shaping business strategies and decisions.

**5. Unforeseen Challenges and Adaptability:

Unprecedented events, like the COVID-19 pandemic, highlight the necessity for businesses to be adaptable in the face of unforeseen challenges. Geopolitical uncertainties introduce complexities that demand agility and strategic flexibility. Businesses need to proactively assess and adjust their operations to navigate the evolving geopolitical landscape.

**6. Global Confidence and Trade Dynamics:

The changing geopolitical scenarios influence global confidence in trade dynamics. Nations and businesses alike closely monitor geopolitical developments to anticipate potential impacts on international trade agreements, tariffs, and cross-border collaborations. Fluctuations in diplomatic relations can directly impact the ease of conducting international business.

**7. Strategic Reassessment and Risk Management:

Businesses are compelled to undertake strategic reassessments and enhance risk management practices. Understanding the geopolitical context becomes integral to developing resilient business strategies that can withstand the shocks emanating from geopolitical uncertainties.

In conclusion, the impacts of changing geopolitical scenarios on business are multifaceted, affecting economic stability, global supply chains, investment decisions, and the overall confidence of businesses. Navigating this intricate landscape requires a strategic approach, adaptability, and a keen awareness of the geopolitical factors influencing the international business environment.

Topic 192: Understanding the Basic Dimensions of Geopolitical Analysis

In the intricate realm of geopolitics, grasping its basic dimensions is paramount for businesses navigating the international landscape. These dimensions provide a comprehensive framework for analyzing the geopolitical forces at play. Let's delve into the fundamental dimensions that shape the geopolitical analysis:

1. Place Dimension:

The "Place" dimension revolves around geography and strategic location. A nation's geographical attributes, such as proximity to key trade routes or access to resources, significantly impact its geopolitical standing. For instance, Singapore, despite being a small country, strategically positioned itself as a global business hub, showcasing the influence of geographic decisions on economic success.

2. Time Dimension:

The "Time" dimension encompasses history and past decisions, playing a pivotal role in shaping the present geopolitical landscape. Historical events and decisions made by nations echo through time, influencing their economic, educational, and political trajectories. A comparative analysis of nations like India and Singapore highlights how past decisions impact their current economic positions and developmental paths.

3. Human Dimension:

The "Human" dimension encapsulates factors like politics, education, and economic development. The nature of politics, level of education, and approaches to economic growth form crucial elements in geopolitical analysis. Understanding how political systems and educational policies shape a nation's economic prospects provides invaluable insights for businesses operating on the international stage.

4. Military Capabilities Dimension:

The "Military Capabilities" dimension is a modern addition, reflecting the importance of a nation's military strength. It involves assessing factors such as nuclear capabilities, military manufacturing capabilities, and dependencies on external sources for defense equipment. Nations with robust military capabilities wield influence, and understanding these dynamics is essential for comprehending geopolitical shifts.

Significance of the Four Dimensions:

Holistic Picture: These dimensions collectively offer a holistic view of geopolitical changes worldwide.

Strategy Formulation: For international traders, analyzing geopolitical developments through these dimensions aids in strategic decision-making.

Profitable Insights: By scrutinizing international news through the lens of these dimensions, businesses can gain profitable insights into changing geopolitical contours.

In conclusion, a nuanced understanding of the "Place," "Time," "Human," and "Military Capabilities" dimensions provides a strategic advantage for businesses operating in the dynamic arena of international trade. Geopolitical analysis, viewed through these dimensions, equips businesses with the foresight needed to navigate evolving geopolitical landscapes and make informed decisions conducive to sustainable growth.

Topic 193: Chapter Conclusion: Mastering the International Business Environment

Congratulations on successfully completing this chapter on the International Business Environment (IBE). Your dedication to understanding the intricacies of this dynamic landscape marks a crucial step toward becoming a successful exporter.

Throughout this section, my goal was to empower you with a comprehensive understanding of every facet of the IBE. The knowledge you've gained serves as a key tool, enabling you to navigate the complexities of international business independently. While collaboration and information-sharing are vital, the ability to draw insights directly from the wealth of global information available positions you as a self-reliant global player.

If you've grasped the concepts presented here, you're now equipped to decipher global events, geopolitical shifts, and business activities. Understanding the "why" behind these occurrences and anticipating their impacts on your strategies is the essence of being a prolific global entrepreneur.

In the upcoming section, we will delve into the various avenues and sources for obtaining critical trade and business information. I'll share insights gained from extensive experience in this field, providing you with practical knowledge to enhance your decision-making capabilities.

Expect discussions on obtaining business intelligence, exploring different sources, understanding the tools available, and uncovering the avenues that lead to success in international trade. Additionally, I will present case studies to illustrate practical approaches when initiating your business, selecting markets, and identifying potential buyers.

I look forward to continuing this journey with you, sharing valuable insights, and further empowering you on your path to becoming a successful exporter to your chosen destination.

Bonus Chapter 3: How to Generate Trade Leads

Topics 194-195: Overview

Welcome back to this bonus section of the course, where we'll delve into the intricate process of generating trade leads in the export business. As you may already know, this is a critical step for any aspiring exporter, and it often consumes a significant portion of an entrepreneur's time.

In this chapter, we'll explore fundamental knowledge about the art of generating trade leads. By the end of our discussions, you'll gain awareness of common methods and approaches used in the industry. The journey of generating trade leads is filled with multifaceted challenges, and together, we'll navigate through them.

From understanding the competitive landscape to unraveling the complexities of transforming inquiries into concrete business transactions, we'll cover a myriad of methods and strategies essential for success. We'll explore both traditional approaches, such as participation in trade fairs and exhibitions, and modern techniques like leveraging online platforms, social media marketing, and the power of networking through industry-specific associations and business networks.

Generating trade leads is a crucial aspect of becoming a successful exporter. It's a challenging process, primarily due to the intense competition in the international market. The potential for profitability in international trade is immense, attracting numerous players and making it difficult to stand out. This chapter aims to equip you with insights and practical ideas to effectively generate and convert trade leads.

Stay tuned as we dive into the strategies, methods, and practical considerations that will enhance your ability to identify potential customers, partners, and lucrative overseas markets. The goal is to provide you with the right knowledge and strategies needed for successful trade lead generation in the complex world of international business.

Let's embark on this journey together, uncovering the secrets to successful trade lead generation in the export business.

Topic 196: Different Approaches and Effective Methods for Generating Trade Leads

Generating trade leads is a nuanced process that involves a combination of strategic approaches and effective methods. Let's explore some essential approaches and methods that can significantly contribute to the success of your export business.

1. Market Research:

Conduct extensive market research to identify countries or regions with a demand for your products or services. Utilize market reports, industry publications, and online databases to understand market trends, consumer preferences, and analyze competitors.

2. Participation in Trade Shows and Exhibitions:

Attend relevant trade shows, exhibitions, and industry events both domestically and internationally. These events provide valuable networking opportunities to connect with potential buyers, distributors, and partners.

3. Online Marketing and Social Media Activities:

Establish a strong online presence through websites, social media platforms, and online marketplaces. Create compelling content such as product videos, blogs, and infographics to attract and engage potential trade leads.

4. Trade Missions and Delegations:

Participate in trade missions or trade events organized by government agencies or industry associations. These missions offer opportunities to meet potential business partners and explore new markets.

5. Networking and Business Associations:

Join industry-specific associations, chambers of commerce, or business networks. Attend meetings, seminars, and networking events to connect with industry professionals and potential clients.

6. Collaboration with Export Promotion Agencies:

Collaborate with export promotion agencies in your country or target markets. Subscribe to their trade lead bulletins and announcements for market insights and connections to potential buyers.

7. Direct Contact and Outreach:

Use direct marketing strategies, such as email campaigns, direct mailing, or phone calls, to reach out to potential leads identified through research. Focus on building relationships rather than immediate sales.

8. Focus on Agents or Distributors:

Identify and collaborate with local agents, distributors, or representatives in target markets. They can act as intermediaries with established networks and expertise in the industry.

9. Utilize Export Platforms and Databases:

Explore online platforms and databases specializing in international trade to find potential leads and partners. These platforms provide a centralized hub for connecting exporters with importers.

10. Offering Samples or Trials:

Consider offering samples or trials of your products or services to potential clients or distributors. This approach allows you to showcase product quality and capabilities, encouraging potential buyers to make actual purchases.

By combining these methods and customizing your approach based on your industry, target market, and products, you can effectively generate trade leads, expand your export opportunities, and increase the chances of success in international business.

Topic 197: Tips for Generating Trade Leads Effectively

In the pursuit of expanding your export business, here are some valuable tips to enhance your trade lead generation efforts:

1. Understand Your Value Proposition:

Study your product thoroughly and conduct competitor analysis. Identify the unique value your product provides in terms of quality, functionality, price, and associated services. A compelling value proposition is a key factor in attracting international customers and effectively generating trade leads.

2. Focus on Landed Cost for Overseas Buyers:

Instead of solely focusing on your product's price, consider the landed cost for overseas buyers. This includes your price, logistics expenses, transportation, insurance, freight charges, and import duties or taxes. Buyers are concerned with the overall landed cost, so focus on markets with fewer border controls, taxes, and import duties to make your product more attractive.

3. Optimize Cost of Generating Leads:

Be strategic in your approach to lead generation. Avoid indiscriminate spending on activities such as providing expensive free samples or participating in costly international trade fairs. Optimize your strategies to ensure cost-effectiveness in generating trade leads.

4. Simplify Transaction Complexities:

Identify and address complexities involved in the transaction process. Depending on your industry, there may be challenges such as high transportation costs or logistical difficulties. Finding ways to simplify these complexities can significantly increase the value proposition for international buyers and expedite the trade lead generation process.

5. Utilize Artificial Intelligence and IT Tools:

Embrace the power of artificial intelligence and IT tools to enhance your marketing campaigns. Leverage these tools to create compelling messages and offers, accelerating your marketing efforts. Stay updated on the latest technologies to remain competitive in the ever-evolving landscape of international trade.

6. Build Relationships:

Cultivate strong relationships with potential buyers, distributors, and partners. Networking plays a crucial role in trade lead generation. Attend industry-specific events, join business associations, and actively engage in networking opportunities to build meaningful connections.

7. Customize Marketing Messages:

Tailor your marketing messages to resonate with the specific needs and preferences of your target audience. A personalized approach demonstrates a genuine understanding of your potential buyers and enhances the effectiveness of your trade lead generation efforts.

8. Utilize Export Platforms and Databases:

Explore online platforms and databases specializing in international trade. These platforms can serve as valuable resources for finding potential leads and partners. Stay active on these platforms to expand your reach and visibility within the global trade community.

By incorporating these tips into your trade lead generation strategy, you can navigate the complexities of international business and position yourself for success in the global market.

Topic 198: Online Platforms and Databases for Generating Trade Leads

To effectively generate trade leads in the digital era, it's essential to leverage various online platforms and databases. Here are some widely used resources by exporters worldwide:

1. Alibaba.com:

Overview: One of the largest online marketplaces connecting manufacturers and suppliers with global buyers.

Focus: Covers a broad range of industries and products.

Tips: Study the features and facilities of Alibaba.com, explore associated websites like JungleScout.com for transaction insights.

2. Global Sources (globalsources.com):

Overview: An online B2B marketplace connecting buyers worldwide with suppliers, especially from Asia.

Focus: Emphasizes electronics, fashion, and gifts.

3. TradeKey (tradekey.com):

Overview: A global trade platform connecting buyers and sellers across various industries, including agriculture, machinery, and textiles.

4. IndiaMART (indiamart.com):

Overview: Focused on connecting Indian suppliers and manufacturers with global buyers, covering diverse industries.

5. Kompass:

Overview: A reputed global business directory providing profiles of international buyers and importing companies in the US and European countries.

Access: Available offline and online; often found in American centers.

6. ExportHub (exporthub.com):

Overview: An international B2B marketplace connecting exporters and importers worldwide, spanning industries like agriculture, electronics, and textiles.

7. go4WorldBusiness (go4worldbusiness.com):

Overview: An online platform connecting global traders, importers, and exporters, offering a wide range of products and industries.

8. Trade India (tradeindia.com):

Overview: Connects Indian manufacturers, suppliers, exporters, and overseas buyers from various industries, including machinery, engineering, textiles, and chemicals.

9. Panjiva:

Overview: Specializes in providing data for global suppliers and manufacturers, aiding businesses in finding potential partners based on import-export activities.

10. eWorldTrade (eworldtrade.com):

Overview: An online B2B marketplace connecting global traders, manufacturers, and suppliers across various industries.

Exploring these platforms involves assessing their features, membership plans, and user reviews to choose the most suitable one for your specific business needs. Delve deeper into each resource to identify overseas trade leads, potential partners, customers, and markets cost-effectively. Consider the characteristics of each platform to align with your business objectives effectively.

Topic 199: Other Online Communities for Trade Leads

In addition to dedicated online platforms and databases, exploring social media communities can also be a cost-effective way to find buyers and suppliers. Here are some noteworthy platforms:

1. Facebook Trade Groups:

Overview: Facebook hosts numerous trade groups covering a wide range of industries.

Search Strategy: Utilize common tags such as export, import, global trade, textile exports, commodities trade, European trade, US trade, and UK trade.

Participation: Join relevant trade groups and engage with members. These groups often have thousands of participants, including buyers, sellers, business partners, and customers.

2. LinkedIn Trade Groups:

Overview: LinkedIn offers various trade groups catering to diverse industries.

Search Strategy: Use tags like China export-import, fruit exports, European trade groups, or export manager to discover relevant trade groups.

Engagement: Participate actively in these LinkedIn groups to connect with professionals, share insights, and explore potential trade leads.

Chapter Takeaway:

Generating international trade leads is undoubtedly challenging but remains a critical aspect of global business success. By tapping into various online platforms, databases, and social media communities, you can uncover valuable opportunities. Here's a recap of key takeaways:

Diversify Your Approach: Explore a combination of online platforms and social media communities to maximize your reach.

Utilize Tags and Keywords: Employ specific tags and keywords relevant to your industry and trade focus to discover niche communities and groups.

Engage Actively: Joining these groups is not enough; active engagement is crucial. Interact with members, share insights, and build meaningful connections.

Cost-Effective Strategies: While generating trade leads can be challenging and expensive, leveraging online communities presents a cost-effective way to connect with potential partners.

Remember, effectively generating and converting trade leads not only opens doors to profitable opportunities but also acts as a significant entry barrier for competitors. Best of luck in your efforts to navigate the dynamic landscape of international trade and convert inquiries into successful business transactions.

Bonus Chapter 4: Harnessing AI Power in Export Operations and Business

Topic 200: Overview

Welcome to the fourth bonus chapter in the VJ Export Mastery series – "Harnessing AI Power in Export Operations and Business." In this section, we will delve into the fundamental understanding of how Artificial Intelligence (AI) can be harnessed effectively in the realm of export business.

The course is taking a leap into advanced territories, exploring the transformative capabilities of AI in the context of international trade. This chapter focuses on creating a strong foundation by understanding the basics of integrating AI into export operations. We'll walk you through the process of developing AI-enabled models tailored for specific export-related tasks.

The upcoming Topics within "All About How To Become A Successful Exporter | Any Origin" are designed to provide practical insights into the strategic use of AI in the global business landscape. This marks a significant shift toward advanced applications, discussing AI's role in international trade within the practical framework of the VJ Export Mastery series on Udemy.

Our emphasis will be on unlocking the power of AI in international trade and business, catering to diverse industries. We aim to decode AI algorithms, explore their functionalities, and showcase practical applications relevant to various facets of international business. The Topics will cover key AI applications, including risk assessment, supply chain optimization, trade finance automation, compliance, market intelligence, translation tools, predictive analytics, customer service, and more.

These applications serve as real-world illustrations of AI's transformative potential in enhancing decision-making, improving efficiency, managing risks, and gaining market insights. The objective of this section is to equip you with both knowledge and practical examples, enabling you to harness the power of AI effectively in international business scenarios.

Join us as we unravel the intricacies of AI in the export landscape, offering valuable insights and strategies to stay at the forefront of innovation and success in the dynamic world of global trade.

Topic 201: How and Where to Use AI in Export Operations?

Welcome back, friends. In this part of the course, we're diving into the exciting realm of advanced applications – specifically, the role of Artificial Intelligence (AI) in international trade, exports, and import operations. This course, a part of the VJ Export Mastery series on Udemy, aims to unravel the potential of AI in the practical context of global business.

Let's start by understanding how and where AI can be employed in international trade. At the heart of AI applications lie diverse algorithms, each contributing to innovative solutions for international business. In this section, we'll explore some key areas where AI can make a significant impact:

Risk Assessment and Fraud Detection:

- AI-powered algorithms analyze vast amounts of data to identify patterns and anomalies.

- Enhances risk management and assessment for international transactions.

- Detects potential frauds and compliance issues, improving overall security.

Supply Chain Optimization:

- AI optimizes supply chain management by predicting demand, suggesting efficient shipping routes, and reducing delays.

- Foresees potential issues, allowing proactive measures to maintain supply chain efficiency.

Trade Finance Automation:

- Automates trade finance processes, analyzing credit risks and automating document verification.

- Facilitates quicker and more efficient transactions, improving overall efficiency in financial operations.

Customs and Compliance:

- AI assists in automating customs and compliance procedures, ensuring adherence to regulations.

- Reduces errors in paperwork, expediting customs and border control clearance processes.

Market Intelligence:

- AI tools gather and analyze vast amounts of market data, aiding in making informed business decisions.

- Provides insights into market trends, consumer behavior, and supports strategic decisions in entering new markets.

Language Translation and Communication:

- AI-powered language translation tools overcome language barriers in negotiations and business agreements.

- Facilitates smooth communication between international stakeholders.

Predictive Analysis for Trade Trends:

- By analyzing historical trade data, AI predicts market trends, commodity prices, and trade patterns.

- Enables businesses to make informed decisions regarding imports, exports, or portfolio management.

Customer Service and Support:

- AI-driven chatbots and customer service tools provide round-the-clock support to international clients.

- Addresses queries in different languages, enhancing customer support efficiency.

Trade Compliance Monitoring:

- AI tools continuously monitor changes in international trade regulations, ensuring businesses stay compliant.

- Keeps businesses updated with evolving trade laws and policies of target markets.

Automated Contract Management:

- AI-enabled contract management systems streamline the creation, negotiation, and management of international trade contracts.

- Improves accuracy and efficiency in dealing with complex contracts.

In the upcoming sections, we'll delve deeper into each of these areas, providing practical insights on creating AI-enabled models for specific tasks in the realm of international trade. Stay tuned as we uncover the transformative power of AI in export operations and business.

Topic 202: Role of AI Algorithms in AI-Enabled Export Operations Models and Their Types

To delve into the advanced applications of AI in export operations, it's crucial to understand the foundational element that drives this innovation – algorithms. The backbone of each AI model lies in the diverse types of algorithms employed. Let's explore some popular types and their roles:

1. Machine Learning Algorithms (ML Algorithms):

Nature and Role: ML algorithms analyze vast amounts of structured and unstructured data, identifying trends and patterns not immediately apparent to humans.

Application: By learning from historical data, ML algorithms make predictions about future market movements, aiding international traders in making informed business decisions.

2. Natural Language Processing (NLP) Algorithms:

Nature and Role: NLP algorithms analyze and interpret unstructured data, such as news articles and social media posts, to gain insights into market sentiments and trends.

Application: Essential for understanding and adapting to the dynamics of international markets, especially in interpreting diverse sources of information.

3. Predictive Analytics Algorithms:

Nature and Role: These algorithms use statistical modeling and machine learning techniques to predict future market movements by analyzing historical data and identifying patterns.

Application: In international trade, predictive analytics aids traders in anticipating market movements, facilitating more informed decision-making.

4. High-Frequency Trading Algorithms:

Nature and Role: Used in specific applications like commodity trading, these algorithms execute rapid international trade transactions, capitalizing on small price movements.

Application: Particularly beneficial in commodities futures and derivatives trading, where quick and precise transactions are crucial.

5. Automated Decision Making Algorithms:

Nature and Role: Employed to automate processes like report creation and document generation, as well as for automatic trading.

Application: Enhances efficiency by automating repetitive tasks, allowing traders to focus on higher-level decision-making tasks for more informed choices.

Understanding the nature and functions of these algorithms forms the basis for creating AI models tailored to specific applications in international trade. In the following sections, we'll delve into practical examples of how to apply these algorithms to enhance efficiency, decision-making, and overall performance in the realm of export operations and business. Stay tuned for insights into the transformative potential of AI in international trade.

Topic 203: Risks and Limitations of Using AI Models for Export-Related Specific Tasks

As we delve into the potential of AI models for export-related tasks, it's imperative to understand and mitigate certain risks and limitations associated with these advanced applications. Awareness of these factors allows for better control and minimization of their impact on the overall performance. Let's explore some key risks and limitations:

1. Bias:

Nature of Risk: AI algorithms are inherently influenced by the data used for their training. If the data is biased, the algorithms will exhibit the same biases, potentially leading to skewed results.

Mitigation: Ensuring that the training data is representative and diverse is crucial. A broad and inclusive dataset helps avoid biased outcomes in both structured and unstructured data.

2. Accuracy:

Nature of Risk: AI algorithms are not infallible and can encounter errors or mistakes. Continuous testing and validation are essential to maintaining the accuracy of predictions.

Mitigation: Regularly testing and validating AI algorithms is imperative to guarantee reliable predictions, enabling human intervention when necessary to uphold accuracy.

3. Regulations:

Nature of Risk: The use of AI in international trade is a rapidly evolving area with limited established regulations. Traders need to navigate and comply with diverse and evolving legal frameworks in different countries.

Mitigation: Staying informed about relevant laws and regulations in host countries, partner countries, and home countries is essential to ensure compliance and mitigate legal risks.

4. Limited Understanding:

Nature of Risk: AI algorithms lack the depth of understanding and reasoning abilities possessed by humans. In complex or nuanced decisions, AI may require constant human oversight and intervention.

Mitigation: Recognizing the limitations of AI's understanding, businesses should integrate human expertise for nuanced decision-making, particularly in situations where a deep understanding is crucial.

5. Dependence:

Nature of Risk: Over-reliance on AI models may lead to a diminished ability to make independent, informed decisions. Traders may become overly dependent on technology.

Mitigation: Striking a balance between using AI as a valuable tool and maintaining human skills and expertise is vital. Businesses should avoid excessive dependence and ensure that technology complements, rather than replaces, human decision-making.

Understanding and proactively addressing these risks and limitations will contribute to the effective and responsible utilization of AI in international trade and export operations. In the following sections, we'll explore strategies and best practices to harness the power of AI while mitigating potential pitfalls.

Topic 204: Advantages of Using AI Models for Export-Related Specific Tasks

As we explore the realm of AI applications in international business, it's crucial to understand the significant advantages that AI models bring to export-related tasks. These advantages contribute to improved decision-making, increased efficiency, enhanced risk management, quicker transaction execution, and reduced costs. Let's delve into each of these advantages:

1. Improved Decision Making:

Benefit: AI enables the analysis of vast amounts of real-time data, identifying trends and patterns beyond human capability. This empowers international traders to make more informed decisions about buying, selling assets, and optimizing portfolios in the dynamic landscape of international trade.

2. Increased Efficiency:

Benefit: AI automates repetitive tasks and processes, such as report and document creation, allowing traders to focus on high-level tasks. This automation enhances the overall efficiency of international trading firms, streamlining operations and reducing the time spent on routine activities.

3. Improved Risk Management:

Benefit: AI algorithms analyze data to identify potential risks in international markets. This equips traders with valuable insights to proactively manage and mitigate risks, protecting assets and minimizing losses. Enhanced risk management is a crucial advantage in the unpredictable world of global trade.

4. Enhanced Speed:

Benefit: AI algorithms execute international transactions almost instantly. This swift execution is especially valuable in fast-moving markets, allowing traders to capitalize on market movements as they happen. The speed offered by AI is a competitive advantage in time-sensitive trading environments.

5. Reduced Costs:

Benefit: AI models automate tasks like report creation, freeing up human resources for more strategic activities. This reduction in manual workload leads to cost savings as international traders can allocate their workforce more efficiently. The overall cost of management is thereby reduced.

Incorporating AI into international business operations provides a strategic edge, offering a blend of efficiency, accuracy, and agility. As we progress, we'll explore how to harness these advantages effectively and address any challenges that may arise in the implementation of AI models for export-related tasks. Understanding both the opportunities and limitations is essential for a comprehensive approach to AI utilization in the context of international trade.

Topic 205: How to Prepare AI Models for Export-Related Specific Tasks

Now that we've discussed the significance of AI models in international trade, let's delve into the practical steps of creating and implementing them effectively. Preparing AI models for export-related tasks involves a structured process that aligns with your specific business objectives. Here's a step-by-step guide:

1. Define the AI Model:

Objective: Clearly define the objective of your AI model. Identify the input data you need and the specific output you aim to achieve.

Example: As an international commodities trader, you might want to monitor and predict price movements. Inputs include historical price data, supply and demand, macroeconomic indicators, and more.

2. Fine-Tune Based on Factors:

Considerations: Fine-tune your model based on market needs, competitor activities, regulatory considerations, technical requirements, and budget constraints.

3. Specify Users and Accessibility:

Details: Define who will use the model. Determine whether it's for proprietary use, public access, or limited use among associates. Understand your audience and users.

4. Choose Code Infrastructure:

Options: Decide on the code infrastructure, whether it's a client-server model, peer-to-peer (P2P), hybrid, or distributed ledger technology (DLT) like blockchain.

Context: Consider the nature of interaction and the security implications of each infrastructure type.

5. Select and Prepare Algorithms:

Approach: Choose algorithms based on the nature of your data. For international trade, you might use machine learning (ML), predictive analytics, and natural language processing (NLP) algorithms.

Customization: Tailor algorithms to suit your specific business needs.

6. Choose Machine Learning Techniques:

Options: Select machine learning techniques, such as supervised learning for structured data, unsupervised learning for diverse data, and reinforcement learning for decision-making with rewards and punishments.

Alignment: Align the techniques with the complexity and diversity of your data.

7. Test AI Models:

Methods: Employ testing methods like split testing, back testing, simulation, and live testing.

Purpose: Ensure accuracy, reliability, and effectiveness. Test how well the model performs under various conditions and scenarios.

8. Software Development:

Team Selection: Develop the software either in-house or through outsourcing. Select a team based on expertise, experience, cost-effectiveness, and collaboration skills.

9. Implementation:

Design AI Platform: Create the user interface, architecture, and workflow. Design a scalable, reliable, and secure platform aligned with your business objectives.

Algorithm Integration: Integrate tested algorithms into the platform. Ensure seamless connections with the user interface and other systems.

Monitoring and Updating: Continuously monitor and update algorithms as new data emerges and market conditions change.

Launch: Finally, launch the model, adapting it based on user feedback and continually updating it to align with changing conditions.

By following these steps, you can develop and implement AI models tailored to the specific demands of international trade, providing a valuable edge in decision-making and strategic planning. The journey doesn't end at launch; continuous monitoring and updates are essential for staying ahead in the dynamic landscape of global commerce.

Topic 206: Tips and Tricks for AI-Based Application Development in International Trade

In the realm of advanced AI application development for international trade, there are essential tips and tricks to enhance the effectiveness and reliability of your models. These insights aim to address challenges, optimize performance, and ensure regulatory compliance.

1. Continuous Learning and Testing:

Importance: Make continuous learning and testing a cornerstone of your AI algorithm development.

Benefits:

Improved Accuracy: Regular updates and retraining on new data enhance prediction accuracy.

Adaptability: Algorithms evolve with changing market conditions, ensuring relevance.

Risk Mitigation: Identify and mitigate potential risks associated with algorithmic decisions.

2. Continuous Evaluation:

Significance: Regularly test and evaluate algorithms to identify and rectify issues promptly.

Advantages:

Stability: Ensures the reliability and stability of algorithms in a live trading environment.

Bug Detection: Early identification of bugs prevents problems in real-world applications.

3. Ensuring Regulatory Compliance:

Awareness: Be cognizant of local regulatory oversights, especially for platforms deployed in the public domain.

Requirements:

Demonstrable Accuracy: Continuous learning and testing assist in showcasing accuracy and reliability.

Compliance: Align algorithms with regulatory requirements to ensure adherence.

4. Optimizing for Performance:

Focus: Prioritize optimization of algorithms and models for peak performance.

Considerations:

Efficiency: Strive for efficient execution of international transactions with minimal latency.

Resource Allocation: Optimize resource utilization for cost-effective and high-performance outcomes.

5. Cybersecurity Measures:

Prioritization: Emphasize robust cybersecurity measures to safeguard sensitive data.

Implementation:

Encryption: Utilize encryption techniques to protect data during transmission and storage.

Authentication: Implement multi-factor authentication to enhance access control.

6. User-Friendly Interface:

Design Focus: Ensure the AI platform has a user-friendly interface for ease of use.

Considerations:

Visualization: Incorporate visual elements for better understanding of data and predictions.

Intuitive Navigation: Prioritize intuitive navigation to enhance user experience.

7. Scalability and Flexibility:

Planning: Design the platform with scalability and flexibility in mind.

Benefits:

Growth Readiness: Accommodate increasing data volumes and user demands seamlessly.

Adaptability: Easily incorporate updates and changes as the business landscape evolves.

8. Ethical Considerations:

Mindful Development: Embed ethical considerations into the AI development process.

Guiding Principles:

Fairness: Ensure unbiased algorithms and fair treatment across various scenarios.

Transparency: Strive for transparency in algorithmic decision-making processes.

9. Feedback Mechanism:

User Input: Establish a feedback mechanism for users to report issues and provide insights.

Benefits:

Continuous Improvement: Leverage user feedback for ongoing improvements and refinements.

User Satisfaction: Enhance user satisfaction by addressing concerns promptly.

Incorporating these tips and tricks into your AI-based application development strategy ensures a robust, compliant, and user-friendly platform for international trade. Regular assessment, adaptation, and attention to ethical considerations will contribute to the sustained success of your AI models in the dynamic landscape of global commerce.

Topic 207: Chapter Conclusion: Harnessing Artificial Intelligence for International Trade

In the exploration of this course section, we delved into the transformative power of artificial intelligence (AI) in reshaping the landscape of international trade. The core takeaway from this journey is the profound impact AI models, applications, and platforms can have in automating and optimizing critical decisions within the realm of global commerce.

Key Achievements and Insights:

Automation and Optimization:

AI has proven instrumental in automating complex decision-making processes associated with international trade, be it in trade, business, or marketing decisions.

Data Analysis and Prediction:

The capability of AI algorithms to analyze extensive datasets, identify intricate patterns, and make predictions regarding financial markets, commodity movements, and diverse international markets stands out prominently.

Informed and Effective Trades:

International traders are empowered to make more informed and effective trades through the insights provided by AI models, ensuring strategic decisions align with market trends and patterns.

Risk Reduction:

The demonstrated ability of AI in minimizing risks associated with human error underscores its significance in enhancing the reliability and accuracy of international trade operations.

The Strategic Edge of AI in International Trade:

In the dynamic and competitive landscape of global commerce, embracing AI technologies offers a strategic edge. The models developed in this course section showcase the potential for AI to augment decision-making, mitigate risks, and foster efficiency in international trade scenarios.

Continuous Evolution:

Recognizing the dynamic nature of international markets, the chapter emphasized the importance of continuous learning, testing, and evaluation of AI algorithms. This iterative approach ensures the adaptability of models to changing market conditions, thereby enhancing accuracy and reliability.

Looking Ahead:

As we conclude this chapter, it becomes evident that the integration of AI into international trade is not just a trend but a transformative force. The demonstrated benefits in informed decision-making, risk reduction, and efficiency set the stage for a future where AI will play an increasingly pivotal role in shaping the global business landscape.

In the next chapter of this course, we will further explore advanced topics, emerging trends, and practical applications, providing a comprehensive understanding of the evolving intersection between artificial intelligence and international trade.

Bonus Section 5: Simple Ways of Using ChatGPT to Reveal Rare Market Intelligence

Welcome back to this bonus section – the fifth in our series. In this segment, we embark on a practical exploration of leveraging AI Language Model (LLM) assistants, specifically ChatGPT, to uncover elusive market intelligence. Our objective is to equip you with insights into employing AI for generating trade leads and conducting efficient market and desk research.

Topics 208-209: Chapter Overview:

Unveiling Hidden Market Insights: By the end of this section, you'll gain a valuable understanding of how simple interactions with AI LLM assistants, like ChatGPT, can unveil hard-to-find market intelligence. We'll demonstrate how these tools can become indispensable for exporters seeking to generate trade leads and navigate international markets.

Topic 210: Initial Focus: Desk Research for a Manufacturer in Gujarat, India:

Our journey begins with a straightforward exercise focused on a manufacturer based in Gujarat, India. This manufacturer specializes in toners and developers for photocopiers and laser printers, and aims to extend its reach into global markets. Through interactions with ChatGPT, we will delve into the manufacturer's queries and witness the AI's responses, guiding us through industry directories, trade associations, and online B2B marketplaces.

Unpacking the Exercise:

Manufacturer's Queries and AI's Responses:

Explore how the manufacturer initiates queries to ChatGPT and witnesses the AI's responses. This will include uncovering industry directories, trade associations, online B2B platforms, and potential importers and exhibitions.

Refining Prompts for Specific Insights:

As the exercise progresses, observe how the manufacturer refines prompts to extract specific information about trade shows, potential importers, and competitive manufacturers on a global scale.

Unraveling the Power of ChatGPT:

Join us in unraveling the power of ChatGPT as a valuable tool for businesses venturing into international trade. This exercise serves as a foundational step, providing a glimpse into the simplicity yet effectiveness of AI-powered desk research.

What Lies Ahead:

This initial exercise sets the stage for deeper explorations into advanced AI applications in subsequent Topics within this course. Stay tuned to discover how AI can be harnessed for more intricate tasks, providing you with a comprehensive toolkit for success in international trade.

Initial Efforts to Trigger ChatGPT: Guiding the Conversation

In the early stages of the exercise, the manufacturer initiated a conversation with ChatGPT, providing essential details about their toner and developer manufacturing business. They emphasized the high-quality standards, international certifications, and cost competitiveness of their products. The manufacturer sought ChatGPT's assistance in identifying large importers and their locations.

1. Leveraging Initial Ideas:

As ChatGPT responded with initial ideas, it refrained from providing specific importer names or countries but steered the manufacturer toward actionable steps:

Industry Directories and Associations:

Mentioned directories like GIRA, ISC, and the ITC, emphasizing the importance of industry-specific platforms.

Trade Shows and Exhibitions:

Highlighted the significance of participating in trade shows related to printing, imaging technology, and office supplies.

Online B2B Marketplaces:

Suggested platforms such as Alibaba, Global Sources, TradeKey, and MadeInChina.com for online engagement.

Research and Targeting:

Encouraged the manufacturer to research and target specific importers, indicating a proactive approach.

2. Refining Questions for Specific Insights:

To progress the conversation, the manufacturer refines their questions, seeking more specific insights:

Specific Industry Directories:

Asks for recommendations on industry directories specifically focused on toners, developers, and imaging technology.

Upcoming Trade Shows:

Inquires about information on upcoming international trade shows specifically related to printing and imaging.

Targeting Importers:

Seeks guidance on targeting large importers in specific countries or regions.

3. Building on Industry Knowledge:

The manufacturer can enhance ChatGPT's responses by providing additional context and industry-specific details:

Contextual Information:

Shares insights into the target audience, preferences, or key competitors to refine suggestions.

Certifications and Standards:

Emphasizes specific international quality checks and certificates obtained, showcasing commitment to high standards.

4. Navigating the Iterative Process:

Recognizing that obtaining specific names may require an iterative approach, the manufacturer continues to refine questions based on the guidance received.

5. Continuous Guidance for Actionable Information:

The manufacturer's role is pivotal in steering the conversation toward actionable information. By asking specific questions, they guide

ChatGPT to provide more targeted insights.

6. Preparing for Further Exploration:

This initial exchange sets the stage for further exploration. As the manufacturer continues to interact with ChatGPT, the focus will be on extracting detailed market intelligence to support their global expansion endeavors.

Stay tuned for the unfolding of this exercise, revealing how simple interactions with AI can pave the way for valuable market insights.

Topic 211: Refining Prompts for Precision: Unveiling Targeted Insights

In the ongoing interaction between the manufacturer and ChatGPT, a strategic shift is observed as the manufacturer refines their prompts to extract more specific and valuable insights. Recognizing the importance of precise questioning, the manufacturer seeks information tailored to their business needs.

1. Initial Inquiry: Names of Important Trade Shows and Exhibitions

Building upon the initial ideas suggested by ChatGPT, the manufacturer crafts a question aimed at obtaining specific recommendations for trade shows and exhibitions to showcase their toners and developers. ChatGPT responds by providing a list of globally recognized events:

- Drupa (Germany)

- Remax World (China)

- Paperworld (Germany)

- Photokina (Germany, Cologne)

- GITEX Technology Week

- Consumer Electronics Show (CES)

- Print and Digital Expo (South Africa)

- Graphics Canada (Toronto, Canada)

2. Further Refinement: Focus on Office Supplies and Consumables

Encouraged by the initial response, the manufacturer refines their inquiry, seeking trade shows and exhibitions specifically centered around office supplies and consumables. ChatGPT, adapting to the refined prompt, presents a more targeted list:

- Paperworld (Germany)

- Office Expo Asia (Singapore)

- London Stationary Show (UK)

- Remano Expo at Paperworld (Germany, Frankfurt)

- SALTEX (Tokyo, Japan)

- Hong Kong International Stationary Fair (Hong Kong)

- ReChina Asia Expo (Printing and Consumables)

- Office Print Expo (South Africa)

3. Observations and Strategic Adjustments:

The manufacturer notes the importance of crafting precise prompts to guide ChatGPT effectively.

By aligning inquiries with specific business requirements, the manufacturer gains insights tailored to their industry niche.

4. Utilizing ChatGPT as a Strategic Research Tool:

The evolving conversation showcases ChatGPT's capacity to offer targeted information based on nuanced prompts.

The manufacturer leverages ChatGPT not just as a generic information source but as a strategic research tool, refining the focus for better results.

5. Continuous Iteration for Deeper Insights:

The manufacturer acknowledges the iterative nature of the process, continually fine-tuning questions to unearth deeper market intelligence.

The dialogue emphasizes the symbiotic relationship between the manufacturer's guidance and ChatGPT's responsive capabilities.

6. Preparing for Next Steps:

Armed with insights into relevant trade shows and exhibitions, the manufacturer is better positioned to plan their entry into international markets.

This exercise sets the stage for exploring additional dimensions of AI assistance in market research within the course.

As the dialogue progresses, the manufacturer's refined prompts showcase the evolving dynamics of utilizing AI, demonstrating its potential for providing targeted and valuable market intelligence. Stay tuned for further insights and advancements in this exploration of AI applications in international trade.

Topic 212: Testing ChatGPT: Uncovering Global Trading Hubs for Office Consumables

Buoyed by the insightful responses received thus far, the manufacturer, in this evolving AI-driven dialogue, refines their prompts further. Aiming for more targeted information, the manufacturer now directs ChatGPT to identify the countries that serve as prominent trading centers and world hubs for office consumables and supplies.

Manufacturer's Inquiry:

Which countries are recognized as the primary trading centers and world hubs for office consumables and office supplies?

ChatGPT's Responses:

1. United States, China, Germany, Japan, UK, South Korea, Singapore.

2. United States, China, Germany, Japan, UK, South Korea, Singapore, United Arab Emirates (UAE).

Strategic Evaluation and Decision:

Common Countries in Both Responses:

- United States, China, Germany, Japan, UK, South Korea, Singapore.

Additional Country in the Second Response:

- United Arab Emirates (UAE).

Significance of UAE for Indian Exporters:

The absence of UAE in the first response highlights the dynamic nature of ChatGPT's answers.

Considering the geographical proximity of UAE to India and its status as a known trading center, this addition holds strategic relevance.

Manufacturer's Decision:

Given the strategic importance of UAE, the manufacturer opts for the second response from ChatGPT.

Observations:

Precision in AI Responses:

ChatGPT not only provides a list of countries but also imparts additional insights, such as Dubai's role as a major trading center in the Middle East.

Strategic Decision-Making:

The manufacturer leverages the AI responses not merely as a list but as actionable intelligence for market entry.

Key Takeaways:

Dynamic Nature of AI Responses:

The iterative process allows for evolving and dynamic responses, emphasizing the need for precision in questioning.

Strategic Utilization of AI Insights:

The manufacturer strategically assesses the information provided by ChatGPT, making decisions based on the relevance of additional details.

Geographical Proximity and Trade Centers:

Proximity to trading centers like UAE becomes a crucial factor for the manufacturer, showcasing the nuanced considerations in AI-assisted decision-making.

Moving Forward:

The exercise sets the stage for further testing and exploration, with the manufacturer gaining confidence in ChatGPT's ability to provide nuanced and valuable market intelligence.

As the manufacturer delves deeper into refining prompts, the AI responses continue to unveil nuanced insights, highlighting the potential of AI in facilitating strategic decision-making in international trade. Stay tuned for further developments in this exploration of AI applications in market research.

Topic 213: Hitting it Hard: Capitalizing on AI Insights for Strategic Business Growth

Emboldened by the wealth of valuable insights gleaned from ChatGPT, the manufacturer enters a phase of heightened exploration and innovation. The manufacturer, now more confident in the capabilities of the AI model, seeks to extract even more precise and pertinent information to fuel strategic decision-making.

Manufacturer's Innovative Prompts:

Inquiry about Importers in UAE:

- Can you suggest me names of some large importers or dealers of office supplies and consumables in UAE?

Expanding to Singapore and UK:

- Can you suggest me names of some large importers or dealers of office supplies and consumables in Singapore?

- Can you suggest me names of some large importers or dealers of office supplies and consumables in the United Kingdom (UK)?

Exploring E-commerce Platforms:

What are the online trading platforms where I can set up an online e-commerce portal to sell my products globally in both B2B and B2C formats?

Costing for Trade Shows:

How much does it cost to participate in a typical international trade show like Paperworld for an exporter from India?

Specific Questions about ITPO and Trade Shows:

- Does ITPO participate in any trade shows or exhibitions that we have discussed?

- Can you tell me who are the companies that are very active in manufacturing and selling the kind of products my company manufactures, and which countries do they belong to?

AI-Driven Responses and Strategic Insights:

Importers in UAE:

Office Rock, Al Masam, Office One LLC, AAB Tools, Altimus Office Supplies, Speedex Group.

Importers in Singapore:

Office World Supply, Stamford Office Supplies, AOS Online, Rubber Stamp Dot Com Singapore, Singapore Office Supplies, Teco Buy Singapore.

Importers in the UK:

Viking Direct, Office Depot UK, Lyreco, EuroOffice, Amazon Business UK, Staples UK, Ryman.

E-commerce Platforms:

Amazon, eBay, Alibaba, Shopify, Magento, BigCommerce, WooCommerce, Global Sources, TradeIndia, MadeinChina.com.

Costing for Trade Shows:

Detailed breakdown provided, covering booth space rental, design, travel, logistics, marketing, and more.

ITPO and Trade Shows:

Suggested that ITPO may participate in trade shows, emphasizing the need to check ITPO's official website for specific information.

International Competitors:

Highlighted major multinational companies in the industry, including

HP, Canon, Epson, Brother, Xerox Corporation, Ricoh, Kyocera, Samsung.

Manufacturer's Excitement and Strategic Planning:

As the manufacturer witnesses the richness of information flowing from ChatGPT, the excitement grows. The AI model is no longer just providing answers; it is becoming a strategic ally in the exploration of international markets. The manufacturer starts envisioning collaborations with potential importers, targeting specific countries, and contemplating participation in trade shows with a newfound confidence.

Key Takeaways:

Precision in Inquiry Yields Strategic Insights:

By refining questions and prompts, the manufacturer obtains precise and relevant information crucial for strategic decision-making.

AI as a Strategic Ally:

ChatGPT evolves into a valuable ally, guiding the manufacturer through market exploration and strategic planning.

Nuanced Costing Information:

The AI's ability to break down costs for trade shows provides the manufacturer with insights for meticulous planning.

Informed Decision-Making:

The manufacturer's ability to extract nuanced and hard-to-find information positions them for informed decision-making and effective market entry.

Continued Exploration:

The manufacturer's journey with ChatGPT serves as a testament to the potential of AI-driven insights in international trade. As the exploration continues, the manufacturer is poised to delve into more complex and specific aspects of market intelligence, leveraging ChatGPT's evolving understanding and responsiveness. Stay tuned for further advancements in this exciting exploration of AI applications in the realm of international trade.

ABOUT THE AUTHOR

Dr. Vijesh Jain is *a corporate trainer, management consultant, and instructor of* VJ Export Mastery Courses Series on UDEMY. He already has more than a quarter million of student enrollments on Udemy. He is an MIB, IIFT, New Delhi, B.E.BITS, Pilani, Phd from University of Mysore and a Certified Global Business Professional by NASBITE, USA. He is the first ever recipient of the best PhD thesis award conferred by BIMTECH, Delhi NCR. He has written several books in the areas related to international trade, management and business. He has also contributed several research papers, those are published in top international research journals. He is widely travelled abroad, having worked with top multinational companies involved in global business and has attended several international conferences and presented papers there. He has trained 1000s of working executives in India and abroad in the area of Global Management, Foreign Trade, Blockchain and Metaverse applications in international trade operations. With a total work experience of more than 35 years with global companies, he has also worked as Dean/Director with several reputed B Schools.